The

BSAT

Official Study Guide

350 Questions You'll *Never* See on the SAT

By John Forster and Marc Segan

RUNNING PRESS
PHILADELPHIA · LONDON

9 8 7 6 5 4 3 2 1
Digit on the right indicates the number of this printing

Library of Congress Control Number: 2009924901

ISBN 978-0-7624-3647-7

Cover and interior design by Jason Kayser
Typography: Helvetica and Times

Running Press Book Publishers
2300 Chestnut Street
Philadelphia, PA 19103-4371

Visit us on the web!
www.runningpress.com

Dedications

For my son Will, cheerleader and critic rolled into one
—J.F.

To my test subjects, Thing 1 and Thing 2
(aka Samantha and Max)
—M.S.

Photo Credits

p. 51 (pencil): ©iStockphoto.com/Christophe Teste; p. 51 (pills): ©iStockphoto.com/Don Wilkie; p. 51 (snacks): ©iStockphoto.com/Brent Shetler; p. 51 (water): ©iStockphoto.com/Marie-france Bélanger; p. 51 (astrolabe): ©iStockphoto.com/Vitaly Shabalyn; p. 51 (bag): ©iStockphoto.com/Andrew Johnson; p. 51 (calculator): ©iStockphoto.com/Marcel Nijhuis; p. 51 (phone): ©iStockphoto.com/Jaroslaw Wojcik; p. 93 (woman): ©iStockphoto.com/Alexander Yakoulev; p. 126 (log): ©iStockphoto.com/Sebastian Knight; p. 230 (puppet): ©iStockphoto.com/Cole Vineyard; p. 249: ©iStockphoto.com/Lev Olkha; p. 251 (drunk): ©iStockphoto.com/Giorgio Fochesato; p. 251 (prayer): ©iStockphoto.com/Andrea Laurita

TABLE OF CONTENTS

PART I

THE BSAT—
COLLEGE TESTING
GROWS A PAIR

The BSAT is . . .

A) the new and better alternative to the SAT and ACT.

B) the test that rewards BS.

C) the test that doesn't make you throw up with anxiety.

D) the test that was not created by academics with their heads up their asses.

E) ALL OF THE ABOVE.

How to Use This Book

JUST OPEN IT

Linear is over. Start on any random page. Take the Diagnostic Test and find out how you did.
Refine your BS abilities with the richly rewarding and thoroughly filthy *Study Guide.* Soon you'll
realize there's more to life than getting into an Ivy just to please your over-involved parents.

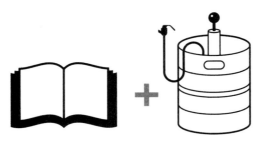

PARTY WITH IT

Use this book with a group of friends, band members, or fellow inmates.
Read the questions out loud. Work together on solutions or just take turns guessing blindly.
Group participation increases your chances of getting laid. Amazingly, you don't have to solve
the problems—or even understand them—to enjoy the benefits of the BSAT.

WRITE ON IT

We mean it. Scrawl all over this book. A lot. In ink. Deface it. That way, anyone who wants to
borrow it will have to buy his or her own damn copy. You'll be doing us all a favor.

Now you're ready to . . . begin.

WTF???

Like we really need another college admissions test? If it's the BSAT . . . yes, yes, YES! To understand why, look at how college testing became the cruel and demoralizing joke it is today.

A Short, Ugly History of College Admissions Testing

Until the mid-1930s, the principal requirements for admission to a Harvard or Yale were wealth, whiteness, and maleness. But one day the president of Harvard wondered, "Might there be a few smart, deserving youngsters out there who *aren't* rich, white, or male? If only there were a test that could separate the gold from the slag . . ."

Thus was born the SAT, a well-intentioned attempt by the smug elite to level the playing field, even if the game being played was still polo. To be sure, the early test questions hinted at a slight cultural bias:

- Train A leaves Hyde Park at the same time Train B leaves Oyster Bay . . .
- If 15 percent of your income is from inherited B&O Railroad preferred stock . . .
- The latest date in the season it's permissible to wear white is . . .

After World War II, with the influx of students on the GI Bill, the requirements relaxed a little and it became possible to have both a Harvard degree and a Mediterranean last name. The SAT changed, too, in keeping with the times:

- Commuter Train A leaves Housing Development A at the same time Commuter Train B leaves Housing Development B . . .
- The Pentagon employs 5,035 Loyal Americans. If 15 Communists infiltrate . . .

During the Culture Wars of the 60s, the SAT's lily-white orientation came under attack. For example, the Black Panthers fought (unsuccessfully) for more questions like:

- The A-Train leaves 125th Street in Harlem carrying 72 soul brothers. At 59th Street it picks up 95 white honky muthafuckahs . . .
- There are 1,250 hippie protesters in Grant Park and 300 pigs in full riot gear with tear gas. If it takes 3 pigs to drag a protester to the paddy wagon . . .

When disco-mania struck in the 70s, leading seamlessly into the 80s stock market boom, people awash in money and cocaine stopped obsessing about the inequity of the SAT. Now free of outside scrutiny, the *educationistas* of the College Board quietly set about imbuing the test with the most vicious bias of all—a bias in favor of geniuses who excel in every endeavor. The SAT that evolved in that dark era—one full of trick questions and opportunities for assholes to show off—is essentially the SAT that exists today.

The SAT's tilt in favor of raw smarts was quickly detected, and remedies were sought. For example, the ACT started to gain ground as an alternative. But with its emphasis on acquired knowledge over brain power, the ACT only made the situation worse. Now the keys to the academic kingdom were being handed to any insufferable grind who was willing to work his ass off memorizing the Totality of Human Knowledge (i.e., Asians). Yet there was still no relief for the 99 percent of normal teen slackers who would rather learn a new ollie than cram vocabulary words like *succubus*. Until the BSAT.

Why the College Board Sucks

Here at the BSAT, we hear heartbreaking stories from the admission wars, stories of wonderful kids who've been screwed over by the Standardized Testing Establishment (especially by those bastards at the College Board). Midwest high school senior Simona Guelph writes:

> *Not only do I have a respectable 3.15 GPA, but I'm also president of 12 clubs and I've single-handedly wiped out syphilis in Zimbabwe. (Letter of Commendation from Ban Ki Moon attached.) Too bad I suck at algebra and rocked a 360 on my Math SAT, so next year I'll be a communications major at Burpee Community College. Curse you, SAT!*

Miami high-schooler Hector Cruz-Rivera:

> *I am an artist. My creative drive is almost insatiable. It is so strong that at least once per hour I must stop everything and choreograph a dance piece. Unfortunately, this means that I cannot sit still for a 3-hour test. Oh God! How will I ever get into Oberlin? ☹ g2g now (to choreograph a piece called 'Not Going to Oberlin').*

These stories bear witness to an arrogant testocracy bent on jamming our country's beautiful polygonal pegs into round holes. Not since the days of the Soviet gulag have the twin tools of boredom and terror been so effectively used to subjugate a population of innocent Sims, who only want to be left alone to text their buddies about where to meet to buy tees. The situation is disgraceful and monopolistic, but . . .

Help Is on the Way

Enter the BSAT. Finally, a test for the rest of us, who may not be smart enough to understand Einstein's Theory of Relativity but who are definitely smart enough not to bother trying. The BSAT is a test that relies on whatever's left when you take away brilliance and book learning. It relies on a type of intelligence that we call BSIQ. We believe that the BSAT is destined to overtake and ultimately replace the old, barbaric college testing rituals.

BSAT FAQs

How Is the BSAT Different from Those Other Tests?

Many students do poorly on the SAT and ACT tests—not because they're stupid, but because the questions are so deeply boring and irrelevant that their minds go numb before arriving at an answer. However, when challenged by a BSAT question, the mind is instantly energized, as if it had jumped naked into a vodka-spiked fountain of Jell-O.

What Do the Various Tests Test?

- The SAT tests *critical thinking*, a skill allegedly needed to succeed in college.
- The ACT tests *academic knowledge*, which you allegedly gained in high school.
- The BSAT tests *ability to bullshit your way through life*, an aptitude that, when fully developed, can propel you further than you have any right to go.

Handy comparison between SAT and BSAT

	SAT	**BSAT**
Sucks or not	Sucks	Doesn't suck
Terror factor	Scary as shit	Chill
Humor comparison	Sunday school	*South Park*
Offensiveness	Sunday school	*South Park*
Great website	Not	Definitely—visit *www.bsatworld.com*
Attracts opposite sex	ha	Do me!
Attracts same sex	ha	Cool!
Test prep book makes a great gift	You're kidding, right?	What a great idea!

I'm Not That Smart. Can I Still Do Well on the BSAT?

Yes. The BSAT measures a different kind of intelligence, known as BSIQ. When you're in deep doo-doo, it is BSIQ that digs you out. And the best way to cultivate BSIQ is to prepare for the BSAT.

Can Being Smart Hurt My BSAT Score?

Don't worry! Real intellect or encyclopedic knowledge won't *hurt* you on the BSAT! But they're optional. By reducing the unfair advantage held by those who have actually prepared for this critical time in their young lives, the BSAT gives even the Noble Slacker a shot at glory.

Are There Any Drawbacks to Taking the BSAT?

Only one. The BSAT is currently accepted at fewer than 100 institutions. A lot fewer. OK, 1 or 2, tops. Maybe not even. However, someday the priggish educational establishment will pull the poker out of its ass and embrace the BSAT. Of course, until then, you're pretty much just strumming your own banjo.

So the BSAT Is a Complete and Utter Waste of My Time?

Whoa! What do you call spending all night on Facebook?

Can the BSAT Help Me Prepare for Tests that Aren't Pure Fantasy?

Definitely. For 3 reasons:

1. The BSAT has answers and study guides, just like the SAT or ACT. Every question on the BSAT can be figured out just like the more "widely recognized" SAT or ACT questions.
2. The BSAT's questions teach you to expect the unexpected. They prepare you not only for the SAT and ACT but also for this warped and bewildering world.
3. Even the SAT and ACT reward the student who can cut corners. This is ten times truer of the BSAT, which has more corners than Amsterdam's red-light district. The more corners you cut, the better you get at cutting corners.

 Always remember, there are no shortcuts to learning how to cut corners.

If I Don't Do Well on the BSAT, Does It Mean I'm Stupid?

Stupid is such a harsh word. But it's probably the right one. Remember, though, many of the happiest, most successful people on the planet are stupid. Isn't it best to find out now and plan accordingly for a happy and successful future?

How Difficult Is the BSAT?

Our test questions offer a range of difficulty, serving genius and cretin alike.

If Success on the BSAT Relies on Plain Common Sense, Why Should I Buy this Test Prep Book?

Excellent question. Very BSAT. Here's your answer, smart-ass: getting a new test accepted by colleges requires a multi-pronged media onslaught, lobbyists, junkets, bribes, the works. This takes big bucks. So when you buy our book, you're helping kids everywhere. Let's get the BSAT recognized. Do it for the kids.

What if I Have 12 College Applications Due Tomorrow and I Haven't Even Started?

Never mind that. Here's a good exercise. Concentrate on all the opportunities you've missed, time you've wasted, and ignorant blunders you've made so far in your life. Now think about how much work lies ahead of you to fix the mess you've created.

Notice that feeling in the pit of your stomach, the tightness in your upper back, your throat? That's ANXIETY. We believe that anxiety is positive because it forces you to confront yourself with important questions like, "Is it possible that, even at my young age, I've already ruined my life?" The answer is yes. It's possible.

 When you buy this book, you are taking a positive step toward sorting out the mess you've made. You should feel proud of yourself. If, by the way, you're still just thumbing through it in the aisle of the bookstore, you need to bring it to the cashier and get on with the healing.

Why Should I Care about College or Any of that Stuff?

Try visualizing your future. Close your eyes and imagine college—a place where your room can be as gross as you want, where you can behave like a slut, where your clothes can stink, and you can sleep all day and drink and play cards all night and no one can tell you not to. Usually someone else is paying the bills, and the college protects your privacy and independence, just as if you were behaving responsibly—you know, like an adult.

Are you starting to care? Good! Don't blow it.

What's My Next Step?

A) You can all of a sudden study hard and expect, against all odds and human experience, to do brilliantly on a test like the SAT or the ACT.

B) You can use what nature and dumb luck have thrown your way.

C) You can cultivate your BSIQ.

D) You can take the BSAT.

E) ALL EXCEPT A)

PART II

THE DIAGNOSTIC TEST—
FINDING OUT
IF YOU'RE A MORON

The BSAT Diagnostic Test requires about an hour to complete, depending on your literacy level, etc. The test is not timed, because life is not timed (with some exceptions, like the Indy 500, Minute Rice, and the sadistic little Saturday morning quizzes inflicted by those bastards at the College Board).

So rip out the BSAT bubble sheet on the next page, whip out your #2 pencils, pop open a brewski or whatever testing aids you've adopted (See *Test-Taking Strategies,* p. 249) and begin.

BSAT Diagnostic Test

Answer Sheet

Answers on p. 36

1351

Section 1

1 (A) (B) (C) (D) (E)
2 (A) (B) (C) (D) (E)
3 (A) (B) (C) (D) (E)
4 (A) (B) (C) (D) (E)
5 (A) (B) (C) (D) (E)
6 (A) (B) (C) (D) (E)

Section 2

1 (A) (B) (C) (D) (E)
2 (A) (B) (C) (D) (E)
3 (A) (B) (C) (D) (E)
4 (A) (B) (C) (D) (E)
5 (A) (B) (C) (D) (E)

Section 3

1 (A) (B) (C) (D) (E)
2 (A) (B) (C) (D) (E)
3 (A) (B) (C) (D) (E)
4 (A) (B) (C) (D) (E)
5 (A) (B) (C) (D) (E)
6 (A) (B) (C) (D) (E)
7 (A) (B) (C) (D) (E)
8 (A) (B) (C) (D) (E)
9 (A) (B) (C) (D) (E)

Section 4

1 (A) (B) (C) (D) (E)
2 (A) (B) (C) (D) (E)
3 (A) (B) (C) (D) (E)
4 (A) (B) (C) (D) (E)
5 (A) (B) (C) (D) (E)

Section 5

1 (A) (B) (C) (D) (E)
2 (A) (B) (C) (D) (E)
3 (A) (B) (C) (D) (E)

Section 6

1 (A) (B) (C) (D) (E)
2 (A) (B) (C) (D) (E)
3 (A) (B) (C) (D) (E)
4 (A) (B) (C) (D) (E)
5 (A) (B) (C) (D) (E)

Section 7

1 (A) (B) (C) (D) (E)
2 (A) (B) (C) (D) (E)
3 (A) (B) (C) (D) (E)
4 (A) (B) (C) (D) (E)
5 (A) (B) (C) (D) (E)
6 (A) (B) (C) (D) (E)

Section 8

1 (A) (B) (C) (D) (E)
2 (A) (B) (C) (D) (E)
3 (A) (B) (C) (D) (E)
4 (A) (B) (C) (D) (E)
5 (A) (B) (C) (D) (E)
6 (A) (B) (C) (D) (E)
7 (A) (B) (C) (D) (E)
8 (A) (B) (C) (D) (E)

Section 9

1 (A) (B) (C) (D) (E)
2 (A) (B) (C) (D) (E)
3 (A) (B) (C) (D) (E)
4 (A) (B) (C) (D) (E)
5 (A) (B) (C) (D) (E)
6 (A) (B) (C) (D) (E)
7 (A) (B) (C) (D) (E)
8 (A) (B) (C) (D) (E)
9 (A) (B) (C) (D) (E)

Section 10

1 (A) (B) (C) (D) (E)
2 (A) (B) (C) (D) (E)
3 (A) (B) (C) (D) (E)
4 (A) (B) (C) (D) (E)

NO TEST MATERIAL ON THIS PAGE

1 1 1

SECTION 1

Sentence Completions

DIRECTIONS: The following sentences all contain one or more blanks. Below each sentence are five alternatives to fill in the blanks. Pick the one that seems the least screwed up.

1. The psychotic seven-year-old subjected his puppy to repeated acts of -------.

   A) Hamlet
   B) bravery
   C) sadism
   D) coprolalia
   E) Congress

2. "-------, Theodore!" shrieked Alvin, "Every time you come out of there it smells -------!"

   A) How lovely . . of daffodils
   B) Close that door . . like something died
   C) Eat my shorts . . fresh and clean as a whistle
   D) It's getting better all the time . . better, better, better
   E) Shoes . . like familiar old shoes

3. Deeply suspicious of one another, President Grbzck and Prime Minister Oeuai each brought along ------- to the other's embassy reception in case of -------.

   A) extra vowels and consonants . . Scrabble
   B) suitcase nukes . . a breakdown in talks
   C) toilet paper . . the runs
   D) tasters . . attempted poisoning
   E) an umbrella . . rain

4. After -------, Grace decided to change her major to -------.

   A) losing her virginity . . Biology
   B) after experimenting with her Biology prof . . Religion
   C) trying celibacy . . Women's and Gender Studies
   D) six months with Louise . . Biology again
   E) all of the above, one after another

5. The freshman realized it was time to do his laundry when -------.

   A) he opened the laundry bag and the carbon-monoxide detector went off
   B) his jeans jumped up from the floor and wrapped themselves around his neck
   C) his roommate moved into a hotel
   D) Campus Security cordoned off his room as a biohazard
   E) he heard the wailing and grinding of zipper teeth from the floor of his closet

6. Ursula's vocation offered her a lot of customer contact, but left her vulnerable to an occasional case of -------.

   A) mistaken identity
   B) Ebola
   C) Budweiser
   D) voodoo
   E) crabs

GO TO NEXT PAGE >

2   2   2

SECTION 2   Reading Passage

> DIRECTIONS: Read the passage below and then answer the questions that follow. The correct response may be stated outright in the text or merely suggested.

A Vestal Virgin was a teenage girl who served in the temple of Vesta, the Greek goddess of hearth and home. The following passage is excerpted from PULP MYTHS: Sleaze and the Ancient Greeks, *collected and edited by Joseph Campbell III.*

There was a Vestal Virgin whose name was Dildo. Though she was pious and chaste, she was also proud. One day, while disporting with her companion Nympho, she declared, "Men!
(5)   What good are men? There is no man on Earth who can satisfy me as I satisfy myself." Dildo's arrogant boast fell upon the ears of Herpes, God of Forbidden Love, who flew down to investigate. With one glance Herpes fell in love with
(10) Dildo and vowed to possess her.

The next day he appeared to her as a beautiful youth and importuned her. But she rejected his suit, saying:
      "Dare not to tempt me from my vows. Get
(15) thee from this sacred house."
      The second day he came disguised as a rich merchant, proffering jewels and fragrant lotions. But again she demurred.
      "Who cares a fig for trinkets or perfume? No
(20) man will ever breach my ante-room."
      On the third day Herpes appeared to Dildo as a middle-aged philosopher with a large bulge in his toga. Again he pressed his suit, this time with suggestive poetry:
(25) "How about some slap-and-tickle, Rumpy-pumpy or hide-the-pickle?"
      This intriguing proposition stopped the maiden in her tracks, but before Herpes could pounce, Nympho intervened, whisking her back
(30) to the temple.
      That night Dildo prayed to Vesta, begging for strength. But Vesta was distracted by the Trojan

War, and instead, Dildo's prayer was overheard by Vesta's mischievous half-brother, Transvesta,
(35) God of Hidden Surprises. Smitten, like Herpes, by Dildo's beauty and virtue, Transvesta vowed to bed her.
      But Transvesta was sly. He came to Dildo as a comforting old lady (albeit with a suspicious
(40) bulge in her robe). Dildo confided in the old lady, who dried her tears and kissed her cheek. That went well, so he nibbled her earlobe and stroked her bottom. But then Dildo felt the bulge and she jumped back. At that moment
(45) Transvesta dropped his robe. Dildo's eyes widened in astonishment and curiosity. Within moments she had become a woman, and not only that, one with a little demigod on the way. Transvesta's trickery had triumphed!
(50)   When Dildo's disgrace became visible, her father, King Mediocrates, sailed home from the Trojan War, abandoning thirty-two triremes, a phalanx of hoplites, and a nubile catamite.* The king offered a sacrifice to Chlamydia, Goddess
(55) of Unintended Consequences, who, it turns out, was the wife of Herpes and the mother of his divine children, Zoster and Simplex.
      Hearing the king's prayer and seeing Dildo's swollen belly, Chlamydia flew into a jealous
(60) rage, believing that the defilement had been performed by her own philandering Herpes. She contrived to teach him a lesson: From that day forward each of Herpes' paramours would suffer suppurating pustules, occurring randomly,
(65) and infecting loved ones and casual hook-ups alike.
      But the punishment was lost on Herpes, who philandered his way through all eternity, leaving a bitter trail of burning and itching.
(70)   Today, the mini-constellation of Herpes can

---

* *Thirty-two ships that try to ream out other ships, a company of foot soldiers, and a cute young boyfriend.*

GO TO NEXT PAGE ⟩

be found in the Crotch of Orion as an angry cluster of cosmic sores that come and go at random, bringing minor discomfort to astronomers since the time of Galileo.

1. What is the best paraphrase for "he pressed his suit" in line 23?

   A) He ironed his toga.
   B) He bought two tickets for *Oedipus Rex*.
   C) He raised his partner's "4 no-trump" bid to "6 clubs."
   D) He tried to get laid.
   E) He took Dildo to court.

2. What is the relationship between Transvesta and Chlamydia?

   A) it's complicated
   B) half siblings
   C) full goddess and demi-god
   D) friends with benefits
   E) no relationship, at least in this passage

3. In line 45, "Dildo's eye's widened in astonishment and curiosity." Why?

   A) She had just sat on a jellyfish.
   B) She was getting her first lesson in the meaning of "Olympic-sized."
   C) Transvesta was doing his impersonation of naughty Greek vases.
   D) Transvesta's member was the size of a naughty Greek vase.
   E) B, C, or D

4. In line 3, what is the meaning of "disporting" in this context?

   A) a misprint for "distorting"
   B) wrestling Greco-Roman style
   C) biathalon
   D) watching *My Big Fat Greek Wedding*
   E) enjoying Greek life

5. If the ancient Greeks had cars, which of the following bumper stickers would King Mediocrates have been LEAST likely to display?

   A) Proud Parent of a Vestal Virgin
   B) Catamite On Board
   C) Gods Bless our Hoplites
   D) Change You Can Believe In
   E) HONK If You've Been Deflowered by a Deity!

GO TO NEXT PAGE

3   3   3

SECTION 3   Mathematics

DIRECTIONS: For each problem in this section there are five possible solutions offered. Choose the correct one. Use any blank space on the page for doodling.

Math Facts

- The circumference of a circle is $\pi \times$ Diameter.
- The volume of a pyramid is Base area $\times$ Height $\times \dfrac{1}{3}$.
- The cross-sectional area of Ruben Studdard is determined by π and more π.

1. Twenty-four years ago, Father O'Malley was 4 times as old as Little Mikey. Last week in criminal court, Mike, as he's now called, reflected that today he is precisely half as old as the aging priest. How old was Little Mikey when he was an altar boy?

   A) 12
   B) 13
   C) 21
   D) 2
   E) π

2. Richie is sick of pushing his brother Leo's wheelchair. Based on the diagram below, what is the number of complete rotations of the large rear wheel needed for Richie to get Leo's small front wheel past the edge of the cliff?

   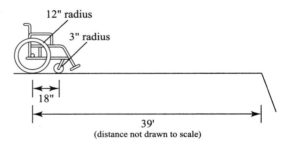

   12" radius
   3" radius
   18"
   39'
   (distance not drawn to scale)

   A) 4
   B) 5
   C) 6
   D) 7
   E) Instead of calculating, Richie could just put some wet paint on the wheel, give Leo a shove, and count the dots on the ground.

GO TO NEXT PAGE

3. Jim has to bring his date Monique (who is drop-dead gorgeous and already a little buzzed), his best friend Steve (who is a drunk and has no morals or loyalty), and a huge honkin' keg of Heineken from the liquor store to the dorm in his 1994 Mazda Miata. The car can only hold Jim plus Monique, the keg, or Steve. If Steve and Monique are left alone, Steve will screw Monique. If Steve and the keg are left alone, the keg will be empty in five minutes. How many one-way trips are required so that Jim gets Steve, Monique, and the keg back to the dorm without incident?

A) 3 trips
B) 4 trips
C) There is no solution. Either Monique or the keg gets tapped.
D) 6 trips
E) 7 trips

4. Lucy, a freshman in high school, hates her nose. To save up to fix it, she works 20 hours a week after school at the Hair Haven and earns $7.45 per hour (less 15% in taxes). If she wants her nose job in time for her graduation in 182 weeks, which nose can Lucy afford?

A)   The St. Tropez: $14,500

B)   The East Hampton: $9,750

C)   The South Beach: $5,475

D)   The Kansas City: $1,595

E)   The Hoboken: $99

5. It is known that 15,000 volts will kill you in 5 minutes, and 10,000 volts will kill you in 15 minutes. James Earl Spitt is to be executed at the Waco State Penitentiary at midnight. Due to a midsummer brownout, they have only 11,500 volts available. Which of the following times is *not* too late for the governor to call in his reprieve for Mr. Spitt?

A) 12:14 a.m.
B) 12:17 a.m.
C) 12:11 p.m.
D) 3:15 a.m.
E) None of the above.

GO TO NEXT PAGE

3   3   3

6. Pharaoh Tsurris II wants to build the pyramid shown below using the Israelite workforce he holds in bondage. It takes one Israelite an average of one year to carve and schlepp a stone of 8 cubic cubits. If Tsurris wants his pyramid completed in 15 years, how many Israelites must he assign to the project?

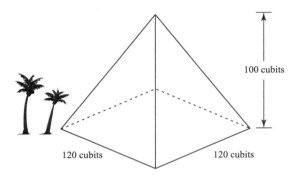

120 cubits   120 cubits

100 cubits

A) 80 Israelites
B) 800 Israelites
C) 4,000 Israelites
D) 12,500 Israelites
E) None. The Israelites turned down the work because they don't do stone. But they did recommend the Ionians and warned against the Carthaginians who estimate low and never finish a job.

7. Mr. Demaroni, the health teacher, says that smoking pot kills brain cells. To illustrate, he presents the below chart to the class. JPD means "joints per day."

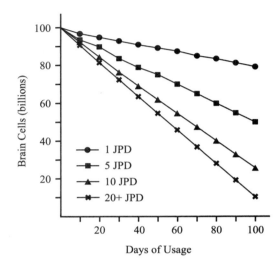

A normal person has approximately 100 billion brain cells. According to Mr. Demaroni, around how many should a typical 10-joint-per-day pothead expect to have left after 3 months of blowing weed?

A) 35
B) 35 billion
C) 50 billion
D) 50 × 1,014
E) Oh my God, this is really scary but I don't understand the question.

GO TO NEXT PAGE

8. Mr. Demaroni says that the formula for calculating your IQ after using pot is the following:

$$IQ_{final} = IQ_{initial} \times \frac{\text{\# Brain Cells}}{100 \text{ Billion}}$$

Based on the chart, if you started with an IQ of 100, what is your estimated IQ after using 20 JPD for 120 days?

A) 80
B) 60
C) 40
D) 20
E) -20

9. Beginning at point A in the diagram below, four Racists carrying tire irons chase an unarmed Minority down the block at 20 feet per second. At point B the Minority makes a left turn. The Racists, reaching point B and observing a group of heavily armed Minorities, stop, turn around, and return to point A at 30 feet per second. If the entire trip takes exactly one minute, how long do the Racists stop at point B to rethink their plan?

A) 0 seconds
B) 5 seconds
C) 10 seconds
D) It seems like an eternity.
E) Until their moms call them home for dinner.

GO TO NEXT PAGE

4   4   4

SECTION 4   Improving Sentences

> DIRECTIONS: The underlined portions of the sentences below may contain errors, from the piddling to the egregious. In some cases the entire sentence is underlined because the whole thing may be messed up. Figure out which of the five alternatives straightens things out the best. Choose answer A) if you still prefer the original.

1. Having been fixed that morning, Natalie drove the car to the Planned Parenthood meeting.

    A) [just the way it stands]
    B) Natalie drove the car, which had been fixed that morning, to the Planned Parenthood meeting.
    C) That morning Natalie drove the car to the Planned Parenthood meeting, which had been fixed.
    D) Natalie had been fixed that morning, so she didn't need to drive to the Planned Parenthood meeting.
    E) At the Planned Parenthood meeting, Natalie suggested that everyone else get fixed, too.

2. Ain't no sunshine when she's gone.

    A) [as is]
    B) There ain't no sunshine when she's gone.
    C) There isn't any sunshine when she's gone.
    D) There isn't any sunshine when she's absent.
    E) She only goes out at night.

3. Being the cream of the crop didn't inoculate him against stepping on his own dick.

    A) [no change]
    B) inoculate him against rabies
    C) protect him against lactose intolerance
    D) guarantee that he would rise to the top
    E) mean he wasn't a big doodoo head

4. I have a little dreidl.
   I made it out of clay.
   And when it's dry and ready,
   Then dreidl I will play.

    A) [perfect]
    B) I have a little dreidl.
       It's boring as can be.
       Let's fire up the X Box
       For Grand Theft Auto 3.
    C) I had a little dreidl
       That came from Toys 'R Us.
       Unfortunately, it got
       Run over by a bus.
    D) I have a fancy dreidl,
       A gyroscope within.
       You try and knock it over
       And still it's gonna spin.
    E) I have a little dreidl
       And one that's pretty big.
       My sister's got a whopper
       That crushed my guinea pig.

5. You touch my cottage cheese again and I'll rip your motherfucking head off, you goddamn motherfucking limp-peckered son of a one-eyed trouser worm.

    A) [perfect as is]
    B) motherfucking one-eyed trouser worm
    C) needle-dicked bug fucker
    D) motherfucking motherfucker
    E) gun

GO TO NEXT PAGE

5   5   5

SECTION 5   Improving Paragraphs

DIRECTIONS: The passage below is an unedited draft that needs help. Read it carefully and try to improve it by answering the questions that follow.

[1] Being a brain surgeon takes brains. [2] In fact it takes two different kinds of brains: the ones needed to do brain surgery and the ones that need the surgery. [3] And never the two shall meet because, as the saying goes, anyone who is his own surgeon probably has a dead patient. [4] My uncle is a brain surgeon and although he must be smart, the way my father talks, he sounds like the dumbest guy in the world. [5] Dad says Uncle Rob can't get the marriage thing straight at all because he's on his fifth wife and seventh kid. [6] (We have cousins leaking out of our ears.) [7] And the wives keep getting younger and younger and the boats bigger and bigger. [8] But how dumb could you actually be if you're short, bald, and round like Uncle Rob and you've got a beautiful young wife and a big yacht? [9] It doesn't take a brain surgeon to figure that you must be pretty smart.

[10] Dad isn't a brain surgeon. [11] He's an accountant for the IRS, which, as the saying goes, isn't brain surgery. [12] Dad says that the whole tangle of wives, kids, and yachts is nothing but a big headache of which he'd never want any of. [13] Wouldn't it be ironic if all a brain surgeon got from his hard work and brains was a big headache? [14] Dad gets headaches all the time. [15] Dad says it's because of guys like Uncle Rob who hide their assets in the Cayman Islands. [16] Dad says the only reason he doesn't send a whole team down there to do a Roto-Rooter audit on Uncle Rob is what if his headaches turn out to be a brain aneurysm?

1. Which of the following best describes Dad's feelings toward Uncle Rob?

   A) ludicrous
   B) envious
   C) obvious
   D) odious
   E) odorous

2. What is the best improvement of the underlined portion of sentence 12?

   [12] *Dad says that the whole tangle of wives, kids, and yachts is nothing but a big headache of which he'd never want any of.*

   A) [no change]
   B) stands in sharp contrast to his own noble devotion to home and family.
   C) sounds fantastic except for the kids.
   D) is nothing but a big headache and who needs it?
   E) is nothing but a big headache but he sure smiles a lot when Aunt Trudy's around.

3. Which of the following would MOST improve the passage?

   A) [It's perfect as is.]
   B) Include photos of the hot young wives.
   C) Fewer instances of "Dad says." This kid needs to start thinking for himself.
   D) Provide link to www//realhotwivesofreal-brainsurgeons.com.
   E) Translate the passage into Spanish and change the font to CHIMICHANGA.

GO TO NEXT PAGE

6   6   6

SECTION 6   Reading Passage Pair

> DIRECTIONS: Read the two short passages below and then answer the questions that follow. The correct response may be stated outright in the text or merely adumbrated.

Passage 1:

This email was sent to a father by his 17-year-old daughter.

Dad--

OK, I just got your Facebook friend request and my finger is still down my throat. WHAT ARE YOU THINKING?? Let me make this
(5) clear—YOU are not allowed on Facebook—maybe legally, OK, but really NOT. You will not WRITE ON ANYBODY'S WALL. You will not POKE ANYBODY—you don't even know what it means and you wouldn't get it even if I
(10) explained it to you. If you don't deactivate your Facebook account THIS MINUTE I swear I'll get pregnant and drop out of school. YOU HAVE BEEN WARNED!!!

                                    Mindy

Passage 2:

This essay was included on the College Common App of Roberta X. She is currently taking a gap year and revising her plan to pursue biological sciences.

(15) I've always believed in Darwin's Theory of Evolution because it explains perfectly how I got to be so beautiful and popular. My mom was beautiful and popular and so was her mom. My ancestors only dated people who were as
(20) cool as they were, refining their genes and passing all that on to me. I'm co-captain of both field hockey and volleyball and have probably the best overall body in the school. Mr. Aptherp, our bio teacher, calls me the poster
(25) child for Natural Selection.

Why I'm upset is, Natural Selection fails to explain Adelaide Barker. She is plain and dumpy, her parents are plain and dumpy, her lower teeth are crooked, her hair has no body,
(30) she has no fashion sense and no friends, let alone a BFF. Adelaide is a runty straggler from the herd, just waiting to be picked off by jackals. Yet she was elected President of Student Council over me. The unfittest triumphed over
(35) the fittest and, what's worse, with this dark victory on her résumé (along with some minor academic honors, like Student of the Century) she might keep succeeding in ways she really should not.

(40) I'm pretty sure there's something going on here besides Darwinism and that something is what I call Unintelligent Design, a malicious force that rebels against Natural Selection and, evidently, sometimes wins. It's like this primal
(45) battle, where Unintelligent Design is always threatening to undo the truth and justice of Natural Selection.

Nature is always coming up with unintelligent designs: frogs with three legs, people who
(50) bungee-jump, the PT Cruiser, Coke Zero. These novelties cause a lot of splash, but soon people get sick of them because they're so unintelligent. Just the way people will start to get sick of Adelaide's gross lower teeth in combination
(55) with that perpetual dorky grin. *Eww.* And then Natural Selection will bring everything back into proper balance.

It's too bad the process involves people like Adelaide Barker. But the good news is that I
(60) challenged the election results, forcing a runoff, which—believe me—this time I will take a lot more seriously. And sooner or later it's only natural that I get selected over Adelaide.

GO TO NEXT PAGE >

1. Why is the author of Passage 1 upset?

    A) Her hair has no body but her body has hair.
    B) Her father tried to friend her.
    C) She's about to get her period.
    D) She's not upset. It's just that her CAPS LOCK key tUrns ON at ranDOM.
    E) The social networking jungle is getting to her.

2. Why is the author of Passage 2 upset?

    A) Her mother dated Adelaide's father so she and Adelaide may be sisters.
    B) Mr. Aptherp put his hand on her ass.
    C) There is a disturbance in the Force.
    D) Though she loves Natural Selection, it fails to explain the existence of Adelaide.
    E) A Student Council President experiencing a major acne attack should temporarily hand over power to the VP (but Adelaide refuses).

3. Based on the passages, which of the following do the two authors have MOST in common?

    A) impotent outrage at people who violate the order of the universe
    B) difficulty in handling conjunctions and adverbs
    C) the willingness to use pregnancy as a weapon
    D) scars from botched wax jobs
    E) cramps

4. All of the following are examples of Unintelligent Design EXCEPT:

    A) the inflatable neck stretcher
    B) Adelaide Barker
    C) a frog with three legs
    D) the Department of Homeland Security
    E) the Large Hadron Collider in Geneva, Switzerland

5. What does Author 2 mean by her ancestors "refining their genes"?

    A) They reproduced using only Extra-Virgin sperm.
    B) They stone-washed and then dry-cleaned their genes.
    C) They stopped reading the *National Enquirer* or believing in UFOs.
    D) They never bred with anyone less cool than themselves.
    E) None of the above

GO TO NEXT PAGE

7   7   7

SECTION 7   Analogies

> DIRECTIONS: In each question below you are given a pair of words, phrases or whatevers that are somehow related. From the choices offered, complete the second pair so that they are related in the same way as the first pair.

1. whatchamacallit : Alzheimer's :: goddamfuckingcocksucker : -------

   A) Parkinson's
   B) Asperger's
   C) Tourette's
   D) Trader Vic's
   E) Orville Redenbacher's

2. testicles : clangers :: breasts : -------

   A) nabba-nacka-wappers
   B) fazools
   C) doozers
   D) bazongas
   E) all of the above

3. Spirit : Opportunity :: R2D2 : -------

   A) R3D3
   B) WD-40
   C) 300 SL
   D) 10,000 BC
   E) C3PO

4. drop : bucket :: Prius : -------

   A) global warming
   B) energy independence
   C) pious
   D) sanctimonious asshole
   E) Hummer

5. school : prison :: marriage : -------

   A) heaven
   B) prenuptial
   C) adultery
   D) a bullet to the head
   E) root canal

6. belch : vomiburp :: fart : -------

   A) fudge your gutchies
   B) gild the lily
   C) buy the farm
   D) roto-rooter
   E) whoop-ass

GO TO NEXT PAGE

8   8   8

SECTION 8   Identifying Sentence Errors

DIRECTIONS: Each of the following sentences contains either a single error or no error at all. Select the underlined portion that contains the foozle or, if none, choose *E) No error.*

1. Although <u>they</u> share many physical features, <u>it</u>
        A   B

   doesn't take a highly trained <u>birder</u> to distin-
                         C

   guish the plaintive warble of the Brown-nosed

   Suckup <u>and</u> the shrill cry of the Pinch-beaked
          D

   Titwringer. <u>No error</u>
              E

2. <u>Like</u>, I mean, you can say what you want, but
   A

   it's, <u>like</u>, a bad thing not to pick that bag up
        B

   when you and Becky agreed to because it's <u>like</u>
                                     C

   sitting out there and <u>like</u> anyone could find it and
                   D

   turn it in to the cops. <u>Like, they're all wrong</u>.
                      E

3. <u>From</u> the moment Mrs. Mellon <u>learned</u> the
   A   B

   meaning of MILF, she <u>began</u> to look at her
                     C

   son's wrestling team buddies just a little

   <u>different</u>. <u>No error</u>
      D   E

4. Rabbi Shpilkes named the family parakeet

   Onan <u>insofar</u> as <u>he</u> always spilled <u>his</u> seed
         A   B   C
   <u>upon</u> the ground. <u>No error</u>
     D   E

5. <u>Chinese</u> fortune cookie: "<u>Blown</u> fuse <u>await</u>
     A   B   C

   bed-wetter sleeping <u>under</u> electric blanket."
                  D

   <u>No error</u>
     E

GO TO NEXT PAGE ▷

8   8   8

6. The Free Range food movement has resulted in
                                     A
   some barbarian practices, including the "Iowa
          B
   Sleigh Ride," in which chickens are harpooned
                 C   D
   from a moving tractor. No error
                          E

7. The boys understood that at a bar called The

   Kennel Club they should not expect to hook up

   with Scarlett Johansson's twin sister, but this
         A
   milling horde of skeevy skanks were nonethe-
                    B   C   D
   less disappointing. No error
                       E

8. In his victory speech, Sen. Smith thanked the

   Almighty for his campaign's miraculous
              A
   revival, which pundits ascribed to the unusually
                   B   C
   high turnout of dead voters. No error
        A   E

GO TO NEXT PAGE

9   9   9

SECTION 9   Mathematics

DIRECTIONS: For each problem in this section, there are x possible solutions offered, where $x = \sqrt{25}$. Choose the correct one. Use any blank space on the page for doodling.

Math Facts

- Chuck Norris can divide by zero. But you can't.
- Chuck Norris can multiply by infinity. You can't.
- You *can* divide by infinity or multiply by zero. But only if Chuck says it's OK.

1. If

   and

   and ,

   what is  ?

   A)

   B)

   C)

   D)

   E)

2. Scout Troop 188 found a wallet full of money in the park. They spent 74% on reefer, 18% on a bong, and the remaining $21.60 for munchies. How much money did they find?

   A) $113.60
   B) $120.00
   C) $270.00
   D) $1,200.00
   E) Wallet? What wallet?

GO TO NEXT PAGE ⟩

3. The following table lists a group of college friends and the numbers of their piercings.

	Ear	Nose	Tongue	Lip	Brow
Rhea	3	0	1	1	1
Sela	2	0	0	0	0
Tania	3	1	4	4	1
Uma	12	2	2	2	2
Valda	5	0	1	0	1

Not counting nostrils, mouths, and ears, how many total holes do these five girls have in their heads?

A) 44
B) 46
C) 48
D) 90
E) Wait a minute—what about nose pores?

4. Uma's Dad got her a summer job at a law firm on the condition that she not be seen sporting more than the average number of hanging ornaments her four friends wear. How many must she remove to get the job?

A) 10
B) 12
C) 13
D) 15
E) Zero—she'll just move them to her belly button where her father won't see them.

5. Jim, a philosophy major, tried out the following logic on his first date with Stacy:

If I'm in love with a girl, I want to sleep with her.

I want to sleep with you.

Therefore, I'm in love with you.

How should Stacy characterize Jim's reasoning?

A) specious
B) phallusy
C) an elegant syllogism
D) Nice try, Socrates!
E) A, B, and D

6. A cookie jar in the school nurse's office contains x number of condoms. The chart below shows the distribution of the five types on offer. In terms of x, how many more Ribbed than Flavored are available for the schoolchildren?

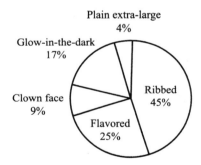

A) $\dfrac{9x}{5}$

B) $20x$

C) $\dfrac{x}{5}$

D) $\dfrac{x}{10}$

E) $\dfrac{\text{Plain medium with extra cheese}}{x}$

GO TO NEXT PAGE

7. Jose, a star center fielder, expects a random drug test on Saturday at 11 a.m. His current blood level of STP, an illegal performance-enhancing steroid, is 16 micrograms/milliliter, which is 16,000 times the legal limit. He knows that by drinking beer, he can piss away half the STP in his blood every hour. When must he stop juicing and start chugging to pass the drug test?

A) Friday at midnight
B) Friday at 8 p.m.
C) "It's Miller time!"
D) What the hell does C) mean?
E) Doesn't matter, he's on a home-run streak.

8. Ashley is twice as popular as Brittany, but half as popular as Desiree. Camille is three times as popular as Desiree, but actually would love to have long straight hair. How much more popular is Camille than Brittany?

A) 6 times as popular
B) 12 times as popular
C) Camille would actually love to have long straight hair.
D) 3 times as popular
E) Is this math? That is *so* not popular!

9. In the figure below, circle X represents the set of all students who begin freshman year as virgins and circle Y represents the set of students claiming to be virgins at the end of the year. Which of the below cannot possibly describe a student represented by region C of circle Y?

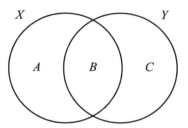

A) an amnesiac
B) a prevaricator
C) a hymen transplantee
D) a miracle
E) a virgin

GO TO NEXT PAGE

10   10   10

SECTION 10   Reading Passage

DIRECTIONS: Read the passage below and then answer the questions that follow. The correct response may be stated outright in the text or merely insinuated.

This "appreciation" first appeared at alternative kids' music website www.waaahh.com. It was widely reprinted in the establishment music press and anthologized in Snuffed. *For historical context, Tot-Rock is a genre of feedback-driven thrash music whose devotees are mainly under the age of 3.*

My best friend in the world was Scottie Kulik. Right, *that* Scottie Kulik, lead singer of Twisted Mittens, the pioneering hard-core tot-rock band. Scottie's tragic death last week at the

(5) age of 28 has shaken the world of children's music to its core. I was there from the edge, when the college sophomore hooked up with our classmate Dominick Milgrom and they wrote their first song, "I Play With Myself." In

(10) fact, I introduced them to their first bass player, the one who tanned to death during the "Set a Bad Example" tour.

It was I who suggested making "A Pot to Piss In" the first single off their second CD (*Up Your*

(15) *Nose with a Rubber Hose*), and in fact, the idea of actually pissing in a pot on stage was my idea, too. I still feel kind of bad that Beef-O-X got electrocuted during the show but I told them to make sure the mike was grounded and they

(20) obviously didn't. Plus it gave Scottie the idea for "Toaster in the Tub," so something good came out of it anyways.

I won't lie. Scottie was controversial. Parenting orgs kind of PHREAKED when "Toaster in

(25) the Tub" was first posted for download. And "Let's Drink Paint Thinner" and "The Doctor Is In" didn't help. But overprotective grownups are no match for spoiled 5-year-olds who want their MTV, as I told Scottie the day TwiMitt's

(30) third album *You're It! (Razor Tag)* crossed over to become the first kids' record to break the Alt

Rock Top 63 when it went to #62.

And when the shit hit the fan with the Attorney General and everything, I helped them

(35) come up with the whole "free speech" thing, which worked for a while, until the release of "Strap on Your Kevlar—This Puppy's Loaded," which got the FBI involved.

I'll never forget the morning I got that call.

(40) I'd been free-basing all night so I was a little jumpy but really alert. When Dom told me Scottie had been drawn and quartered by four soccer moms in SUVs, I was like, "Whoa, dude! Whatever happened to restraining

(45) orders?" And I'll never understand the note they stapled to his back: "Someday when you have kids of your own, maybe you'll understand." The irony is that Scottie loved kids and would have made a great dad, if they'd just given him

(50) a chance.

The real tragedy is that my best friend was just coming into his own as an artist. With "Daddy's Acetylene Torch" he'd opened up a new vein of creativity. At the time of his death

(55) he was totally psyched about a new rock opera he was working on, *Things to Do With Broken Glass*, based on the life of our beloved but troubled nursery school teacher, Miss Oliphant. I believe it would have been a masterpiece. But I

(60) guess we'll never know.

GO TO NEXT PAGE

1. All of the following statements show the author's pathetic need to take credit for Scottie's so-called accomplishments EXCEPT:

   A) He says he was there "from the edge."
   B) He claims that the stage piss was his idea.
   C) He and Scottie both had an undescended testicle.
   D) He introduced Scottie to his first bass player.
   E) He supposedly came up with the "free speech defense" thing, whatever that is.

2. The statement "Scottie had been drawn and quartered by four soccer moms in SUVs" is best described as:

   A) an objective account of what actually happened
   B) an attempt to gross the reader out
   C) a way to build empathy for Scottie
   D) a sophisticated reference to medieval customs
   E) probably a crock of shit

3. Which of the following song titles could not possibly be from the rock opera *Things to Do With Broken Glass*?

   A) "My Beautiful Pony (Got Hit by a Truck)"
   B) "The Sippy-Cup Drug Song"
   C) "In-a-Gadda-Piñata"
   D) "Let's Fill the World With Love"
   E) "Pick that Scab"

4. What makes the author think that Scottie would have been a great dad?

   A) Scottie always provided sound advice to children.
   B) Scottie had worked through his issues and was ready for the next stage.
   C) Scottie was infantile, so he'd be great with infants.
   D) The author is an expert on child rearing.
   E) The author has been free-basing.

GO TO NEXT PAGE ⟩

11   11   11

SECTION 11   Essay

DIRECTIONS: Map out and write an essay in which you develop your views on the assigned issue. Support your position any way you choose. Make it *amazing*.

Think Box

People are loath to generalize about racial characteristics. But some have suggested that what this country needs is a more open and frank discussion about race. If it is indeed time for that discussion, what are the most pressing questions to be addressed?

ASSIGNMENT: Why aren't white people cool? Would it help if they could jump?

_____

_____

_____

_____

_____

_____

_____

_____

_____

_____

GO TO NEXT PAGE

_____
_____
_____
_____
_____
_____
_____
_____
_____
_____
_____
_____
_____
_____
_____
_____
_____
_____
_____
_____
_____
_____
_____

STOP
Don't even *think* of turning the page.

BSAT Diagnostic Test   Answer Key

Section 1

1 C
2 B
3 D
4 E
5 C
6 E

Section 2

1 D
2 E
3 E
4 E
5 D

Section 3

1 A
2 C
3 E
4 A
5 E
6 C
7 B
8 E
9 B

Section 4

1 B
2 A
3 D
4 A
5 B

Section 5

1 B
2 D
3 A

Section 6

1 B
2 D
3 A
4 D
5 D

Section 7

1 C
2 E
3 E
4 B
5 E
6 A

Section 8

1 D
2 E
3 D
4 A
5 E
6 B
7 D
8 E

Section 9

1 D
2 C
3 C
4 C
5 E
6 C
7 B
8 B
9 E

Section 10

1 C
2 E
3 D
4 E

So How'd I do?

Time to score your Diagnostic Test. It's going to involve doing some arithmetic, though nothing harder than figuring out how to score a spare in the middle of the tenth frame. We'll walk you through it, but first you'll need to…

Score Your Own Essay

A perfect score on the BSAT Essay is 20. Ideally, you'll use the "Score Your Own Essay" table below to honestly and unflinchingly judge your attempts at self-expression. However, if you're a typical narcissistic mall rat, you'll find it extremely difficult to objectively grade your own writing. So just award yourself a 20 and move on.

"Score Your Own Essay" Table

	4	3	2	1
Approach to the Topic	Stunningly original	A mish-mash, but doesn't put you to sleep	Painfully trite and obvious	Approach? What approach?
Reasoning & Essay Structure	Solid as a brick shit house	Doggedly competent	Intellectually lazy and flaccid	An utterly random sequence of ideas
Level of Vocabulary	The next Oscar Wilde	Sophisticated, if not that surprising	Crude and rudimentary	Neanderthal
Grammar and Usage	Nary an error	The occasional error	Rife with errors	The occasional non-error
Overall	The work of a consummate master	Kind of just what you'd expect	Clueless and a little sad	An intellectual hellscape

How Many Right Answers?

Now check your answers on your Bubble Sheet against those in the Answer Key on p. 36. You may disagree with some of our answers or find others unfair. Tough shit.

Calculate Your Raw Score

Use this work sheet to arrive at your "raw score" for each of the three sections of the test.

Critical Reading:

Section 1:   Number Correct = _____; Number Incorrect = _____

Section 2:   Number Correct = _____; Number Incorrect = _____

Section 6:   Number Correct = _____; Number Incorrect = _____

Section 10:   Number Correct = _____; Number Incorrect = _____

                Total Correct = _____;   Total Incorrect = _____

_____ − (_____ ÷ 4) = _____
Total Correct   Total Incorrect   RAW SCORE A

Writing Skills:

Section 4:   Number Correct = _____; Number Incorrect = _____

Section 5:   Number Correct = _____; Number Incorrect = _____

Section 8:   Number Correct = _____; Number Incorrect = _____

Section 11:   Essay Score × .4 = _____;

                Total Correct + Essay = _____;   Total Incorrect = _____

_____ − (_____ ÷ 4) = _____
Total Correct + Essay   Total Incorrect   RAW SCORE B

Math & Reasoning:

Section 3:   Number Correct = _____; Number Incorrect = _____

Section 7:   Number Correct = _____; Number Incorrect = _____

Section 9:   Number Correct = _____; Number Incorrect = _____

                Total Correct = _____;   Total Incorrect = _____

_____ − (_____ ÷ 4) = _____
Total Correct   Total Incorrect   RAW SCORE C

Arriving at your Real Scores

Use the *Raw-to-Real Conversion Chart* below to obtain your Real Scores. Simply locate your three raw scores on one of the first two columns to obtain those three familiar numbers between 200 and 800. A perfect 800 on each of the three sections yields a perfect composite score of 2400, an outstanding achievement. A composite of 600, the minimum possible, still places you at a higher level than the tomatoes growing in your garden. And diligent perusal of the Study Guide will raise that score pretty quickly. (And don't forget to subscribe to the BSAT Question of the Day at BSATWorld.com.) So . . . with your Real Scores in hand, you now know where you stand.

Though maybe not. Because the BSAT Diagnostic Test is so short—consisting of a mere 60 questions—it is subject to random factors like luck and sunspot disturbances. In practice this means that, on any given day, a cretin could pull down a 2310, while a card-carrying Mensa blow-hard could take a 1250 acid bath. In fact, a bottle-nosed dolphin we know by the name of Ace rocked a 2400 his first time out.

"Why don't you guys just make the test more reliable?" you may wonder. Because at the BSAT we believe that even reliability itself is not all that reliable. The truth is, life is a raw deal and a cold douche. And the sooner you stop pleasuring yourself with illusions like fairness, merit, and hard work, the better.

Raw-to-Real Conversion Chart

Raw Score A	Raw Scores B & C	Real BSAT Score
0 to 1.5	0 to 1.75	200
1.75 to 3.25	2 to 3.75	250
3.5 to 4.75	4 to 5.75	300
5 to 6.5	6 to 7.75	350
6.75 to 8.25	8 to 9.75	400
8.5 to 9.75	10 to 11.75	450
10 to 11.5	12 to 13.75	500
11.75 to 13.25	14 to 15.75	550
13.5 to 14.75	16 to 17.75	600
15 to 16.5	18 to 19.75	650
16.75 to 18.25	20 to 21.75	700
18.5 to 19.75	22 to 23.75	750
20	24	800

What Your Scores Mean

Now that you've got your BSAT scores, there are many exciting things you can do with them.

- You can frame them.
- You can fold them four ways and make a beautiful origami cootie catcher.
- You can send them to colleges where you're applying. (Good luck with that.)
- You can use them to gain invaluable insights about your future. Check out our predictive "How-I-Did vs. How-I-Will-Do" Chart below.

HOW-I-DID vs. HOW-I-WILL-DO CHART

200–299	Don't panic. A score this low does not (necessarily) mean a life of vile servitude. But you're going to need a great body. Join a gym. Now.
300–399	How to put this nicely? You basically lack the sense God gave geese. However, you may have automotive aptitude, but "body shop" only—nothing with moving parts. You may also have a future in a field involving blows to the head, like professional wrestling. The beauty of being in the 300s is that, should your career stumble, you don't have far to fall.
400–499	At this level, you're not exactly stupid, just kind of dense. Many options are open to you, few of them interesting. Consider TV traffic reportage, the beauty sciences, or international banking.
500–599	You landed smack in the middle of the BSIQ bell curve (right where the clapper is, which is why you find yourself surrounded by dingdongs). You're able to fool roughly half the people, but sadly, you can be fooled by the other half. However, just because you're crushingly average, you may not need to settle for an average career. Did you ever consider trampoline repair? Bounty hunting? Script continuity on a soap opera? Go for it.
600–699	Watch out—you're smart, but not that smart. The BSAT 600 Club is home to Nigerian email scammers, K Street lobbyists, and other members of the petty criminal classes. America has a GDP of $12.4 trillion. You've got enough smarts to get some appropriately tiny share of it. Just remember, the 700 Club eats the 600 Club for breakfast.
700–799	OK, hotshots, you're probably great at selling, cajoling, extorting—in short, getting your way. You can think on your feet, you have the gift of gab. You're qualified for the most demanding careers, including improv comedy and Somali pirate. Remember to always take the low road and life will be good to you.
800	You've risen to the top (where the scum always collects). You can do or be whatever you want. However, with your sky-high ability to hustle, you are most suited to the "undermining professions," such as arch-evildoer or revolutionary. Congratulations on admission to a very small club of quasi-uber-gods.

Learning from Your Mistakes

You've taken a big step forward. Don't feel bad if you missed a lot of questions. The very next part of this book is our get-smart-quick Study Guide. If you really blew the Diagnostic Test, we recommend that you also examine the Advanced Test-Taking Strategies in Appendix 1. Pay special attention to the sections on Cheating and Pharmacological Aids.

Beyond the Study Guide

Each question on the BSAT focuses with laser-like precision on a specific skill or intellectual function—such as logarithms, or the ability to visualize famous people stark naked. Therefore any question that you bungle is a wake-up call from your BSAT front desk, telling you where to concentrate your efforts. This table provides suggestions for supplemental study.

If you blew a lot of:	You should study:
Sentence Completions	*Mad Libs 25th Anniversary Bonanza Book*
Reading Passages	*Anything with writing on it—street signs, cereal boxes, all the books in the Library of Congress, whatever . . .*
The Essay	*Plagiarism for Dummies*
Improving Sentences/Paragraphs	*The Snoop Dogg Style Manual: My Flows Don't Suck*
Sentence Errors	*Badass Punctuation: Fucks Jerks and Shits*
Math Problems	*Alexander and the Terrible, Horrible, No Good, Very Bad Polynomial*
Analogies	*Kids Compare Things to the Darndest Other Things!*
Of General Interest:	*The Other 90%: How I Found the Rest of My Brain,* by Britney Spears *Retain More! Plaxico Burress Memorizes the 2002 San Antonio Phonebook*

In choosing a career, bear in mind that not all professions correlate with specific BSAT score ranges. For instance, doctors, lawyers, and academics are spread pretty evenly across the BSAT spectrum. Any asshole can be one. This is also true of rednecks, hypochondriacs, and saints. In other words, a high IQ is no guarantee of a high BSIQ.

Don't Forget the Answer Explanations

Finally, make sure to read the Answer Explanations, especially to the questions where you got schooled good. If you read an explanation twice and still don't understand it, let it go. Yes, you'll want to let a little air out of your ego. But, as noted elsewhere, stupidity is not the curse it's cracked up to be.

ANSWER EXPLANATIONS

SECTION 1: Sentence Completions

1. The key here is knowing a little bit about psychotics, your main context clue. For starters, psychotics don't usually go to the theater so cross off A) Hamlet. They do run for public office but seven is too young, so good-bye E) Congress. Forget B) bravery because although psychotics sometimes do things that seem brave, they're really just crazy. D) coprolalia is a really great word meaning dirty, filthy, disgusting language. But wait a second! Puppies don't understand English. So if you didn't already know that C) sadism is exactly what a little lunatic would inflict on a small animal, now you do. **Answer: C.**

2. Context clue: Alvin is shrieking, which suggests "PU" rather than "mm mm." That eliminates all positive smells: A) daffodils, C) fresh and clean and D) better, better, better. Answer E) familiar old shoes could conceivably smell nasty, but would they provoke a shriek? No. That leaves B) like something died. **Answer: B.**

3. The big context clue is deeply suspicious, which suggests that whatever these heads of state bring along is for the prevention of treachery. Like D) attempted poisoning. **Answer: D.**

4. Here's a Rocky Road problem—it's all about logic. (See Study Guide, Chapter 4.) Each answer appears to be an exciting new chapter in Grace's development. String them together, one after another, and you get a vivid portrait of a young, intellectual sex addict. **Answer: E.**

5. OK, dirty laundry could only behave as in B or E if our freshman were on acid. As for A, let's get real: B.O., no matter how strong, cannot set off the carbon monoxide detector. And even the scuzziest underpants aren't in the same league as a real D) biohazard, like anthrax. So that leaves C) his roommate moved into a hotel. **Answer: C.**

6. Reality evaluation time. Let's think: What might Ursula get an occasional case of? There's no such thing as a "case" of D) voodoo. A case of B) Ebola is fatal, something you only get once, not occasionally. That narrows it down to A, C, or E. A case of C) Budweiser, is a lot, even for Ursula. And since by now you may have an idea of what she does for a living, you know that for Ursula, A) mistaken identity is a lot less likely than E) crabs. **Answer: E.**

SECTION 2: Reading Passage

1. Any of these answers except B and D would make sense to a foreigner with say, three years of English instruction. Only in the fourth year would he learn that "he pressed his suit" just meant D) He tried to get laid. **Answer: D.**

2. Let's see . . . Transvesta boinked Dildo. Chlamydia was married to a guy who didn't boink Dildo. Pretty thin relationship. In fact, nothing there. **Answer: E.**

3. Once you rule out any jellyfish-related answers, your knowledge of Greek pottery (which is basically pornography you can drink from) should quickly lead you to all the remaining choices—every one of them size-based. **Answer: E.**

4. Notice that "disporting," contains the word "sport," as in "having fun." So what did this girl named Dildo do for fun? Don't guess—it must be supported by the text. Since there's no specific text to suggest B) wrestling, C) biathalon, or D) watching DVDs, just go with the general E) enjoying Greek life. **Answer: E.**

5. From reading the passage and the footnotes,* you now know quite a lot about King Mediocrates and Greek things, like, for example, A) Vestal Virgins, B) Catamites, C) Hoplites, D) Change You Can Believe In . . . oops. How'd that get in there? **Answer: D.**

* Always read the footnotes.

SECTION 3: Mathematics

1. If you wanted to do this right, you'd use algebra, setting up and solving the following simultaneous equations, where P is the priest's current age, and M is Mikey's:

$$P - 24 = 4 \times (M - 24)$$

$$M = \frac{1}{2} \times P$$

If these equations make you nauseous, try the Low Road. First of all, C and D are wrong because altar boys aren't 2 or 21 years old. As for E, the number π is irrational. If you think that's the answer, so are you. That leaves just A) 12 and B) 13, both nice altar boy ages. Let's try "plugging in" *A) 12*. If Little Mikey was 12, then Father O was 4 × 12 = 48 and so today he's 48 + 24 = 72. And today Mike must be 12 + 24 = 36. And since 36 is indeed $\frac{1}{2}$ of 72, we're done! Little Mikey was 12 and the pederast prelate is going up the river. Amen. Answer: A.

2. For gravity to do the rest of the job, Richie has to get just the <u>front</u> wheel of Leo's chair past the edge of the cliff, not the rear one. That distance is 39 feet <u>minus</u> the 18" ($1\frac{1}{2}$ feet) separation of the wheels, or $37\frac{1}{2}$ feet. The circumference of a circle is π times the diameter. Here, the radius of the rear wheel is 12" (1 foot) and the diameter is therefore 2 feet. So each full rotation of the wheel takes Leo 3.14 × 2 feet = 6.28 feel closer to his destiny. Now do some plugging in. 5 rotations won't do it: 5 × 6.28 = 31.4 feet—not far enough. But 6 works: 6 × 6.28 = 37.68 feet, or just over $37\frac{1}{2}$ feet. Bon voyage, Leo. **Answer: C.**

3. This is an old-fashioned logic puzzle originally having to do with a fox, a chicken, some grain, and a rowboat. We prefer brew, bros, and babes. There's a simple trick: Just keep Steve away from the keg and Monique. That means the goal of the first trip must be to get Steve away from trouble:

> Trip 1. Jim takes Steve back to the dorm and leaves him there.
> Trip 2. Jim returns to the liquor store carrying nothing.
> Trip 3. Jim brings either the keg or Monique back to the dorm.
> Trip 4. For the return trip, Jim throws Steve into the Miata (keeping him out of trouble).
> Trip 5. Jim leaves Steve at the liquor store and takes whatever's left (either Monique or the keg) to the dorm.
> Trip 6. Jim returns to the liquor store carrying nothing.
> Trip 7. Jim finally brings Steve to the dorm to stay.

That's 7 trips. Having a friend like Steve cost Jim at least two extra trips and a lot of thinking. Let that be a lesson to you. **Answer: E.**

4. First, notice that the costs of the various nose jobs are all very far apart. That should suggest estimating. So Lucy makes *around* $7.50 an hour × 20 hours a week = *around* $150 per week. But remember, she loses 15% to taxes, so make that *around* $125 per week. She's got 182 weeks left. Round that to 200 and multiply:

200 weeks × $125 = $25,000

(If you were an obsessive who wants the exact answer, your calculator would give you $23,205.) Lucy can get any nose she wants. She could even buy herself 2 East Hamptons plus a Kansas City and have change left over! But what would she do with them? **Answer: A.**

5. First figure out how long 11,500 volts takes to fry you. Try making a simple graph (see below). Notice how at 11,500 volts you're done in 12 minutes. Therefore any time between midnight and 12:12 a.m. Mr. Spitt would remain in this world, although kind of smoky in the later minutes. So now you realize that A, B, C, and D are all too late. But if you'd been clever enough to note that we're in Texas, you already knew he was toast. **Answer: E.**

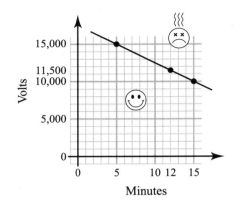

6. If you're offended by this question, get over it. The question writer is hoping to make you mad and thereby fuck you up. Don't fall for it. Use that anger to figure out the total volume of stone to be cut.

   From the Math Facts you know the volume of any pyramid $= L \times W \times H \times \frac{1}{3}$.

   So Tsurris will need $120 \times 120 \times 100 \times \frac{1}{3} = 480{,}000$ cubic cubits of stone.

   How many Israelite man-years will that take to cut and schlep?

   Since one Isrealite cuts 8 cubic cubits per year, it will take $\frac{480{,}000}{8} = 60{,}000$ man-years.

   If it's spread out over 15 years you need just $\frac{60{,}000 \text{ man-years}}{15 \text{ years}} = 4000$ Israelites.

That's a lot of schlepping. **Answer: C.**

7. If he can focus for a moment, even the 10 joint-per-day guy can see that his graph line is the one with the little (they aren't actually moving around) triangles. Three months is around 90 days, right? So just look at the triangle above the 90 and see on the vertical axis how many brain cells are left. Around 35, right? But remember—that's in *billions*. (Just plain 35 would be very bad news.) The answer is 35 billion, which is bad *enough* news. Mr. Demaroni will be showing *Reefer Madness* next class. **Answer: B.**

8. If you extend the 20 JPD line to where it seems to want to go, it looks like you end up with about *minus* 20 billion brain cells, and therefore, a -20 IQ, answer E. But what is a *negative* IQ? Maybe Mr. Demaroni has been blowing a little Marrakesh Mellow himself. **Answer: E.**

9. If you're a Minority you may be familiar with this type of problem. You will immediately realize that your job is to figure out how long each trip lasted, add them together, and then subtract that sum from the total round trip of 60 seconds.

   The first trip is Racists running at 20 feet per second from point A to point B:

   $T_1 \times 20 \text{ ft/sec} = 660 \text{ ft}$
   $T_1 = 33 \text{ sec}$

   Second trip, back to point A:

   $T_2 \times 30 \text{ ft/sec} = 660 \text{ ft}$
   $T_2 = 22 \text{ sec}$

Since $T_1 + T_2 = 55$, the time between trips is 5 seconds (60 − 55 = 5). Since that's an awfully long time to stand there staring at disaster, answer D may seem right. But B is the more specific answer, and therefore correct. Choice E is charming but too goofy. **Answer: B.**

SECTION 4: Improving Sentences

1. The original sentence leaves the strong impression that Natalie has been neutered like a stray cat rather than having had her car repaired. D and E also partake of this idiotic notion. And the meeting has not been "fixed," like some horse race, as in C. So it's got to be . . . **Answer: B.**

2. The original sentence *A) Ain't no sunshine when she's gone* is like a delicious soup prepared by a world-class chef. To alter one word of this sentence would be like pissing in a world-class soup. So don't. **Answer: A.**

3. This poisonous brew mixes together <u>three</u> metaphors: cream of the crop, inoculation, and stepping on your own dick. Answers B and E persist with the madness, while C is just randomly inane. D gets us down to one only slightly far-fetched metaphor. It's the best you're going to get. **Answer: D.**

4. You're being asked to "improve" the lyric of the Chanukah classic, "The Dreidl Song." We strongly recommend that you leave this one alone, unless you want the great and terrible God of the Old Testament to smite you. That would hurt. **Answer: A.**

5. This sentence qualifies as AMAZING. But could it be even more AMAZING? We say yes! So let's have a sophisticated discussion about balance and tone. If your sentence already has two instances of "motherfucker" in it, should you add a third? A fourth? At what point might you have too much of a good thing? Let's work backward: *E) gun*, doesn't work; it's just anti-climactic and boring. D, with its back-to-back motherfucking motherfucker, feels like too many motherfuckers, while C, though strong, feels like too few. B is the Goldilocks scenario—just the right number of motherfuckers. **Answer: B.**

SECTION 5: Improving Paragraphs

1. This is a trick question. It becomes ludicrously easy if you ask yourself which of these words denotes an actual *feeling* (as opposed to an adjective that happens to end in "ous")? Only *envious* qualifies. **Answer: B.**

2. The author has employed too many "ofs." Answers B, C, and E all solve that problem but pile on extra baloney about kids, devotion, Aunt Trudy, etc. When improving a sentence, always choose the one that's just like the original, only better, and without a lot of extraneous shit. **Answer: D.**

3. At first blush, this question appears highly subjective. Sure, bring on the hot young wives, wow, I LOVE that font, etc. But the truth is, those are just frills. What about improving the actual text? Your choice is between *A) It's perfect as is* and *C) Fewer instances of "Dad says."* But when you get rid of those Dad-sayses, it turns out this kid has nothing to say. So never mind. **Answer: A.**

SECTION 6: Reading Passage Pair

1. This passage asks you to draw global conclusions, which may have you saying, "Shit, you mean I have to read this whole passage?" Yes, you do. But it's only 12 lines long, for Chrissakes. And every one of those lines is a cry of protest against her father's Facebook presence. **Answer: B.**

2. This question is much more specific than the previous one. In fact, the answer is perched on line 26, staring up your nostrils. **Answer: D.**

3. There's certainly a lot of yelling and complaining from both authors. Why? What can have dismayed them both? Botched wax jobs? Heavy periods? Or could it be the clowns who are ruining their young lives? **Answer: A.**

4. We already know from the text that B and C are Unintelligent Designs. And A seems like a no-brainer, in every sense. So, of D and E, which design is <u>more</u> unintelligent? Would it be *E) the Large Hadron Collider*, the most sophisticated piece of machinery ever built by mankind? Or would it be that ill-considered, politically motivated, bureaucratic clusterfuck known as *D) the Department of Homeland Security*? **Answer: D.**

5. You worked so hard to understand all about the Large Hadron Collider that we'd now like to reward you with a little party favor, a freebie hiding in plain sight on line 20. **Answer: D.**

SECTION 7: Analogies

1. Test sentences:

> People with Alzheimer's say "whatchamacallit" a lot.
>
> People with ------- say "goddamfuckingcocksucker" a lot.

That would be a textbook diagnosis of . . . **Answer: C. Tourette's**

2. Test sentences:

> <u>Clangers</u> is a rude nickname for <u>testicles</u>.
>
> ------- is a rude nickname for <u>breasts</u>.

Try all the answers, one by one. It's really fun and they ALL work. Especially nabba-nacka-wappers. **Answer: E. all of the above**

3. Test sentences:

> <u>Spirit</u> is a robot with a companion robot named <u>Opportunity</u>.
>
> <u>R2D2</u> is a robot with a companion robot named -------.

Never mind that Sentence 1 is real robots and Sentence 2 is movie robots. A robot is a robot. **Answer: E. C3PO**

4. Note that it's irrelevant that sanctimonious assholes drive Priuses or, for that matter, that arrogant assholes drive Hummers. Instead, focus on the test sentences:

> <u>Drop</u> is the tiniest step toward <u>bucket</u>.
>
> <u>Prius</u> is the tiniest step toward -------.

Careful here. *A) global warming* is the problem, not the goal we're taking a step toward. That goal would be . . . **Answer: B. energy independence**

5. Test sentences:

> <u>School</u> is an institution that often feels as bad as <u>prison</u>.
>
> <u>Marriage</u> is an institution that often feels as bad as -------.

The two feel-bad candidates are *D) a bullet to the head* or *E) root canal*. But how to choose? Just pick the one that seemed like a good idea at the time but now goes on and on forever WITH NO WAY OUT AND MAKES YOU WANT TO SCREAM, "DEAR GOD, PLEASE LET IT END!" **Answer: E. root canal**

6. Test sentences:

> When your intention is to <u>belch</u>, but some solid material accidentally comes along for the ride, you <u>vomiburp</u>.

> When your intention is to <u>fart</u>, but some solid material accidentally comes along for the ride, you -------.

In case you didn't know, "gutchies" means underpants, in Pittsburgh. **Answer: A. fudge your gutchies**

SECTION 8: Identifying Sentence Errors

1. Faulty idiom. We distinguish one thing <u>from</u> another, not one thing <u>and</u> another. Even Suckups and Titwringers. **Answer: D.**

2. Um, if you had, like, to pick one "like," um, which one would you, like, pick? It's like they're all, like, the same. You know, alike. **Answer: E.**

3. Adjective vs. adverb. <u>How</u> exactly did Mrs. Mellon look at the boys? Differently. And how did they look at her? Hornily. That's what adverbs are all about. **Answer: D.**

4. Faulty diction. "Insofar as" means "to the extent that." "Because" is a better choice. Or, if you insist on being all fancy, "inasmuch as." (By the way, the rabbi's kids call the bird Wanker.) **Answer: A.**

5. This is a fine example of correct Fortune Cookie English. Adding extra words like "the" and "a" would just screw it up. Don't mess with a winning formula. **Answer: E.**

6. Faulty diction. "Barbarian," when used as an adjective, refers to actual barbarians—like Attila the Hun or Genghis Khan. OTOH, when you act <u>like</u> a barbarian, for instance, harpooning chickens, the proper adjective would be "barbaric." Neither would be a good adjective to describe Babar the Elephant, who is gentle. **Answer: B.**

7. Verb agreement problem. A milling horde, whether of skeevy skanks or bodacious beauties, is singular. So, although the skanks (plural) <u>were</u> disappointing, the horde <u>was</u> disappointing. Better luck next time, guys. **Answer: D.**

8. Nothing wrong here . . . except zombies in the voting booths. **Answer: E.**

SECTION 9: Mathematics

1. This is a straightforward function problem that happens to involve brutally abusing a cute puppy. Don't let that get in your way.

Notice that the first operation performed on the puppy is putting an arrow through his little head, so eliminate any answer with no arrow. Goodbye, B) (puppy-in-a-cauldron) Next, there has to be a hole made by the pistol shot. Out go A) (stupid graphic puppy) and C) (shishkebab puppy), leaving just D and E. Choice E can't be right, because there's some sort of puppy duplication thing going on and anyway all three heads seem firmly attached. And we're still missing the axe/decapitation function. The only correct answer can be D: (separated single head, with arrow, plus bullet hole in the chest). Nice puppy. **Answer: D.**

2. This one should be easy, even if you're as wrecked as Cheech and Chong on Grace Slick's birthday, which is about how wrecked Scout Troop 188 is.

Check it out, man, the weed and the bong constitute what percentage of the whole score?

> 74% + 18% = 92%? Right on, bro.

So what percentage of the stash is $21.60, dude? 100% − 92% = 8%? Groovy!

Finally $\dfrac{\$21.60}{.08} = \$270.00$ Oh wow, man!

Out–f–ing–rageous!! **Answer: C.**

3. This is easy, no tricks. Just add them up, all the ear, nose, tongue, lip, and brow piercings for all the girls—total 48. **Answer: C.**

4. We have to average the number of rings of the other four girls. Rhea 6 + Sela 2 + Tania 13 + Valda 7 = 28. Divide by 4 girls to get the average of 7. Uma has 20 piercings by herself, which is 13 more than the average. That's a lot of empty holes. **Answer: C.**

5. Jim is offering Stacy what *looks* like a valid syllogism, a three-step piece of logical reasoning. However, Stacy pictures Jim's syllogism as a Venn diagram:

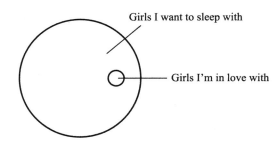

Jim's statement describes only the smaller circle. But Stacy knows that although she falls into the larger circle, there's only a tiny chance she's also in the smaller one.

A) specious means plausible but false, *B) phallusy* is a pun combining words for fallacy (a falsehood) and phallus (penis), *C) an elegant syllogism* is what Jim's reasoning isn't, and *D) Socrates* is a famous ancient Greek philosopher who loved to disprove faulty reasoning. Jim is screwed, but not in the way he was hoping. **Answer: E.**

6. Don't let the "plain extra-large" pie slice confuse you. This is a condoms-in-the-cookie-jar problem, not a pizza problem. Ribbed condoms make up 45% of the total number x, or $.45x$. The Flavored are $.25x$. The difference is the answer:

$$.45x - .25x = .2x = \frac{1}{5}x = \frac{x}{5}. \textbf{ Answer: C.}$$

7. Reminder: Start by eliminating the obviously moronic answers, like C and its idiot sidekick, D. The key to this problem lies in the idea of "half-life." We know that each hour Jose guzzles brew he cuts his STP concentration by half. Starting with 16,000 times the legal limit, simply count how many times you divide by 2 until you get to less than 1 times the legal limit. Write it down—you know: 16,000 / 8,000 / 4,000 and so on. The answer is 14, maybe 15 to be safe. That many hours earlier than 11 a.m. on Saturday means around 8 p.m. on Friday. So *A) Friday at midnight* is too late but *B) Friday at 8* seems OK. But what about E? And what happened to Jose's urine samples? That bumbling old team doctor. Still, Jose should play it safe. **Answer: B.**

8. The quickest way to solve this problem is to put yourself in the girls' mindset:

"OK, so like ignore answer C about Camille and that long straight hair thing . . . OMG . . . if she doesn't shut up about it no one's going to talk to her. Puh-leeeese! But anyway Camille's really really popular (if you ask me, I don't know why). Answer D is *so* wrong, because you can see right away that Camille's *more* than like three times as popular as Brittany because she's already three times as popular as Desiree who we know is much more popular than Ashley or Brittany. (But those two are so *not* popular, I can hardly tell them apart.) So it comes down to A and B. My head hurts! I think it's B. No wait . . . E. No, B." **Answer: B.**

Note: You may be annoyed that this problem perpetuates stereotypes about shallow girls who don't like math. Would you feel better if we told you that these are actually boys with weird names who call each other "she"?

9. Region C is the set of students who finished freshman year claiming to be virgins, but who did not, in fact, begin the year as virgins. What in the world can explain that situation? Here's a list of possible explanations: Forgetting, lying, re-installing virginity, or holy intervention. What do you know? Those exactly correspond to A, B, C, and D! By elimination, **Answer: E.**

SECTION 10: Reading Passage

1. Unfortunately, as in many ALL / EXCEPT questions, the answer depends on the kind of detailed knowledge of the text that you can only get by actually reading. For instance, if you just skim, you might easily imagine reading something about an undescended testicle, when, in fact, you hadn't. **Answer: C.**

2. "Drawing and quartering" is a medieval torture in which each limb of the victim is tied to a different horse. At the signal, each horse gallops off in a different direction. The probability of this happening today is so vanishingly small as to be in the "crock of shit" range. **Answer: E.**

3. You're looking for the one title in this list that wouldn't make your mother uncomfortable (though it might make you gag), the one song that could have been recorded by The Singing Nun in 1966. Right. **Answer: D.**

4. Consider the possibilities one by one. A? No. The only "sound advice" Scottie ever gave was to turn it up to 11. B? No. Remember, "the next stage" included the rock opera *Things to Do With Broken Glass*. C? No. Though Scottie *was* infantile, he was also a danger to infants. D? No. The author's only area of expertise appears to be free-basing, which leads us to the correct answer, E. In line 40, he even admits it. Mystery solved! **Answer: E.**

PART III

THE STUDY GUIDE—
CLEANING UP THE MESS
IN YOUR HEAD

CHAPTER 1

BASIC TEST-TAKING SKILLS

What to Bring on Test Day—We hope you understand, don't you, that no one actually administers the BSAT . . . yet. But on that glorious day when they do, we'll recommend bringing:

a cell phone or Blackberry (life includes Google—why shouldn't the BSAT?)

4 Ticonderoga #2 pencils (they must be #2—we don't know why)

Twinkies, Tic-Tacs, or other nourishment

calculator

meds (see section on pharmacological aids)

bottle of water

airsick bag

astrolabe or autoharp (your choice)

 No one legitimate will ever ask you your PIN# while you're taking the BSAT!

Bubbling In—We won't insult you by telling you how to fill in little ovals with neat black pencil marks. We have more creative ways to insult you. For example, *"Cazzo vai via, stronzo, e scopa tua mamma!"* *

Guessing—The BSAT, just like the SAT, awards you 1 point for a correct answer and subtracts ¼ point for a wrong answer. A blank gets a zero. Just trust us that this formula makes blind guessing yield exactly the same score as taking a nap.

 OTOH . . . Napoleon was once asked whether he preferred his generals to be courageous or brilliant. His answer: Neither. He preferred them *lucky*. So if you are the kind of person who consistently wins at three-card Monte on the street, feel free to ignore our advice.

That said, guessing remains one of the sharpest arrows in your quiver. There are three types of guesses:

a. *Educated guess*—to be used when you understand the question and have a good reason to eliminate one or more answers. (See the Process of Elimination section below.) NOTE FOR MORONS: We mean a *good* reason—not just because you're a Capricorn and "Capricorns are very intuitive."

b. *Uneducated guess*—when you don't understand the question, but you're still able to spot one or more stupid answers to cross off. Lucky for you, the BSAT is full of stupid answers, like "D) I'll get back to you on this one" or "B) the square root of 'suck on this!'"

c. *Wild guess*—a.k.a. "pulling it out of your ass"—always a bad idea. Your ass is no place to be looking for answers. If you have no clue, move on. If you keep finding yourself in this position, you might as well go ahead and take that nap.

In real life one is constantly called upon to make important decisions without having enough information. Which leaves you no choice but to guess. In fact, the world belongs to the really good guessers, those who make great decisions while hardly knowing anything at all! And the best guessers are masters of **Process of Elimination, or POE.**

POE Is your Friend! POE is a miraculous PROCESS in which you ELIMINATE possible answers, one by one, using whatever criteria make sense to you at the time. This tool is BY FAR the most powerful implement hanging from your Test Day toolbelt. You won't believe the results.

SCENARIO	OUTCOME
Best case	You eliminate all answers but the correct one. Slam dunk!
Next best case	You eliminate some, but not all, wrong answers—it's progress.
Worst case	You end up more confused than before. (Rare.)

* *"Get outta here you jerk and go (have relations with) your mother!"*

EXAMPLE:

Which of the following countries was involved in the Thirty Years' War?

A) Narnia

B) Bermuda

C) France

D) Oz

E) Turkmenistan

POE in action:

FIRST, eliminate countries that are imaginary. Say good-bye to *A) Narnia* and *D) Oz*.

NEXT, eliminate any country that, though real, is basically nothing but a Club Med with its own police force. Good-bye *B) Bermuda*.

FINALLY, eliminate countries that are less than 30 years old, like *E) Turkmenistan* (formed, as we all know, when the old Soviet Union broke apart in 1990).

Observe the power of POE: Having not a clue about the Thirty Years' War, you have arrived at the correct answer: *C) France*. Use POE early and often!

SENTENCE COMPLETIONS

In Standardized Testville, Sentence Completions are mysteriously placed under the heading of Critical Reading. Why is it even called *Critical Reading*? Maybe because in order to complete the sentences, you must both *read* and be *critical* at the same time, as if that were some amazing feat, like singing "Stairway to Heaven" while mouthing the words to "Fathers Be Good to Your Daughters." In our opinion, you bring off more impressive feats of multi-tasking every time you text your best friend while carrying on a conversation with your other best friend while watching reruns of *The Simpsons* while updating your blog. But we'll let it go.

The concept of the Sentence Completion is jackass-simple. You're asked to read a sentence that has a blank or two in it and to determine from the context what word or phrase goes in the space. Being aware of your context is always a good survival skill, like keeping your finger on the button of your pepper spray when you walk through South Central at 3 a.m.

A Typical Sentence Completion:

> Given the severity of the snowstorm, it's not surprising that they decided to close the -------.
>
> A) pageant with Hava Nagilah
> B) Panama Canal
> C) open wound before his liver froze
> D) schools
> E) casinos and bars

The sentence will always contain some *context clue* that enables you to zero in on the right answer. In this case, the context clue is: the severity of the snowstorm. Whenever there's a severe snowstorm, what's the first thing they close? (Hint: casinos never close.) Right: *D) schools.*

BSAT Sentence Completions come in two flavors. Let's call them Plain Vanilla and Rocky Road. With Plain Vanilla, we're mainly testing your vocabulary strength. Rocky Road is richer, but also harder to digest; here, we're testing your powers of logic (sometimes topped with Plain Vanilla vocab sprinkles).

Plain Vanilla

Your success on these will depend on knowing what words actually mean (as opposed to how cool they sound in rap songs). But even if your vocabulary contains fewer words than a Cro-Magnon phrase book you can sail through Sentence Completions with flying colors—if you use a little common sense and POE.

Example: The wino passed out in a ------- puddle of his own

regurgitant.

A) brazen

B) malodorous

C) legendary

D) mellifluous

E) superchunky

The major context clues here are <u>wino</u> and <u>regurgitant</u>. Does the word "regurgitate" sound familiar? If no, see the ADVICE TO MORONS sidebar on this page. If yes, then you should entertain the idea that <u>regurgitant</u> may be a noun meaning "vomit." Now consider your options: *E) superchunky* is not a good choice because winos don't eat much solid food. Caution: *D) mellifluous* is a tricky word. It has nothing to do with fluid. It refers to a pleasing sound—probably not retching. Only an idiot would call a puddle *C) legendary* and only a *brazen* idiot would fail to notice the word "odor" in *B) malodorous*, the correct answer. Drunken vomit smells bad (as you'll learn if you end up at a party school).

ADVICE TO MORONS
What if you barely understand any of the words in a problem? First, try plugging in any words you *do* understand. If none of them fits, just pick a word from among the ones you *don't* understand, using either "eeny, meeny, miney, mo" or "one potato, two potato." Do not use "rock/paper/scissors," (too slow) or "A . . . my name is Alice", (for jumping rope only).

Rocky Road

In logic-oriented Sentence Completions, the words are rarely difficult, but the ideas may be. In fact, slogging through all the possible answers of a Rocky Road can be more work than pulling a hamster through a trombone. Example:

We out-of-staters can no more understand the pride Wisconsinians take in their cheese than we can imagine -------.

A) what Michael Jackson sees when he looks in a mirror

B) the joy Icelanders take in their National Penis Museum

C) the instructions Donald Trump gives his barber

D) Winston Churchill as a baby

E) A, B, or C.

The context makes it clear that the blank must be filled with something that's almost impossible for most people to imagine, like *drowning in your own saliva* or *peace in the Middle East*. Of the answers provided, there's only one that's *not* impossible to imagine: *D) Winston Churchill as a baby* (for the simple reason that he looks like a baby in every photo ever taken of him). So the answer must be all of the other three, which is *E) A, B or C.*

Let's Get Systematic!

We've devised a handy-dandy mnemonic acronym that will systematize the process of solving Sentence Completions. We call it: UGLY.

  U Underline the context clues.
  G Give an answer of your own.
  L Look at the given answers and compare.
  Y You're done. Move on.

It is quite common to freak out while you're taking a test that's critical to your parents' willingness to continue subsidizing your leisure. Get a grip.

Let's go though the steps one by one.

U - Underline Context Clues

Let's explore a Sentence Completion for context clues:

> The Admissions Director was confused by the
> discrepancy between the ------- tone of Amy's application to
> Holy Union Seminary and the ------- flavor of her
> Facebook page, particularly the area titled "Hot Hunks I
> Have Known (in the Biblical Sense!)."
>
> A) lofty . . humble
> B) pious . . saucy
> C) off-beat . . purple
> D) creepy . . vanilla
> E) awful . . awful

What are the clues from the context? Let's try underlining them. Remember: Make a big mess. In ink.

> The Admissions Director was confused by the <u>discrepancy</u> between the ------- tone of <u>Amy's application to Holy Union Seminary</u> and the ------- flavor of her Facebook page, particularly the area titled "<u>Hot Hunks I Have Known</u> (in the Biblical Sense!)."

There are two blanks to fill in. And the three context clues should lead you to expect a "discrepancy" between a seminary application and a hot Facebook page. Now look at the answers, trying to find two that go together like Ozzy Osbourne and the Wizard of Oz (i.e., NOT).

Which of these adjectives describe the contrasting, discrepant elements? Only A or B, right? But A has a problem: While the seminary application might be *lofty*, the Hot Hunks part of it wouldn't be *humble*. However, B fits perfectly: Seminary applications are *pious* and a Hot Hunks tribute page would be *saucy* (i.e., hot and hunky) in tone.

G - Give Your Own Answer

Before you look at the answers, read the sentence and supply your own word or phrase—whatever pops into your head. Unless you're clairvoyant, this word or phrase will be wrong. But when you go through this exercise, you'll develop a strong sense of whether you're looking for a *positive* or a *negative* term, which turns out to be extremely helpful.

Create your own answer for the example below:

> When Winona burned down the school library, she was declared -------.

Winona did a bad thing (torching the library), so she was probably declared something fairly negative, like "Public Enemy Number One" or more pretentiously, *"non compos mentis"* (legally nuts). Or perhaps something as simple as "a troubled young woman" or "a real dud." Whatever floats your boat.

ADVICE TO MORONS

If you try the above exercise and come up with nothing, try saying "spoogie spoogie spoogie." Or maybe "Gort! Klaatu barada nikto!" During a real test, this will make you laugh and, if nothing else, distract your neighbors and lower their scores.

L - Look at the Given Answers and Compare

OK, what are the choices that are actually given to you? Are any of them negatives that coincide with your instinctive responses?

> When Winona burned down the school library, she was
> declared -------.
>
> A) soup du jour
> B) persona non grata
> C) potato au gratin
> D) vichyssoise
> E) potato non grata

With your criteria in mind—something negative and judgmental—there is only one candidate: *B) persona non grata*, which means "someone who is not welcome." If you don't know the meaning of that phrase, you can still get there by POE, simply by noting that all the other answers involve potatoes or soup or both, which is dumb.

Y - You're Done. Move On.

Obviously, we had a letter left over in UGLY and just put this one in to fill out our lame acronym. We now follow our own advice and move on.

Tune-up Sentence Completions

> EX1. Pandering shamelessly to its readers, *ADHD for Dummies* is
> composed of thousands of sentence fragments thrown
> together with no discernible -------.
>
> A) theological underpinnings
> B) organizing principle
> C) . . . oh look . . . a camel!
> D) social conscience
> E) chance of finding a publisher

Answer: This is Plain Vanilla and is easier if you know what ADHD is. Any book with "For Dummies" in the title probably doesn't need much in the way of *A) theological underpinnings* or *D) social conscience*. And since it's already been published, cross off E. You can toss *C) . . . oh look . . . a camel!* as a dumb joke from a writer who obviously does *not* have ADHD. Finally, *B) organizing principle*, is *exactly* what would be missing among all those sentence fragments if the book is pandering to its unfortunate . . . hey . . . wow . . . maybe it *is* a camel? No, no, settle down. **Answer: B.**

EX2. Biff wanted to ------- Steph, but not if it ------- Jeff.

    A) boff . . miffed

    B) miff . . meant boffing

    C) play rough with . . if it caused a rift with

    D) reassemble . . meant taking parts from

    E) A, B, or C

Answer: D makes no sense unless we're talking about Frankenstein's lab or the Jawas' robot scavenger transport from *Star Wars*, which we aren't. The rest of the answers all work fine in their own mellifluous, semi-poetic ways. **Answer: E.**

EX3. Meteorology aside, there is a vast difference between "Purple -------" and "Purple -------."

    A) Rain . . Haze

    B) Prose . . Poetry

    C) People Eaters . . Paper Hangers

    D) Magenta . . Amethyst

    E) ha ha . . strange

Answer: You don't have to know anything about music from the '60s or '80s to get this one right. *Meteorology* is the context clue. Which answer includes references to weather? Yes, only *A) Rain . . Haze*. The other answers try to distract you with lots of *Purple* references, but only A features its own five-day forecast. **Answer: A.**

EX4. After twelve drinks, George fumblingly ------- Martha's
------- and proclaimed "-------!"

    A) dialed . . cell phone . . I think I love you

    B) bound and gagged . . roommate . . I think I love you too

    C) unbuttoned . . blouse . . I thought Martha was in here
       somewhere

    D) rowed to . . Vineyard . . Where the fuck am I?

    E) Any of the above

Answer: This Rocky Roader is an example of the *multi-blank shaggy dog story*, a type of question found only on the BSAT. You're seeking the answer that yields a story that makes perfect sense. However, in this case, it turns out that none of them could be called wrong. That happens sometimes. **Answer: E.**

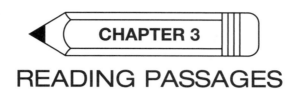

READING PASSAGES

Critical Reading passages on the BSAT resemble those found on the SAT or ACT, except they're shorter, punchier, and grosser. In a word, better.

Whenever you begin reading a passage, your first goal must be to answer the question "What the fuck is going on here?" That means figuring out the subject, which is usually reducible to a short sentence, like "Ambitious men have small peckers," or "Ballet is the new NASCAR racing," or "Secaucus, New Jersey, used to smell really nasty."

Next, you'll need to identify the author's personal slant on whatever is being discussed. For instance, if the subject is pecker size, might the author's thesis be self-serving? Might he have a small pecker that he is hoping will propel him to Napoleonic glory? Maybe he has a big pecker, which is his only consolation for being a loser. If the author is a woman, maybe she's writing simply to take revenge on a small-peckered jerk who ditched her. Or maybe she wants her own pecker. Or his. Get the idea? To better uncover the author's agenda, it may help to know a little about BSAT authors, as a group.

What Kind of Authors Write BSAT Passages?

Most BSAT authors are patently defective human beings—crabby, smug, vapid, egotistical, incontinent, you name it. And as you read the so-called work of these so-called authors, don't be afraid to judge them. They deserve it. In fact, whenever you start a passage, get into the habit of asking yourself a few useful diagnostic questions:

- Is this author an idiot?
- Is this author an asshole?
- Is this author nuts?

If the answer to any of these is "yes"—and it usually is—then you're going to want to use "creative skepticism," part of BSIQ. It's exciting and challenging to go head-to-head with this rogues' gallery—and just one of the many rewards of choosing the BSAT.

Occasionally an author will appear rational and delusion-free. That's nice, but don't let down your guard. Madmen are crafty. The price of 800s is eternal vigilance.

Why do you BSAT people hire these SAD MISFITS?
- SAD MISFITS work cheap.
- SAD MISFITS are more entertaining than real writers.
- SAD MISFITS make us feel superior. Which we enjoy.

Things to Do BEFORE You Read the Passage

Ascertain that the passage is in English, or at least, in a langwizzle you can understizzle. If it's not, you're either in the wrong room or you're having a stroke.

Read the blurb carefully. The blurb is that useful little paragraph *in italics* at the beginning of each passage. It contains tidbits like title, author, historical context, etc. The blurb, like POE, is your friend. Love the blurb.

Often the title will tell you the topic outright: "Invitation to a Three-Way," "The Metaphysics of Warner Bros. Cartoons," or "The Gamma Delta Kama Sutra." Other times you'll have to wait and see: "Mind Over Mama" or "Mice vs. Lice." Any clue? Didn't think so.

Likewise, the author's name and any biographical shards may reveal the passage's point of view. For instance, it could help enormously to know that the author is:

- a famous serial killer
- Geoffrey Chaucer
- a cross-dressing octogenarian gigolo
- Kurt Cobain's psychiatrist
- 10,000 rhesus monkeys with typewriters
- anonymous (loves piña coladas)

Scan the passage for structure. Look for places where the text divides itself into logical sections. Telltale clues: expressions like "Part One" or "First, let's consider the non-lubricated varieties." In the latter, chances are that the next section will take up lubricated varieties. That may be the end of it, or succeeding sections may take up flavors, textures, etc. Stay alert and you may figure out the whole structure without ever having to throw your brain into gear.

Read the questions *first.* That's right—before you read the passage. Here's a magic principle: Once you know the questions, then you know what you need to extract from the passage. Conversely, *until* you know the questions, you're just sucking in a bunch of bullshit *you hope* will be useful. But most of it won't be.

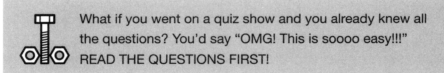

What if you went on a quiz show and you already knew all the questions? You'd say "OMG! This is soooo easy!!!"
READ THE QUESTIONS FIRST!

As you read the questions, put them in categories. Determine if the question is **specific** or **global**. A specific question asks for a small bit of information—a fact, a name, a definition. A global question asks you for a larger idea—a theme, a concept, a conclusion. The answers to specifics are often neatly confined to a line or two of the text, while global answers may be diffused through one or two paragraphs or, God forbid, the whole passage.

ADVICE TO MORONS
Skip global questions. Globals are looking for CONCEPTS, which are really hard for morons. Take the hit and move on.

The specific questions are easier. Answer them first. Be on the lookout for questions that are as pointed as a supermodel's hip. For instance, if the passage is entitled "Mr. Sperm's Journey," look for questions like "What is the third stop on Mr. Sperm's Journey?" Often they'll be asking for a definition, like "In line 6, what is meant by the Fallopian Regional Games?" That question may seem like Greek to you now but, as you read, one tiny factino can make the meaning drop into place. For example, it may turn out that Mr. Sperm is a strong swimmer who is training for both the 5-inch freestyle and the 8-inch medley relay at the Fallopian Regional Games. "Wow, that makes *so* much sense!"

Global questions can be a pain in the ass. Answer them last. Globals are tricky is because it's often hard to see how to cut those corners. Sometimes you just want to say, "Fuck it, I'll read the whole passage." Resist this temptation. Remember, unless you actually like books, *reading should be your last resort.*

Global questions come in a variety of forms. Some examples:

> "What is the LEAST offensive title for this passage?"

> "The author would probably be into all the following perversions EXCEPT -------.''

> "The author's attitude toward 'mayhem and pillage' can be characterized as any of the following EXCEPT -------.''

> "Which of the following most accurately explains why the hero wanted to take his grandmother to prom?"

> "In view of its contextual meaning in both passages, which of the following most nearly captures the spirit of the sentence 'Watch me crank dat Roosevelt, then super soak that ho'?"

Now You're Ready to Read the Passage.

No subject matter is off limits for BSAT passages, with the exception of children's letters to God, which are precious and private. Examples from recent tests:

- a page from the Victoria's Secret catalog
- two versions of "The Aristocrats" joke that were too filthy for the movie
- "The Eunuch's Tale" from *1001 Nights in Hezbollah Captivity*
- an excerpt from *The Da Vinci Code* encoded in C++
- a list of the most popular baby names of 1990

The scope is broad, so be ready for anything. Play hunches, jump to conclusions, try to read the author's mind, no matter how illegible it may be. Remember, the BSAT writers' thinking is often so sloppy that even *they* don't know what they're trying to say. (And that's *after* editing.)

 Never assume the author isn't full of shit.

Sample Passages

Short Passage

When a passage is this short, just go ahead and read it.

From the homepage of a popular Arabic language website:

> Vile infidel dog, may your father's mother fornicate with your mother's father and may their issue
> have testicles like dried raisins. May your gluttonous mother feed on fried pork rinds on the first
> night of Ramadan. May your bankrupt scum-worshipping civilization flay itself to ribbons with
> your evil flag, drenched in $500/barrel oil. And may the muezzin of death amplify this mandate
> (5) a thousandfold through the shitty sound system on his minaret.

What can you deduce about the author's mood and tone? A little angry, maybe? A tad judgmental, even confrontational? Feeling a little put upon, are we? Now let's look at the questions.

EX1. The tone of this passage is all of the following EXCEPT -------.

A) angry

B) judgmental

C) confrontational

D) put upon

E) generous

Answer: OK, this one's a gift to see if you were paying attention. Were you?

EX2. This passage is in the form of a -------.

A) limerick

B) dream

C) roast

D) birthday greeting

E) curse

Answer: The writer is addressing a vile infidel dog with a parallel string of increasingly hostile "suggestions," each one starting with "May." This bears all the earmarks of a curse. If you didn't pick up on the curse-like aroma, you may want to rethink the whole college thing.

EX3. With which of the following value judgments would the author most likely agree?

A) Jesus was a better prophet than Mohammed.

B) Beyoncé is a better singer than Mariah Carey.

C) Israel is a really cool place.

D) Fallujah is a more livable city than Carbondale, Illinois.

E) Separation of church and state is a good thing.

Answer: Given the likely profile of the author, the only possible answers here are B and D. Regarding *B) Beyoncé is a better singer than Mariah Carey.*: They're both awesome singers, but we have no way of knowing our jihadist's taste in music. On the other hand, *D) Fallujah is a more livable city than Carbondale, Illinois* at least seems more relevant—and you can be pretty sure the guy wouldn't feel so at home in Carbondale. So Fallujah beats Beyoncé with a stick. **Answer: D.**

A Pair of Short Passages

Read both passages, then answer the questions.

Passage 1:

From the introduction to The Extreme Hunting Sourcebook, *by Lt. Col. Rip Masters (Ret.):*

If you think that using grenades for big game hunting isn't sporting, I can tell you haven't tried it. The truth is that grenade hunting requires great skill, and shifts a lot of risk from the prey back onto the hunter. Think about timing: There are ten seconds between pin-pull and detonation. That pineapple spends most of it in the hunter's hand. Toss it a few milliseconds too early and your
(5) quarry is gone. Too late and your arm is gone. How about placement of the lob? There's nothing more discouraging than tracking a ten point buck all morning only to watch it splatter all over the foliage due to a careless overthrow.

Some say that technology is ruining the manly art of hunting, feminizing it with laser sights and high muzzle velocities. But as you browse this book I believe you'll come to realize that tech-
(10) nology is exactly what will save modern hunting. Tuna fishing with dynamite, duck hunting with RPG's, these are today's real sports.

Passage 2:

From the introduction to Lettuce Prey, *by Sindhra O'Rourke:*

Two years ago, while enjoying a health salad in the West Village, I suddenly became aware of the screams of agony arising from the iceberg lettuce I was chewing. My jaws were immediately par-alyzed with shame and self-recrimination. It was the last salad I ever ordered. I went home and tearfully gave the contents of my crisper a respectful burial in the back yard.
(5) As a simple matter of conscience, my diet now consists of nuts and only nuts. No fruits, no grains, and of course, no vegetables. There was a time when I, like 99 percent of the world, ate all of these "foods," suffused with vegan arrogance, willfully oblivious to the violence and pain my choices entailed. But all of that has changed.

If this book, an admittedly grim tour through the cruel mechanics of commercial lettuce grow-
(10) ing, accomplishes nothing else, I sincerely hope that it will sensitize the reader to the misery that permeates this nation's over-watered, over-fertilized "lettuce lots." Flora Consciousness is the key not only to curing this shocking situation, but also attaining a truly holistic, loving, and sustain-able relationship with the biosphere.

EX1. What is the MOST likely reason these two essays have been paired?

- A) The essays, taken together, make one wonder if censorship might be a good thing.
- B) They both present deeply felt points of view by thoughtful analysts.
- C) They both present deeply felt points of view by rabid zealots.
- D) Taken together, they present a balanced picture of how we get our food.
- E) They exemplify the yin and the yang, respectively.

Answer: The authors each present a strong, passionate argument for their respective lifestyles. Answers B or C address such "deeply felt points of view." But remember, "never assume the author isn't full of shit." And both of these authors clearly are. **Answer: C.**

EX2. What would be the likely result if Lt. Col. Rip Masters, the writer of the first passage, read the second passage?

- A) The colonel, realizing that vegetables feel pain, takes up veggie-hunting.
- B) The colonel, realizing that Sindhra O'Rourke feels pain, tortures him to death.
- C) The colonel asks Sindhra over for a cup of coffee.
- D) The colonel joins an ashram dedicated to the nutarian lifestyle.
- E) The colonel dies laughing, choking on his fresh venison hot-pocket.

Answer: What kind of person is Colonel Masters? Answers C and D are premised on his being sympathetic to the nutarian lifestyle. If this seems farfetched, which it totally does, you must choose between A, B and E. Eliminate A because the Colonel would hate veggie-hunting (not enough blood). And eliminate B because torture is way too low-tech for the Colonel. So by POE we are left E, where he chokes to death on his own venison. **Answer: E.**

EX3. In the first author's view, why do laser sights and high muzzle velocities feminize the sport of hunting?

- A) Because feminists have high muzzle velocities.
- B) Because real men would use flame-throwers.
- C) Because girls are much more into technology than guys.
- D) Because guys who use high tech gear also wear pantyhose for warmth.
- E) That's not his view. It's what is said by some misguided people.

Answer: It's right there in line 8: "Some say that technology is ruining the manly art of hunting, feminizing it . . ." When the answer is a gift, don't be afraid to take it. **Answer: E.**

A Long Passage

Now it gets tougher. Here is a hefty chunk of pseudo-intellectual drivel. See how many questions you can answer without actually having to read the passage.

This paper was delivered at the Northwest Symposium on Freakish Phenomena. The author, Dr. Sarah Schleppinger, is a philosophical anthropologist who specializes in the morality of the prurient.

Some taboos are culture-specific while others appear to be near universal. Compare cannibalism and incest.

The Korowai tribesmen of Western New Guyana think nothing of feasting on a juicy shank of spit-roasted enemy or dead-relative-liver-stew. Arguing that such practices are far from being in
(5) decline, Bemis speculates (*Journal of Cannibalism*, Vol. 8, 2006) that the growing availability of refrigeration has even fostered a surge in Micronesian cannibalism, now that the sultry climate is no longer an impediment to saving leftovers. Pirate cultures as recent as the 19th century record the lip-smacking, guilt-free consumption of "long pig." Western cultures deliver a surprisingly similar message: people eat people, whether out of necessity, like the Donner Party (The Donner
(10) Party Was No Party, Lippencott, 2008), or for sheer enjoyment ("Sweeney's Meat Pies Top Weekend B.O. Menu," *Daily Variety*, December 17, 2007).

Unlike cannibalism, incest is banned in almost every society, modern or ancient, eastern or western. Some quick examples will prove the point. The anonymous *Codex Eroticus* (from Cisalpine Gaul, c.215 BCE) says, "the amorous property owner is free to wander wherever his divin-
(15) ing rod may lead him, save into his mother's atrium." [Trans. by author] The Buddha's "seventh basket of deep thoughts" includes this remark to a troubled disciple: "I have shown you fourteen ways to become One with the Universe. Why do you need to be One with your Sister, too?" The plight of film auteur Woody Allen, who managed to gross out even Hollywood with merely "the perception of the appearance" of incest, underscores current sensitivities on the subject.

(20) There are noteworthy exceptions to the incest taboo, some of them pretty wild. For instance, although the Old Testament is generally in the "just say no" camp, there is the story of Lot's daughters, who can't get dates because all the cute boys in Sodom and Gomorrah have been brimstoned. These two high-spirited girls hit on the idea of getting their father drunk and "lying with" him (Genesis 19:30-38), which they do and nothing bad happens. In another example, Richard
(25) Wagner allows Siegmund and Sieglinde, his operatic brother and sister duo, to have it off in Act I of *The Valkyrie,* which produces a handsome but idiotic son, Siegfried, who ends up causing the apocalypse (*The Ring of the Niebelungen: Myths We Could Have Done Without,* Lefkowitz and Schwartz, 1994). Montrachet et al. (*Taboo Newsletter*, July 22, 2008) point out the common element in these two trespasses: Both take place in Imaginary Land. Therefore any resulting hemo-
(30) philia or feeble-mindedness is equally imaginary. But these are simply the exceptions that prove the rule, which Nietzsche summed up powerfully in his secret diary: "Niemand hat ein Mutterficker gern." ("Nobody likes a motherfucker." [Trans. by author])

Now we come to a conundrum, as observed by Wyznetsky (*Journal of the Highly Abnormal,*

(35) Vol. 34, 1996). It turns out that incest, while universally prohibited, is practiced much more than cannibalism, which turns out to be rare even among cannibals. For instance, the Yamchuuli of the Flamingo Islands eat each other only during the biennial Feast of the Atawaali (literally "twanger the size of an eggplant"). But there is a Yamchuuli website called www.flamyamwhambam.fla that features titillating videos depicting adolescent males having forbidden full-moon sex *(bombimbo)* with their mothers on a mat of *flatuulo* reeds. This is a very popular site among the Yamchuuli, get-

(40) ting over 3 hits per week. To further complicate the picture, V. Prawabala (*Journal of Savagery*, 2nd Quarter, 2007) has reported incidences of Bulaasi tribesmen fornicating with their relatives and then eating them (a practice dubbed "ingest"). In this case the culture-specific and the universal taboos collide and the result is just plain disgusting. And what about the even more disturbing practices of the Mii, who have been known to cook their relatives and then fornicate with them? Clearly

(45) the biologico-cultural axis of taboo taxonomy is in its infancy. More serious fieldwork will be required if we are ever to understand the complex mechanisms that rule our darker impulses.

Wow. This is a very dense and difficult passage. But before you bail, try putting the strategies we've been talking about into practice.

First, where is the author coming from? Obviously the blurb places her deep into geek territory. It also tells us that she specializes in "the morality of the prurient." Prurient means "inordinately interested in sex." Aha. We're now in possession of the key to Dr. Schleppinger's worldview.

Read the questions and categorize them as specific or global.

EX1. In line 7, what is meant by "impediment"?

A) triangular frieze above a colonnade
B) child molester
C) stimulus
D) obstacle
E) navel orange

Answer: The category is specific. So go to line 7 in the passage. This one's easy—just a few feeble traps to avoid here: *A) triangular frieze above a colonnade* is a pediment, not an impediment. Likewise, *B) child molester* is a pederast or pedophile, not an impediment. *C) stimulus* is the *opposite* of an impediment. However, *D) obstacle* is exactly what an impediment is, which renders *E) navel orange* moot. **Answer: D.**

EX2. In line 38, what is the best definition of "titillating"?

A) wobbling back and forth in pairs
B) suggestively exciting
C) orb-like
D) dressed in a dirndl
E) mammalian

Answer: Ah, another specific. From the BSAT List of Amazing Words (See p. 253), you know that "titillating" has nothing to do with tits. So eliminate all the obvious tit answers: *A) wobbling back and forth*, *D) dressed in a dirndl*, *C) orb-like* and *E) mammalian*. Thus, by POE, the correct answer is *B) suggestively exciting*, not because tits are indeed suggestively exciting, but because that's what "titillating" means. **Answer: B.**

EX3. According to the author, Lot's daughters had nothing to fear
from incest because -------.

A) their father used condoms
B) they were adopted
C) they were imaginary
D) it's in the Bible so it's OK
E) incest hadn't been invented yet

Answer: While not "line specific," this question can be answered by scanning for "Lot" and reading a few lines before and after. You'll find "Lot's daughters" down on line 21. Except that the answer doesn't really come till the end of the paragraph, on line 29, when Montrachet wryly observes that genetic defects are not nearly as devastating to people who are fictional. **Answer: C.**

Note that you've answered three questions without having to read the passage. But if you think you'll never have to read again . . . read on.

EX4. The best title for this passage would be -------.

A) Hot Bombino During the Atawaali
B) Ingest—The Raw and The Randy
C) Siegfried and Madonna: Dueling No-No's
D) The Biological-Cultural Axis of Taboo Taxonomy
E) News, Views, Blues, and Taboos

Answer: You know the passage is scholarly, simply from the citations and the turgid prose. So look for a title that is pretentious and semi-incomprehensible. *A) Hot Bombino During the Atawaali* is more than semi-incomprehensible, even for academia. On the other hand, *B) Ingest: The Raw and the Randy*, though offering that pretentious "Title: Subtitle" thing, is so pop-sounding it could be a gothic bodice-ripper. *C) Siegfried and Madonna: Dueling No-No's* is not only too informal, but a quick scan of the text fails to turn up any reference to Madonna. *D) The Biologico-Cultural Axis of Taboo Taxonomy* should set off your pretension detector, assuming you know that "taxonomy" means "classification" and not "limousine service." And the inappropriate catchiness of *E) News, Views, Blues, and Taboos* should further confirm that . . . **Answer: D.** And you *still* haven't had to read the passage.

EX5. The author would agree with all of the statements below
EXCEPT -------.

A) The Mii are even hornier than the Bulaasi.
B) The Donner Party's cannibalism was justified.
C) The Yamchuuli are a long way from Web 2.0.
D) Incest and Cannibalism are incredibly boring.
E) "Ingest" is no way to treat your mother.

Answer: Damn! These "all...EXCEPT" questions are the worst because you have to understand every possible response. Our bad. You may have to read this constipated crock-pot after all. See how annoying these long passages can be? All right, let's get started.

A) "The Mii are even hornier than the Bulaasi." Well, they'll fuck their relatives even *after* they've cooked them so, yes, that is some powerful lust. Got to agree.

B) "The Donner Party's cannibalism was justified." In line 9, the author says it was "out of necessity." So that's another check.

C) "The Yamchuuli are a long way from Web 2.0." If a popular Yamchuuli site gets three hits per week, they have yet to reach the IT tipping point. Agree.

D) "Incest and Cannibalism are incredibly boring." Wait wait wait—This author *loves* incest and cannibalism. The woman *lives* for incest and cannibalism. Does she find them boring? I think not. Ding, ding! A probable winner, but let's finish it out with….

E) "'Ingest' is no way to treat your mother." The lady *said* it was disgusting, so she agrees.

After all that, **Answer: D.**

IMPORTANT CHANGE OF POLICY: Children's letters to God are no longer off limits. We just received this actual child's letter to God. It's too hilarious not to share.

Dear God—

This letter is private, for Your Eyes only.

The doctor says Jimmy may never walk again. I have an idea. Maybe you could give my legs to Jimmy. Or even better, give Miranda's legs to Jimmy. She's been in a coma for 3 years and I don't think she'll notice. But if You decided to take my legs, could I have a wheelchair with a 5 horsepower motor and 3 speeds, like in the catalog?

Also, can You help us find my dog Othello's body so we can give him a decent burial? We don't know the exact section of the turnpike and all the roadkill looks the same.

Sincerely,
Little Chuckie

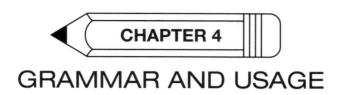

GRAMMAR AND USAGE

Shakespeare's reputation doesn't depend on his correct use of pronouns. And yours won't either. Even so, there are plenty of good reasons not to mangle your grammar.

1. Decent grammar leads to clear communication and minimizes screw-ups. Correct syntax (the rules of how to combine words and phrases) helps to ensure that your rock band's Stonehenge will end up 22 feet high, not 22 inches. Even using perfect English, you'll be misunderstood at least half the time, simply because nobody listens. If you make the situation worse by misplacing your modifiers and mixing your metaphors, your Stonehenge may never get built at all.

2. When you choose the wrong word, people get the wrong idea, not just about your message but about *you*. The idiom makes the idiot. You could end up a pariah just because you defended "the importance of *bondage* between a mother and child." Just because you objected to "some jerk *incinerating* himself into the conversation." Just because you think "comparisons are *odorous*."

3. Above all, here at the BSAT, bad grammar just pisses us off. So if pissing us off is your goal, now you know how. But *your* score suffers, not ours. On the other hand, we want you to express yourself with the bracing clarity of a bag of ice cubes poured down your underwear. We let a lot of grammar mischief slip by on the theory that struggling with fussy rules uses up energy better expended on making your ideas AMAZING. For instance, we don't give a rat's ass about speling. (That's why God invented Spellcheck.) Likewise, we're down with slang, and even words you just make up as you go along, like *garbaginous*.

Now we turn our attention to grammar and usage crimes, starting with misdemeanors and proceeding through felonies.

Sentences That Go On and On and On

These are sentences that string together clause after clause where you'd expect at least a comma or two to help you get your bearings instead of oh my god just rolling on like the mighty Mississippi until you think you're going to lose your mind and by the way don't get me started on another phenomenon which is at least as bad an infraction against good grammar. The fragment. Really not great.

Repetition That Says the Same Thing Twice

Here's an example, along with suggested improvements:

>Always a stickler for editorial economy, he ~~kept on sending~~ [sent] a continuous ~~and steady~~ stream of complaints ~~and criticisms~~ to the newspaper's Department of Redundancy ~~Department~~.

RULE OF THUMB: Once is usually more than enough. If we didn't want to hear it the first time, we certainly don't want to hear it again. However, sometimes repetition can be magnificent, bringing the emotion of a sentence to life:

>   She pestered me and pestered me and pestered me until finally I'm like, OK, chill!

Or:

>   Shit shit shit shit shit!!!

Adjectives That Think They're Adverbs

Wrong:

>   Come quick! The toilet is overflowing!

Right:

>   Come quickly! The toilet is overflowing!

Quick is modifying the verb, indicating the way in which you need to *come*. So it calls for the adverbial ending *–ly*.

Wrong:

>   The prisoner ain't reacting so good to the waterboarding.

Right:

>   The prisoner ain't reacting so *well* to the waterboarding.

Good needs to be in its adverbial form, *well*. It describes the verb *reacting*.

Learn the difference between an adjective and an adverb, or you're not going to do that awesome on this test.

The Late Great Past Participle

Compare "I drank too much" to "I have drunk too much." *Drank* is the simple past tense; *drunk* is the past participle. Don't confuse the two. (Also don't confuse with "I *am drunk* too much," the present inebriated.) Example:

>   You turn me on so much, baby, this is the third time I've came.

This is very wrong. But English teachers say things like this to their students every day. Clearly the past participle is headed for linguistic extinction. We'd stick up for this plucky little part of speech but, frankly, we've got more pressing concerns—global warming, Iran's nuclear ambitions, tomorrow night's Flashmob.

Parallelisms That Make Us Cross

When you have a list of items, it's good to express each item the same way. These are correct:

>   To die, to sleep, perchance to dream. (Hamlet)
>   Wishin' and hopin' and thinkin' and prayin'. (Dusty Springfield)

This one is not:

>   Far from being Mr. Right, Kevin would regularly pick his nose, clean out his earwax, and would
>   be constantly scratching his cooties.

Strict parallelism would call for "would regularly pick his nose, clean out his earwax, and scratch his cooties." (You don't need "constantly" because you've got "regularly.")

Although a list should be parallel, it should not be *boringly* parallel. Knowing how to spice things up often involves BSIQ. We like this sentence:

> He was FUCKED UP, with shit comin' outta his nose 'n shit, pickin' thru the garbage lookin' for his teeth 'n shit.

In fact, we *really* like this sentence. It's AMAZING. But what exactly makes it AMAZING? In this case, it's all about the repeated phrase *'n shit,* which knits the whole thing together and makes it *feel* somehow deeply parallel, even uber-parallel. English is a language in transition, and we predict a big future for constructions like this one.

 The AMAZING sentence justifies itself. AMAZINGness needs no apology. The AMAZING just works.

Dumb Diction & Malapropisms

When you choose the wrong word, you're making a **diction error.** An example:

> I think I can say, without fear of contraception, that The Sex Pistols will outlast Tori Amos.

The above writer is either choosing the wrong word or fomenting anti-Catholic sentiment in an inappropriate context. Another example:

> Abdullah looked very fierce with that turbine on his head.

Unless Abdullah is wearing a turbo-prop beanie, the author probably meant to say *turban.*

You can often get away with diction goofs because most people will blame themselves for not understanding your wit or irony. But here at the BSAT we never blame ourselves; we blame *you,* even for trivial glitches like "I could *of* had a V8" or the phrase "for all *intensive* purposes" (a corruption of "for all intents and purposes") that are more common than sand in your clams.

Idiotic Idioms

An idiom is a gaggle of words that always go together a particular way to yield a distinctive meaning. For instance you can say "he tossed his cookies" or "he threw up," but not "he threw his cookies" or "he tossed up." The following is wrong:

> The a capella group was accused with ten counts of public lewdness, which prevented them of getting to the concert on time.

Correct: . . . was accused <u>of</u> ten counts . . . which prevented them <u>from</u> getting to the concert.

Idiom errors are worse than diction errors, because rather than making you sound creative or ironic, screwed-up idioms just makes you sound foreign. Not bright-foreign, like Julie Delpy, but dim-foreign, like Inspector Clouseau. Before you know it, you're being deported. Heed the wisdom of Chinese philosopher Noh Duh, who said: "Every termite plays a part in bringing down the pagoda." In other words, if your idiom fails, you fail.

Double Negatives

Grumpy grammarians insist that two negatives always make a positive. We disagree:

- 1 negative: You ain't goin'.
- 2 negatives: You ain't goin' nowhere.
- 3 negatives: You ain't never goin' nowhere.
- 4 negatives: You ain't never goin' nowhere nohow.

However, Double Positives are a different story:

16-year-old Girl: Daddy, I'm going out tonight with a 39-year-old biker with awesome tattoos.

Father: Yeah, right.

How to Mangle a Verb

There are several amusing ways to keep a verb from doing its job. One of our favorites is **tense errors.**

> After we rented our shoes, Julia jams her hand in the ball return and there's blood everywhere.

Or:

> Next Tuesday the law to allow rich people to stomp all over poor people was finally approved.

More subtle but equally clumsy are **verb form errors**. For example:

> Life on other planets may shock us or really turning us on.

"Shock us" is in the present indicative tense; "turning us on" is a gerund. Mixing them is something people make fun of foreigners for doing.

Make sure your **subject and verb agree.** Both plural or both singular—take your pick. But not:

> Neither Dr. Phil nor Deepak Chopra think a blow-up doll is the solution to your desperate loneliness.

Correct:

> Neither Dr. Phil nor Deepak Chopra <u>thinks</u> a blow-up doll . . .

Beware also of plural-singular inconsistencies. Example:

> With their extraordinary lungs, Brittany and Tiffany dream of becoming the world's first underwater pole dancer.

Two girls merging into one dancer? Try again.

Pronouns from Hell

Pronouns win the prize for being the most botchable parts of speech. There are several ways to accomplish this feat.

1. Most common is the **error of pronoun agreement:**

> Someone needs to stop sticking their fat nose into my beeswax.

Correct:

> *Someone* needs to stop sticking his or her fat nose into my beeswax.

Notice that *someone* includes the word *one*, which is singular, so it doesn't go with *their*, which is plural. Many people use "their" as a substitute "his or her," thinking it's less cumbersome and more gender-neutral, which it is. It's also wrong, even on the BSAT.

2. The next most common glitch is the **pronoun case error:**

> Me and her got married under the influence, but the influence wore off.

The subject here is "Me and her," right? Yes, but it's wrong, because "Me" and "her" are in the object form. Objects don't do things; things are done to them. For instance, "If she disses me one more time I will slam her through the frickin' wall." Note that here the words that are doing the doing (dissing and slamming) are *I* and *she*. So the corrected sentence should read:

> She and I got married under the influence, but the influence wore off.

Why not "I and she"? Because if him hopes for any chance with she, she comes first.

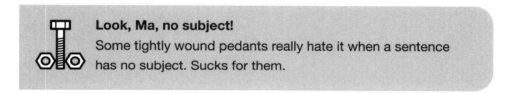

Look, Ma, no subject!
Some tightly wound pedants really hate it when a sentence has no subject. Sucks for them.

3. The **pronoun shift** is also common.

> You know it's time for a facelift when the bags under one's eyes have bags of their own.

Who needs this face lift? Is it "you" or is it "one"? Make a choice.

4. The **ambiguous pronoun** makes it impossible for the reader to figure out who is doing what to whom.

> Bob and Fred went salsa dancing even though he was still in traction.

5. The BSAT can also include tricky **pronoun gender traps**.

> Except when alone, the supervisor was careful never to lift his skirt.

Surprise! There's actually no error here. The supervisor was Scottish.

Messed Up Modifiers

When you **misplace a modifier,** you often end up saying things that get you into trouble:

> The next item up for auction was a grand piano that had belonged to a famous ballerina with thick legs and a beat-up appearance.

Oops. The thick legs and beat-up appearance, which were supposed to describe the piano, got too near the famous ballerina and ended up modifying her (as well as insulting her). Try repositioning the modifier and all will be well:

> The next item up for auction was a grand piano with thick legs and a beat-up appearance that had belonged to a famous ballerina.

No go. The beat-up appearance still belongs to the ballerina. How about:

> The next item up for auction was a famous ballerina's grand piano with thick legs and a beat-up appearance.

Success! The ballerina's dignity has been restored.

Another example:

> As you read *Lassie Come Home,* try to keep a vision of the Scottish landscape in your mind, which is empty and windswept.

Unless it's your mind that's empty and windswept, you'll want to rearrange the sentence like this:

> As you read *Lassie Come Home,* try to keep in your mind a vision of the Scottish landscape, which is empty and windswept.

Get the idea? Fix this one:

> He wrote his award-winning screenplay while flying across the country on a Palm Pilot.

Sometimes a modifier sits between two clauses and you can't tell which one it belongs to. It's called a **squinting modifier** because if you squint at it, it seems to squint back at you. Here's an example:

> Students who sleep with their professors often can improve their grades.

The meaning of this sentence is ambiguous. Shuffle the word *often* around and take your pick of the two completely different, but now unambiguous, statements:

> Students who *often* sleep with their professors can improve their grades.

Or:

> Students who sleep with their professors can *often* improve their grades.

Mixed Metaphors

Only one metaphor to a sentence, please. To make our point, here's a compact little unit stuffed with three different metaphors:

> At the end of the day, his dark night of the soul inaugurated the dawning of a new era.

Even worse:

> Hemorrhoids can be a real pain in the neck.

No. Just, no.

The Faulty Comparison

This is the error where you compare apples to oranges, although, come to think of it, that comparison is perfectly valid. This error is more like comparing Condoleeza Rice to the national anthem of New Zealand. Some examples:

Elton John's lyrics are even more incomprehensible than Norah Jones.

This sentence is unintentionally comparing lyrics to a person, which is silly. The writer probably meant to compare Sir Elton's lyrics (which, by the way, are by Bernie Taupin) to Norah Jones' lyrics. Norah is intriguingly enigmatic, but nowhere near as incomprehensible as the words to "Philadelphia Freedom."

Another example:

A quick fling with Ashton Kutcher appeals more to Laura than Arnold Schwarzenegger.

The intent here is to show Laura comparing a fling with Ashton to a fling with Ahhnold. But curiously, instead it seems to suggest that Arnold might also like to try hooking up with Ashton.

One last example:

Merwin's zits are worse than Larry and Kirby combined.

This is another case of comparing Condi and Kiwi. No matter how bad Merwin's zits are, they're no match for Larry and Kirby themselves, let alone their zits.

Inane Imagery

Imagery can be powerfully evocative. Or not. Make sure yours is nothing like any of the following examples:

- *The stork stood in the pond like a stork-shaped lawn ornament.*
- *George prowled the buffet like a hyena before an array of puddings.*
- *He felt a wave of jealousy like the one the Cubs fans do in the upper deck at Wrigley Field in Chicago.*
- *Her eyes burned with the intensity of a lighthouse, wreathed with syphilitic russet.*

Where to Use All This Information

The grammar and usage principles developed in this chapter will come in very handy for:

- Improving Sentences
- Improving Paragraphs
- Identifying Sentence Errors
- Impressing People Who Think Good Grammar Is Cool

The Last Word on Grammar and Usage

On the BSAT, the natural and haphazard evolution of our language is recognized and even celebrated. We actually *like* sentences like "When she backed over my iPod, I'm like, girlfriend, you better watch your ass." So be adventurous. And above all, be AMAZING.

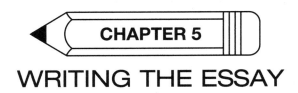

WRITING THE ESSAY

If you've suffered through the 25-minute essay on the SAT or ACT, you may find writing yet another essay as welcome as a case of jock itch. But hang on! The BSAT essay is different. Unlike those other tests that traffic in the warm mush of the safe and the obvious, our essay spurs you to new heights of literary audacity and, above all, *AMAZINGness*.

We don't even care if you're full of shit. We *want* you to be full of shit. In fact, our judges are full of shit themselves. (It takes one to know one.)

Perhaps you question the need for any essay. You may be thinking, "In the 21st cntry y wud any1 even bother writin? y not jst txt?"

We have several answers, some stronger than others.

Lame answer: Writing is an art, among the highest expressions of civilization; texting is a widgety fad.

>**Your rebuttal:** ya so wat. i dont wanna b an artst. i hate artsts.
>**Our rebuttal of your rebuttal:** OK, fair enough.

OK answer: Learning how to write is really learning how to think. If you can't write it, you can't think it.

>**Your rebuttal:** What a crock! Lots of lousy writers have been good thinkers (Homer, Michael Crichton). And lots of successful writers can't think straight (Ann Coulter, Gore Vidal).
>**Our rebuttal of your rebuttal:** Point taken. On the other hand,

Smart Answer: Unbelievable as it may sound, there are vital communications not easily conveyed by txt: your senior thesis, family Christmas letters, eulogies, etc.

>**Your rebuttal:** I don't plan on writing a senior thesis.
>**Our rebuttal of your rebuttal:** Don't be an asshole and make us foresee every reason you may need to write. Maybe you'll need to draft a plea to the governor for clemency. Or an artfully non-committal apology to the voters whose trust you betrayed. Writing-dependent situations arise all the time, even for semi-literate yahoos like you.
>**Your rebuttal of our rebuttal of your rebuttal:** Whatever.

Irrefutable Answer: Writing is a sophisticated and powerful method for getting what you want—wealth beyond the dreams of avarice, desirable sex partners, your own reality show.

>**Your rebuttal:** OK, I'm starting to get it.

The elements that go into writing a great BSAT essay are the same ones that will help you trample your competition, ward off blame, attract praise, worm your way into the affections of the power brokers, and generally shine like the hero you could only ever be in a video game. Now let's break writing down into its two essential components: form and content.

Form Is the Easy Part

Form refers to organization, grammar, punctuation, and the other mechanics of communication that elevate us above the Labrador retriever. Also, stylistic decisions like whether or not to use adjectives. These are right-brain housekeeping skills that any idiot can learn. We're not about to waste our precious time teaching them to you. Buy a copy of *Strunk & White*. Or memorize our pithy review of grammar and usage from the last chapter.

Content Is Trickier

Generating content involves thinking, free association, and left-brain functions like creativity and insight. We *are* willing to waste our time talking about content because that is where the game of life is won or lost.

Most writing tutors suggest that you view writing an essay as the construction of a solid argument. At the BSAT we spit on this approach. Ptooey! We agree with Emerson (or was it Kipling?) when he said, "Arguments convince nobody. They convince nobody because they are presented as arguments." Instead, we encourage literary guerilla tactics. Never mind building a logical case. Your job is to cajole, flatter, intimidate, and if necessary, torture the reader into agreeing with you. The task here is reader manipulation—raw and no-holds-barred.

Facts Don't Matter

When we say "facts don't matter," we're not saying that you don't need facts. Of course you need facts! Communication is based on facts. But they needn't be *true* facts. Make them up or steal them—nobody cares. You have total immunity. If, let's say, your essay involves an honest evaluation of your personal strengths and weaknesses, give yourself the dignity of Aslan, the drive of Junie B. Jones, and the originality of Leonardo Da Vinci. It's all good.

Facts Need Support
Once you've created a fact, treat it with the respect it deserves. Consider writing a Wikipedia article in order to ground it in "reality." Facts need a foundation.

How Do You Structure a BSAT Essay?

Instead of the cast-iron SAT form (See sidebar), we recommend a more flexible, streamlined approach that is composed, like a figure-skating routine, of both mandatory and elective elements.

Required:

- An opening paragraph that sucks the reader in like the undertow of a tsunami.
- A closing paragraph that leaves 'em with either a laugh or a shiver of delight.

Optional:

- One or more middle paragraphs with supporting examples. The danger is that these paragraphs can be like Death Valley, where your reader encounters the desiccated skeletons of your puny original ideas, which couldn't survive the harsh glare of further examination. It's usually better to come up with an idea so strong it doesn't need any pesky supporting examples. (See Essay #2 below.)

The Ugly Truth About the SAT Essay

Why is writing their 25-minute essay as boring as going with your mother to choose paint colors for the den? Because the topics are duller than Occam's Razor after the nth shave.

Tedious SAT strategy in a nutshell: After you decide which side of the question to argue, you grind out an opening statement and then pick your way painfully through two or three middle paragraphs of desperate bullshit that pretends to support something that deserves no support, capped off by a pat, high-fructose, corny closing sentence. We understand why you're not a big fan.

Neither are colleges. The SAT writing score is the most ignored thing since William Shatner's latest CD. However, your BSAT essay, held to the highest standards of AMAZINGness, cannot be ignored.

Let's start breaking down the BSAT essay structure.

Fast Out of the Gate

A skillful BSAT essay begins with what we call the "Two-by-Four." That's a metaphor for a big piece of wood you use to hit your reader over the head to get his attention. The best writers mercilessly club their readers into submission with opening sentences like:

"She floated into my life on the morning tide—bloated, face down."

"Vladimir Nabokov is a brilliant writer, a Nobel laureate, and one sick motherfucker."

"I've never seen the point of wearing panties."

Riveting Your Reader's Attention . . .

. . . is so easy that there's no excuse for not doing it. Humans are hard-wired to respond to stories. If you tell us yours, with lots of juicy personal details, you'll have us at "hello." For instance, in your immigration essay, recall for us how you and your mom, eight months pregnant with your younger sister, swam the Rio Grande on New Year's Day.

Remember, "facts don't matter." So please, no abstract trash about free will or why democracy is good. Give us the good stuff and lay it on with a trowel!

Pulling Into the Station

It's always good to exit with something catchy and energetic. We call this the Happy Ending. It might be a joke:

"And if the Queen had balls . . . she'd be King!"

Or retrofit a good pun to make your point:

"I conclude my survey of prehistoric carnivorous flowers with a question: with fronds like these, who needs anemones?"

Last minute surprise revelations are always effective:

"And I should know . . . because that hopeful little crippled girl was me."

The Topics and Assignments

Here are some prompts from recent BSATs:

- Is there anything really wrong with plagiarism? Isn't it just recycling, a path to sustainable literary output?
- Are ethics a hoax or merely a mass delusion?
- It has been said that rudeness is the weak man's imitation of strength. So when a strong man is rude, what's *he* imitating?
- If you get cirrhosis of the liver, isn't it your own fault?
- Is lust an effective motivator for intellectual achievement?
- If you're really good at talking the talk, is there any point to walking the walk?
- Has any guy ever really changed to please his girlfriend?
- If there is a God, why does She allow TV shows like *Fear Factor*?

The THINK BOX

Sometimes the topic will be preceded by a little discussion to get you thinking. That's called the **Think Box.** Example:

> **Think Box**
>
> Socrates said, "the unexamined life is not worth living." Yet many who examine their lives reach the exact opposite conclusion, leaving suicide notes that say, in effect, "OK, I've examined my life and concluded that it's not worth living, so I'm killing myself. If I'd never examined my life, I'd still be alive. Thanks for everything, Socrates."

This is followed by the **Assignment.** This is the specific question that your essay attempts to answer.

> **ASSIGNMENT:** Paris Hilton has obviously never examined her life. But everyone else has. Does that explain why she's still alive?

Good luck.

So There You Have It

The BSAT essay asks a lot of you. To score well on it, you must internalize the key concept that *writing must never be viewed as an end in itself.* You write in order to get something (in this case, a good score). It follows that integrity doesn't cut it around here—it's just so much dead wood. And sincerity is for losers. There are only four reasons to fire up your word processor: Wealth, Power, Sex, and Fame. If that sounds cynical, then you're beginning to get the idea. 'bout time.

Sample Essays:

Essay #1

DIRECTIONS: Map out and write an essay in which you develop your views on the assigned issue. Support your position any way you choose. Make it AMAZING.

Think Box

Science is on the verge of cloning humans, effectively creating genetic duplicates of ourselves. Cloning could have revolutionary cultural and social implications. Or it could be a big fizzle, like the Segway, that electric scooter that was supposed to change the world.

ASSIGNMENT: If cloning were to become common, would it be a good thing for society? For the individual??

I would like to have a clone. I would like to have a clone for many reasons in fact. A clone is so exactly like me that you could hardly believe it. You know, I could really use a clone because they have to do whatever you want. That's what clones are for.

Things I could make my clone do are:

1. going to class. Lots of us are very busy and I'm one of them. So I could send my clone. Who would know?

2. test things out on it, like does this medical procedure hurt or not? I could wait outside and if I hear him screaming like crazy, there's your answer.

3. also to see if I was going to get some weird genetic thing like Six-Finger Disease where the test is sticking a needle in your eyeball or something. I could make the clone do it instead of me. And that works, because usually everybody is different, but not me and my clone. So if the answer was yes, I'm going to get that disease, then I'd be right to be scared all the time.

I know what you're thinking. "Big shot, what if your clone argues with you about all this?" I argue a lot and so he would probably too. But here's my answer. I just had this idea and I am already 16 so my clone will be younger than me and also smaller. So even if Mr. Cloneboy doesn't want to do what I say, he will have to because I said so.

But now I also again know what you're thinking. If my clone is so much younger than me, how will the going to class instead of me thing work? And that's right. So I take that part back.

Even if we sometimes disagree though, I think my clone and I have a lot in common. It's even better than a twin because even the Olsen twins have their own differences. But a clone doesn't have that excuse. It's me and that's it. But he could learn from me and not screw up all the time. Also I could talk to my clone about really private things (like that rash).

I believe that for the reasons above but also others, clones should become very popular. And you know, my clone might want his own clone but I'd have to see about that.

Essay strengths: This essay develops from a bold premise: the clone as slave. The writer puts forward many provocative ideas, and energetically, if haphazardly, works through their implications. A couple of strong specifics—"sticking a needle in your eyeball" and, of course, the Olsen twins—are always a welcome addition. The informal, conversational tone lends momentum.

Essay weaknesses: Most of the writer's ideas are idiotic. The prose style is pre-Jurassic. Random pronouns float through the piece like ectoplasm in a Stephen King story. The writer seems shaky about word order in the English language ("but now I also again know . . ."). The essay is a poster child for run-ons and redundancies.

Summary: A primitive and highly flawed effort that is, nevertheless, strangely powerful. Score: 16 out of 20.

Essay #2

DIRECTIONS: Map out and write an essay in which you develop your views, etc.

> **Think Box**
>
> The impulse to express one's individuality is powerful and important. Is it more authentic to tattoo your tongue or drive a Smart Car, to play the nose flute for tips or live in a yurt made of recycled tires? And when does self-expression become social transgression?

ASSIGNMENT: What's your keeping-it-real way of saying, "Here I am, world!"?

I own a pit bull because I'm a very alpha-type guy who doesn't take shit from anyone. And my pit bull Jaws helps me get the message out. Of course I keep him in a choke collar that's a welded ring of #4 rebar, and he's been socialized at the Michael Vick K9 Academy, which also trains Jay-Z's Dobermans. But even with all that training, there's still an element of chance — the sudden noise of a dumpster winch or the electric field surge of a lightning bolt could set him off and then, man, you better grab your nuts. I carry a million dollar liability shield and my peeps are on my case to double it.

Don't get me wrong — I'm not gonna let my dog shred your dog into a wet pile of ground chuck, that's not how I roll. But I like to know that he could. I like a dog with power in reserve. Don't gimme a sissy dog that squeaks and yaps and doesn't do shit; gimme a dog that looks all cool and under control but then, BAM! just snaps. THAT's exciting. Jaw-dawg is a time bomb. Everyone respects a guy with the guts to walk around with a bottle of nitro in his back pocket. And that's why I own a pit bull.

Essay strengths: This essay beautifully mirrors its topic by grabbing the reader and not letting go until the owner says "Down, boy." In a strong, stylish voice the writer engages us with a flowing exposition of his inner dialog. Lots of good specifics: Jay-Z's Dobermans, the welded rebar choke collar, the wet pile of ground chuck. And most unusual for an essay like this, there is a high degree of suspense, since every walk this dog takes is potentially a life-or-death situation.

Essay weaknesses: The essay is a simplistic and thoroughly self-aggrandizing statement whose effect is further marred by the fact that both paragraphs end up in exactly the same place: my dog wants you dead. It's not clear whether the writer is refreshingly honest or an appalling sociopath with a mullet. Also, we'd recommend "give me" over "gimme" in this context.

Summary: This essay, while pretty good, falls into the trap of being off-putting. On the BSAT essay, making the reader squirm seldom gets you a higher score. Yes, it's good to write what you know. But first ask yourself if what *you* know is something that *we* want to know. If not, write about something you *don't* know. It worked for Shakespeare; it can work for you. Score: 11 out of 20.

Essay #3

DIRECTIONS: Map out and write . . . (the usual boilerplate)

Think Box

In Chaos Theory, a phenomenon called the Butterfly Effect predicts that tiny changes in the initial conditions of a system like, say, the weather, can produce huge changes down the road. For instance, one flap of a butterfly's wings in a Tokyo garden can shift air currents enough to produce a hurricane that'll wipe out the hemp crop in Jamaica. Or a difference of 2 points on one's BSAT score can mean the difference between a life of triumph and one of bitter oblivion.

ASSIGNMENT: Small things can have large consequences. Do you agree?

History is replete with battles, campaigns, popular movements, and palace intrigues whose all-but-preordained outcomes were flushed down the crapper because of some teeny-tiny wrinkle that seemed trivial at the time. Due to time limitations I will cite one historical example that happens to include many of the types of events mentioned above.

The year was 1881 and Adolf Hitler had been in power since the early Cretaceous period. But sometime in 1880 his enthusiasm for hip-hop music caused him to make the fatal blunder of "suggesting" that the Vienna Philharmonic create a concert series featuring Kanye West. This angered the Valkyrie sisters and prompted them to enter into an alliance with the Swedish resistance, under the command of George Washington. That alliance would ultimately lead to Hitler's humiliating defeat at the Battle of Gettysburg, where Washington was joined at the last minute by a horde of dinosaurs under General Hannibal Lecter, who, ironically, was the former conductor of the Vienna Philharmonic.

But the irony goes further. Cornered like a rabid raccoon, Hitler kidnapped Stephen Hawking and forced him to redirect the Leonid meteor shower, which, as we all know, killed all the dinosaurs, making Hitler believe he'd won, not only at Gettysburg but also at Pearl Harbor. However, the rotting dino carcasses released so much methane gas that they caused global warming, which, even more ironically, caused Kanye West to retire because he hates performing in hot weather.

So, to summarize, Hitler's whimsical love of gangsta muzik caused not only his loss at Pearl Harbor but also the extinction of the dinosaurs, global warming, and, most crucially, the retirement of Kanye West. Little things can indeed have big consequences.

Essay strengths: This is a well-conceived and beautifully executed essay that nails the topic with a masterful command of history and myriad supporting details.

Essay weaknesses: One could quibble with some of the punctuation, but basically . . .

Summary: . . . this essay is a home run! Score: 20 out of 20.

Essay #4

DIRECTIONS: Map, etc.

Think Box

Our world faces huge problems: suicidal reliance on fossil fuels, rising temperatures, plummeting lobster populations, out-of-control talk show hosts. There is no shortage of bold calls to action, yet the tasks are so daunting that the individual is tempted to put his head in the sand, to leave solutions to the so-called experts.

> **ASSIGNMENT:** How can ordinary people get involved in solving global problems?

Call me nuts but I'll say it anyway: AIR is the solution to the world's energy problems. Air is everywhere (except underwater), it's clean and it uses up almost no oxygen. Air is just floating around, waiting to be exploited by someone clever enough to see its huge potential. I know these are big words and I'm just in high school, but this is for real.

I call it "Air-nergy" and the principle couldn't be simpler: Near the earth the air has high pressure. Higher up it has low pressure. Even a schoolchild knows that high pressure always rushes to fill in low pressure, so WHAT ARE WE WAITING FOR? Just put up a bunch of horizontal windmills to catch all that upward airflow and bye-bye OPEC! Heck, the biggest problem we'll face is that it might slow the Earth's rotation a little and we end up with 26-hour-long days. Another possible problem is people and animals being sucked up into the sky and chopped up by those spinning blades. This may sometimes happen, but there's an obvious solution: Velcro.

Can there be bad effects like not being able to breathe near the earth's surface or the long-term reversal of the atmosphere and the stratosphere? If I'm honest about it, maybe yes. But several award-winning people I know, including my English teacher, say that with Air-nergy we won't run out of surface pressure for decades. Or if we do, here's a quick fix: just reverse the system and run it that way for a while!

The Patent Office's refusal to recognize Air-nergy is proof that the Establishment always resists truly revolutionary thought. They say that it defies the laws of physics and is as whacko as the perpetual motion machine or Lester Hendershot's magnetic generator. I chuckle at this because it misses the whole point, which is that Air-nergy frees us from the tyranny of physics! Great inventions, such as this, cannot be ignored or suppressed. The stakes are too high and sometimes you just gotta believe. Like I say, call me nuts.

Essay strengths: The essay displays youthful idealism matched with equal measures of exuberance and easy confidence. A suitable modesty is in evidence ("I'm just in high school"), and the writer shows a willingness to face squarely and then solve inevitable problems (Velcro and reversing the system). He or she shows ample technical creativity and flexibility.

Essay weaknesses: The writer is obviously a flake without the least grounding in science or common sense. This screed goes way beyond making up facts, all the way to declaring independence from the "tyranny" of physics. The reader is tempted most of all to embrace the author's first and last suggestions and, indeed, call him nuts.

Summary: Excellent essay. A tour-de-force of BSAT inventiveness. Score: 19 out of 20.

CHAPTER 6

IMPROVING SENTENCES & PARAGRAPHS

It's a rare sentence that's so clear and powerful that it couldn't use a little improvement. Even the *King James Bible,* widely regarded as revealed truth, has the occasional ambiguous pronoun or misplaced modifier (although, in fairness to God, some of this may be the translators' fault).

The BSAT offers two distinct types of sentence improvement questions: improvements in *grammar* and improvements in *content*. The format is the same for both.

Read the given sentence carefully, and identify which of the five alternative versions of the underlined part MOST IMPROVES the sentence. If none of the alternatives is an improvement, go with Answer A). which is always a variation on "no change necessary."

Type 1—Grammar Improvement

These are straightforward grammar-and-usage exercises where you identify the error and choose a version where it has been fixed. For example:

> Patricia found a letter in her box that really hurt.

> A) [Love it! Don't change a word!]
> B) In her box, Patricia found a letter that really hurt.
> C) Patricia's box really hurt, letter or no letter.
> D) The letter that Patricia found in her mailbox really hurt her feelings.
> E) The stupid asshole she'd been dating left this obnoxious letter in Patricia's box that made her want to nail his nuts to the wall.

The original sentence states clearly, if unintentionally, that Patricia's box hurts because there's a letter in it. Though theoretically possible, it's more likely that the author meant to say that the letter in Patricia's mailbox really hurt her feelings. So which alternate says that? **Answer: D.** As for the rest, answers A, B, and C all are hung up on the box thing, while answer E is way TMI.

Type 2—Content Improvement

This type of question tests your "reality evaluation" skills. Which alternative makes the sentence conform best to reality as we know it? This does not necessarily mean that, all of a sudden, the facts do matter. (See "Facts Don't Matter," p. 77) Rather, you must stay flexible and use your BSIQ to try to determine the "truthiness" of the situation.

Try an example:

> I work on the railroad every day.
>
> A) [perfect as is]
> B) I've worked on the railroad all day long.
> C) I've been working on the railroad all the live-long day.
> D) I am so sick of working on the railroad I could puke.
> E) I'm only working on the railroad to get Dinah to blow
>   my horn.

Sooner or later even a moron is bound to arrive at the correct answer, *C) I've been working on the railroad all the live-long day.* But for you non-morons, beware the temptation to over-think the question, which could lead you to choose E, a penetrating look into the speaker's *motivation* for working on the railroad, but one that goes way beyond the mission of improving the original sentence.

This one's a little harder:

> Best played naked and drunk, Twister is a children's game
> that can be enjoyed by the whole family.
>
> A) [no change required]
> B) naked and stoned
> C) naked in warm mud
> D) naked, drunk, and stoned in warm mud with whipped
>   cream and chocolate sauce with a cherry
> E) any of the above

On this question, you're being asked to search deep within your soul for the absolute best way to play Twister. "But isn't that answer completely subjective?" you ask. "After all, one person's warm mud is another's whipped cream." And you're right. So the answer is E.

Type 1/Type 2—Combo Platter

Some questions will call on both your grammar/usage skills and your reality evaluation skills. For example:

> I'm like, whoa, if me and Mindy would've knew we could
> of vaselined our face before punching out that BEE-OTCH
> we coulda, like, save us 2 black eyz and 3 fat lipz cuz her
> fist wudda slide right off our skin.
>
> A) [This sentence is fantastic just the way it is.]
> B) This sentence is irreparable.
> C) [This answer intentionally left blank.]
> D) [This answer intentionally left blank.]
> E) [This answer intentionally left blank.]

Notice there are only two possible answers on this one. If you simply take a guess, you have a 50-50 chance of being right (another of our little gifts). But which answer is correct? The sentence is arguably not perfect. But is it really irreparable? Or is that a little harsh? The only way to find out is to try to repair it. How about something like this:

> Had Mindy and I but known of the possibility of applying Vaseline to our faces before dispatching that harpy, we might have spared ourselves two black eyes and three swollen lips, since her fist would have slid right off our skins.

Is this new sentence any better? **Pros:** It's certainly easier to understand, less like deciphering the Dead Sea Scrolls. **Cons:** But now it lacks the passion, energy, inventiveness, and exuberant syntax of the original, i.e., it's wimpy. It's like a hospital bubble boy who couldn't possibly survive out in the real world. And worse, it's no fun.

This is an instance of a classic dilemma: Any change you make to the sentence both improves and ruins it. So alas, it does appear to be irreparable. (Sigh.)

Whither Grammar?
The "2 black eyz and 3 fat lipz" example in the text demonstrates an emerging strain of English that is best described as "post-grammatical." It's as if English speakers everywhere are rebelling against their own mother tongue, jettisoning everything from verb conjugations to punctuation like so much useless ballast. We've no idea where this trend will lead, but you can be sure that the BSAT will be surfing the forward edge of this wave.

Tune-up Improving Sentences

EX1: <u>Sizzling on the griddle, Marilyn smelled something delicious.</u>

    A) [Yum!]

    B) Sizzling on the griddle, Marilyn smelled delicious.

    C) Sizzling on the griddle, something about Marilyn smelled delicious.

    D) Marilyn sizzled on the griddle, smelling delicious . . . or something.

    E) Marilyn smelled something delicious sizzling on the griddle.

Answer: This question is straight-up grammar: The problem with the sentence is that, thanks to a misplaced introductory clause, Marilyn appears to be sizzling on the griddle as she sniffs something delicious (probably her own flesh as it cooks). If you try all the possibilities, you'll quickly discover that E is the only answer that places her out of harm's way. **Answer: E.**

EX2:   "Beer, beer, beer," they <u>chanted sloppily swilling the filthy</u>
<u>brew</u> spilling from the dustpans they'd used to gather it
when the keg broke.

   A) [Sounds good to me.]
   B) chanted, sloppily swilling the filthy brew
   C) chanted sloppily, swilling, the filthy brew
   D) chanted sloppily, swilling the filthy brew
   E) B or D

Answer: This sentence is a punctuation nightmare: A is comma free and, as a result, meaning free. B gets the adverb "sloppily" to modify "swilling," which works. C and D go a different route, hooking "sloppily" up with the verb "chanted," also possible. But observe that C is kind of weird and medieval, so it's best to stick with B or D which is the combo offered by E. **Answer: E.**

EX3:   <u>The old captain was especially proud of all the inflatable</u>
<u>children's life preservers.</u>

   A) [Beautiful!]
   B) The old captain was especially proud of all the children
he'd inflated, not to mention their life preservers.
   C) The inflatable old captain was especially proud of all the
children's life preservers.
   D) The old captain was especially proud of all the children's inflatable life preservers.
   E) The old captain was especially inflated by all the proud
children's life preservers.

Answer: A reality evaluation question: The sentence deals with a captain who has apparently provided life preservers to a group of inflatable children. Illogical, Captain. There must be some mistake. Inspecting all the answers, you'll find that D is the only one that gives the life preservers credit for being inflatable. **Answer: D.**

Improving Paragraphs

When it's a whole passage that needs improving, rather than just a sentence, you need to reach down deeper. You're really being asked to think like an editor, to do things like:

- Figure out what the hell the writer is trying to say and help him or her do it better.
- Rearrange anything out of sequence—sentences, paragraphs, ideas (if any).
- Rewrite sentences that meander or stumble or just plain suck.
- Fix punctuation, including semi-colons, ampersands, tildes, and the like.
- Flag any material that's libelous.

To do all this you'll need to implement the grammar and usage principles you reviewed in Chapter 4, as well as harness the BSIQ that's been yours since before you slid down the birth canal.

In the sample passage below, notice a few things:

- The sentences are numbered for easy reference.
- The passage is several paragraphs in length.
- The writing is pretty awful. That's intentional.

Sample passage:

[1] I would like to propose my own personal paradigm for sportsmanship: "Who cares how you play the game? [2] It's whether you win or lose." [3] When you lose, everyone knows perfectly well how you played the game: badly. [4] And when you win, no one cares how you played. [5] As the youngest-ever Olympic hopeful in women's heavyweight power lifting, I recently learned these lessons and more.

[6] The trials were on the campus of Bemidji State University in Minnesota and I knew my main competition was Clarice, the deep-voiced mountain of a woman I was rooming with. [7] For four days we pretended to be all nicey-nice but I could tell she was about to cut me off at the knees. [8] So I struck first, telling her that her boyfriend Don, who's a shot putter, was checking me out during warm-ups, knowing this would unfocus her. [9] But I underestimated Clarice, who sneaks into our bathroom—not sure when, maybe when I'm weighing in—and somehow squirts Tiger Balm into my traveling tube of Preparation H (hemorrhoids are an occupational hazard of power lifters). [10] Have you ever tried to Clean and Jerk 190 kilos when your asshole feels like it's on fire? [11] That day Clarice helped me achieve a Personal Worst.

[12] Strictly speaking, what Clarice did to me was not illegal, not like steroids or anything. [13] OK, it was unsporting, underhanded, and fucked up. [14] But what kills me is that I didn't think to do it to her first. [15] However, I didn't, so she beat me fair and square. [16] By the way, I've taken time off from the Clean and Jerk to concentrate on the Snatch. [17] And in a way I'm grateful to Clarice for expanding my horizons. [18] Next time we meet, she'll probably have forgotten all about me. [19] Until she squirts what she thinks is spermicidal gel onto her diaphragm and pops it into place.

EX1. To maintain a smooth flow of ideas, which sentence should be deleted from the third paragraph?

A) Don't delete anything.
B) (15) . . . she beat me fair and square.
C) (16) . . . to concentrate on the Snatch.
D) (17) . . . I'm grateful to Clarice . . .
E) Cut the whole paragraph.

Answer: Obviously, the author takes a serious detour in Sentence 16, as she digresses about her training priorities. Just delete that. (By the way, sometimes a digression *is* urgently called for. For instance, right now we feel the need to let you know that the Clean and Jerk is the name of a required Olympic lift, as is the Snatch.) **Answer: C.**

EX2. Which of the following is the best way to improve Sentence 9?

  A) Don't suddenly switch to the present: make it ". . . who snuck into our bathroom . . ." and ". . . and somehow squirted Tiger Balm onto . . ." and ". . . maybe when I was weighing in . . ."

  B) Split the big sentence into 5 or 6 baby sentences.

  C) Delete the explanation about hemorrhoids and weightlifters—more than we want to know.

  D) The sentence is too long. Delete every third word.

  E) None of this is going to help.

Answer: We're well aware that Sentence 9 is as long as a five-act play, although there's no law against that. If we delete every third word (answer D), the sentence reads: "But Clarice into not maybe weighing somehow Balm traveling Preparation are hazard lifters," which blows. Splitting it up like so many Balkan countries (answer B) is no better. As for C, don't even think of deleting the hemorrhoids parentheses—that's our favorite part! However, A would be a nice improvement, solving an annoying verb tense error. **Answer: A.**

EX3. Which of the following is the best revision of the underlined portion of Sentence 15?

  However, I didn't so she beat me fair and square.

  A) [as it is now]

  B) fairly and squarely

  C) roundly, soundly, and profoundly

  D) (that huge hairy bitch!)

  E) any of the above

Answer: Let's consider the possibilities. A is the idiom "to beat someone fair and square," which, if slightly less than grammatical, is well-worn and much accepted. B is the same idiom, but with corrected grammar—hard to reject. C is a catchy new idiom, based on the old one—we like it. And D is irresistible. **Answer: E.**

EX4. Which is the best version of Sentence 2?

  It's whether you win or lose.

  A) [as it is now]

  B) weather you win or lose

  C) whether you win, lose, or draw

  D) whether you break her balls

  E) whether 'tis nobler in the mind to win or lose

Answer: It's hard to see what could be wrong with A, but let's check out the other possibilities anyway. B is a dumb spelling of "whether." C creates a variant on the idiom "whether you win or lose" and is even dumber than using "weather." D and E are ridiculous follow-ups to "It's not how you play the game, it's . . ." **Answer: A.**

IDENTIFYING SENTENCE ERRORS

Identifying Sentence Errors is pretty easy, especially if you were raised by humans, as opposed to, say, wolves. You're given a sentence with four possible errors underlined, along with a fifth possibility, usually "no error," but occasionally something more creative. Just pick one. Easy as a scratch 'n' sniff lottery ticket!

You don't even have to say *why* it's wrong. However, if you take Chapter 4 to heart (Grammar and Usage), you'll not only be able to flag the error but also give it a nice fancy name.

> Example: My plans <u>for</u> the future include <u>winning</u> the Nobel Prize,
>   A   B
>
> playing <u>point guard</u> for the Milwaukee Bucks, and <u>to find</u>
>   C   D
>
> my own apartment. <u>No error</u>
>   E

The error is D. This is a parallelism that derailed and burst into flame. If your dreams include "winning" a prize and "playing" a sport, then you'll be "finding" an apartment, not "to find" an apartment.

Tune-up Sentence Errors

> EX1. When Big Bob <u>walked</u> into a room, the floors <u>shook</u>, the
>   A   B
>
> walls <u>heaved</u>, and beer <u>foams</u> up from the baseboards.
>   C   D
>
> <u>No error</u>
>   E

Answer: You can't put "walked," "shook," and "heaved" (all past tense) alongside "foams" (present). So past <u>or</u> present—either one works—but only one to a customer. Since we can only change *one* underlined word, the answer must be "foams," which has to become "foamed." **Answer: D.**

> EX2. Lew knew they'd know he didn't <u>no</u> any more than they
>   A
>
> <u>gnu</u> about what he <u>new</u> and when he <u>nu</u> it. <u>All wrong</u>
>   B   C   D   E

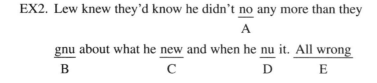

Answer: The writer clearly meant, "Lew knew they'd know he didn't <u>know</u> any more than they <u>knew</u> about what he <u>knew</u> and when he <u>knew</u> it." But he substituted every inappropriate homophone he could find. This behavior must not be rewarded. **Answer: E.**

EX3. That was also the night <u>which</u> our dog <u>Bailey</u> ate a
         A   B

   whole <u>tube</u> of <u>Asian Pussy Tightening Cream.</u> <u>No error</u>
     C   D   E

Answer: Accepting the "facts" of the event as they are, it should be clear enough that *A) which* should probably be *on which*. **Answer: A.**

EX4. The dress-code <u>motion</u> has carried; <u>members</u> of the
       A   B

   Non-Conformist Club <u>is</u> required to wear black <u>turtlenecks</u>
         C   D

   at all times. <u>No error</u>
       E

Answer: It is members (plural) so the turtlenecks (plural) obviously *are* required. **Answer: C.**

EX5. IF <u>YOU'RE</u> REALLY <u>MY</u> BIRTH MOTHER WHY
    A   B

   <u>DON'T</u> I HAVE FOUR CHINS <u>LIKE</u> YOU? <u>No error</u>
    C   D   E

Answer: This *cri de coeur* ("juvenile rant" to English speakers) is the real thing. You can't make this stuff up. **Answer: E.**

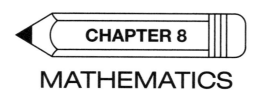

MATHEMATICS

BSAT Math is real-life math, "situation" math that's connected to facts on the ground, not lines on a blackboard. This is the math you use to find out whether your dealer is short-weighting you, whether you're pregnant, whether to hold 'em or fold 'em. No trigonometry, no calculus, no proofs, none of the stuff that made your high school life a *pure living hell*.

BSAT problems are invariably so-called word problems.

So instead of a diagram with angles like these: you get angles like these:

Isn't that an improvement?

When solving BSAT Math problems, you've usually got two options: the High Road (rigorous, thorough, painstaking) or the Low Road (quick and dirty). When faced with this choice in either life or in math, ALWAYS TAKE THE LOW ROAD. Take the High Road *only* when there is no other choice. (And when you do, make sure everyone hears about it.) **The Low Road is The BSAT Way.**

 On BSAT math problems, there are usually a few answers you can ignore, silly little gifts to make your life brighter and make guessing easier. Unless you're a moron in which case you have larger problems.

Types of Math Problems

Sometimes, in life and on the BSAT, you *will* be called upon to solve problems using actual math (the High Road). So let's go over some math topics that will come in handy. This is a review only and is not designed to *teach* you the math you were supposed to learn in school. If you did learn it, great. If you didn't, you're stuck on the Low Road and this review will probably just serve to remind you what a fuck-up you were in school.

Counting

There are many sophisticated methods for counting, above and beyond using your fingers. A few that come up on the BSAT:

- **making a list**—a good way to count your enemies, your shoes, calories, etc.
- **multiplication**—perfect for figuring out how many different "looks" are in your closet
- **Venn diagrams**—useful for surveys and for generalizing about ethnic groups
- **combinations and permutations**—for cracking safes, hacking passwords, etc.

Sample Venn Diagram Problem

Samantha just broke up with her boyfriend Steve. In her search for a new boyfriend, she conducts a survey of the 523 straight guys at her small liberal arts college. Her results:

Sex-crazed Dickheads	491
Beer-soaked Jocks	302
Guys who are both	271

How many guys are neither Sex-crazed Dickheads nor Beer-soaked Jocks?

A) 311
B) 189
C) 23
D) 1
E) 0

Answer: To understand the problem, try a Venn diagram!

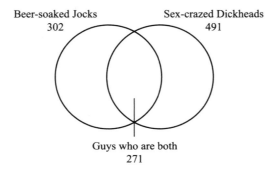

Beer-soaked Jocks
302

Sex-crazed Dickheads
491

Guys who are both
271

We want to find out how many are left over after we take away all the Sex-crazed Dickheads and Beer-soaked Jocks. Look at the diagram. Be careful: If we just add Beer-soaked Jocks and Sex-crazed Dickheads, we end up counting that middle area—guys who are both—*twice*. Solution? Just subtract guys who are both *once:*

491	+	302	–	271	=	522
(Sex-crazed Dickheads)		(Beer-soaked Jocks)		(Guys who are both)		(Guys she won't date)

523 total guys – 522 guys she won't date = 1 eligible guy. The answer is D. Unfortunately, that's Steve, the guy she just broke up with. **Answer: D.**

Algebra

Mega-useful. You'll recall that this branch of math deals with equations that have variables like x and y. And sometimes they have exponents like x^2 or y^3, right? And surely you remember that you can do things to both sides of the equation like adding . . . dividing . . . Is any of this ringing a bell?

Sample Algebra Problem

> Kent farts. Immediately, one-half of the people in the room leave. Then four enter but, getting a whiff, half of those quickly exit. The number remaining is three-halves the original. How many were in the room at the beginning?
>
> A) 2
> B) 3
> C) 6
> D) Depends on the Flatulence Corollary to the Ideal Gas Law.
> E) 8

Answer: The High Road solution involves algebra. First, let's convert the words into an equation. The trick here is to decide what x should stand for. Don't make it stand for something stupid and random, like Kent's inseam. Make it something you really care about, like how many people were originally in the fart chamber. Then just follow along the narrative line. Start with x people and then half of them exit:

$$x - (\tfrac{1}{2})x = (\tfrac{1}{2})x$$

Then, four people enter, making the total:

$$(\tfrac{1}{2})x + 4$$

Next, two of them depart, leaving:

$$(\tfrac{1}{2})x + 4 - 2 = (\tfrac{1}{2})x + 2$$

Since this final number of people needs to equal $(\tfrac{3}{2})x$ (where x was the original number in the room), now we simply solve for x:

$$(\tfrac{1}{2})x + 2 = (\tfrac{3}{2})x$$

We can multiply everything by 2, leaving:

$$x + 4 = 3x$$

Subtracting *x* from both sides, we get:

$$4 = 2x$$

Dividing both sides by 2, we find that:

$$2 = x$$

So the number of people in the room at the beginning was 2. In other words, there was originally only one person in the room with Kent. **Answer: A.**

ALTERNATE METHOD (for those who tend to be lucky): Just pick a number, plug it in, and see what happens. Here's an idea—try 2.

Geometry

Geometry, also quite useful, comes in 3 flavors:

- **Plane geometry**—shapes that are flat: maps, traffic signs, tattoos, etc.
- **Solid geometry**—shapes that have volume: boxes, globes, ice cream cones, etc.
- **Coordinate geometry**—this is useless in real life, except to geometry teachers.

Sample Plane Geometry Problem

Luca, a freelance assassin, has been hired to resolve a problem using his trusty Walther WA 2000 sniper rifle. Referring to the diagram below, if the typical wise guy runs at 15 feet per second from the door to the parking lot, how long on average is each wise guy exposed to Luca's efforts at conflict resolution?

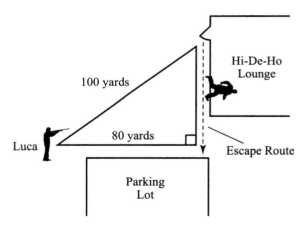

A) 6 seconds

B) 12 seconds

C) 1 hour and 20 minutes

D) 1 minute

E) It cannot be determined.

Answer: Notice that the "escape route" side of the triangle would be the shortest leg of a 3-4-5 right triangle. That would make it 60 yards long or 180 feet. So a wise guy tear-assing at 15 ft/sec would cover 180 feet in 180/15 = 12 seconds. Badda-bing! **Answer: B.**

If you've forgotten all your geometry, note that even a fat, drunken Mafioso can cover the distance we're talking about in less time than *C) 1 hour and 20 minutes* or even *D) 1 minute*. Assuming E is bullshit (which it is), you're choosing between *A) 6 seconds* and *B) 12 seconds*. 50-50 odds are not bad. Good luck.

 In a right triangle, just because one of the angles is "right" doesn't make the other two wrong. And even if they were wrong, it still wouldn't make the first one right.

Sample Solid Geometry Problem

A mathematician named Hall
Has a hexahedronical ball.
The cube of its weight
Times his pecker, plus eight
Is his phone number. Give him a call!

A hexahedron is a cube. If one edge of Hall's ball (need we say testicle?) is 34 millimeters and it weighs 1 milligram / cubic millimeter and his pecker weighs 54,065 milligrams, what is the professor's phone number? You may use your calculator.

A) 911
B) 011 44 (0) 20 7405 7686
C) (212) 497-0768
D) 1-900-HOT-BABE
E) (818) 354-4321

Answer: To calculate the weight of Hall's ball you'll need to multiply its volume by its density (which, strictly speaking, is physics—but hey, stuff happens.) If his ball is 34 mm on a side, the volume of his cube is $34^3 = 39{,}304$ cubic mm. Multiply that by his ball's density of 1 milligram/mm^3 gives a ball weight of 39,304 milligrams. Multiply that by his pecker weight (provided): $39{,}304 \times 54{,}065 = (212)\ 497\text{-}0760$. Add 8 to get (212) 497-0768, or **Answer: C.**

If you have a cheesy calculator that only goes to 8 places, don't panic. You're golden once you see that 212 area code come up. USEFUL TIP: Most ball-and-pecker problems use the metric system.

Sample Coordinate Geometry Problem

By the spring of their freshman year, which was spent drunk, twin brothers Jock and Jack stare blankly as their academic advisor, Professor Quilch, tells them that they're on a "slippery slope." So Prof. Q offers them some "pointers." Jock gets (1,2) and (2,0) and Jack gets (2,2) and (4,1). If by Tuesday they can tell him which one of them is on the slipperier slope, Quilch will let them return to their college "careers" in the fall.

Which brother is in worse shape?

A) Jock

B) Jack

C) Their slopes are equally slippery.

D) Neither slope is particularly slippery.

E) Does the slippery thing have something to do with beer?

Answer: If the brothers notice that Prof Q's "pointers" are points on a coordinate plane, they *may* be able to answer the problem. Each pair clearly defines a line. These are represented on this graph:

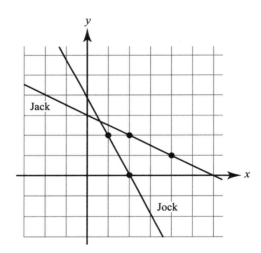

Now all they need to know is the difference between a positive slope and a negative slope, and they can resume their scholastic decline in September. (A positive slope wouldn't be slippery since you can't slide upwards.) Ironically enough it's Jock who recalls that down and to the right is negative and that "downer and righter is negativer." And he's the one in worse trouble! **Answer: A.**

Interpreting Data: Tables and Graphs

Charts, tables, and graphs are visual ways to present a bunch of data to make it understandable. They're also used to propagate some of the world's biggest lies. For instance, tables of cell phone calling plans are gorgeously laid out to cleverly conceal the horrible reality that once you go over your limit, you're paying $2.99 per minute.

Knowing how to read a table is your best defense against such crimes against humanity. So even though this type of question can seem insultingly easy, this is the math that'll save your ass when you're being stalked by MasterCard, Capital One, and other usurious scum.

Sample Table Problem

To help them decide which film to see first this weekend, Ethan and Karl have put together a table based on information available at www.slasherdork.com.

Type of death	Points per Occurence	Number of occurences per film		
		I Know What You Did Last Friday the 13th on Elm Street—Director's Cut	*Saw 17: Cordless and Recharged*	*Bad Prom*
Power tool (note 1)	5	3	12	0
Non Power tool (note 2)	2	5	3	4
Non-tool deaths, boring (note 3)	1	4	1	6
Non-tool deaths, interesting (note 4)	4	1	7	3
Elaborate accidents (note 5)	3	1	0	5
note 1: drills, electric & gas saws, etc. note 2: axes, screwdrivers, augurs, pliars, etc. note 3: electrocutions, strangulations, shootings, defenestrations, etc. note 4: head explosions, flayings, acid or glass swallowings, etc. note 5: threshers impalements, plate-glass truck beheadings, scarf/axle entanglements, etc.				

If they base their decision on the highest point total, which film should they choose?

A) *I Know What You Did Last Friday the 13th on Elm Street—Director's Cut*

B) *Saw 17: Cordless and Recharged*

C) *Bad Prom*

D) *Return to Pee-Wee's Playhouse*

E) It doesn't matter. Every one of these films is a cinematic masterpiece, the work of a visionary auteur at the peak of his filmic potency.

Answer: Even though the table looks complicated, the problem is actually easy and might give you ideas for your Netflix queue. All we're doing here is adding up points. That double-digit entry for *Saw 17: Cordless and Recharged* should immediately light up your phone banks, especially since power tool deaths are worth a whopping 5 points per occurrence, for a total of 60 points. When you add in the 28 points from interesting non-tool deaths, answer *B) Saw 17: Cordless and Recharged*, opens up an unerasable lead over the others. **Answer: B.**

Sample Graph Problem

It is well-known that mobile homes attract tornadoes. The
graph below shows the annual incidence of tornadoes alongside the number of trailer homes in Oklabraska County,
Arkansas during a recent 8-year period.

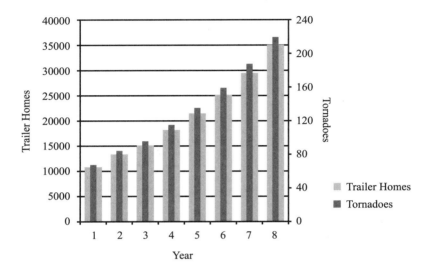

If the growth in the number of trailers continues at this rate,
the effect on the weather will be disastrous. By what year
will Oklabraska County see a tornado strike every day?

A) year 9

B) year 10

C) years 12–18

D) years 30–40

E) It'll never happen. Way before then Oklabraska County
    will be wall-to-wall trailers.

Answer: This is an extrapolation problem. First, notice that both tornado growth and trailer growth appear roughly
linear. So let's find the growth rate of tornadoes. From Year 2 to Year 8, tornadoes grew from around 80 to around
220, a growth rate of 140 tornadoes in 6 years, or 23 new tornadoes a year. In what year will the tornado freqency
hit 365, or one per day? 365 – 220 = 145 tornadoes. At 23 new ones per year, that's 6 or 7 years away, which is year
14 or 15. **Answer: C.**

Probability

If you ever went with your uncle to the race track or watched Men "the Master" Nguyen bluff it out with Amarillo
"Slim" Preston on the World Series of Poker, you have as firm a grasp as you need on probability.

Sample Probability Problem

Everyone knows that automobiles are dangerous. Just driving to the grocery store you have a 2 in 1,000 chance of getting into an accident. Talking on a cell phone as you drive increases those odds by a factor of 15, while getting a blowjob behind the wheel bumps them up by a factor of 33. What are your chances of crashing if you drive, talk, and get blown all at once?

A) Very low, I'm a really good driver.
B) 10%
C) .01%
D) 99%
E) Oh . . . yes . . . ooh . . . just like that . . . YES . . .

Answer: C is out; if driving to the grocery store gives you a 2 in 1,000 chance of crashing, how could DWB (driving while being blown) be 20 times safer (1/10,000)? And, of course, A and E are nonstarters, leaving just *B) 10%* or *D) 99%*. Starting with 2 out of 1,000 and increasing those odds by a *factor* of 15 and then by a *factor* of 33, should strongly suggest *multiplication*, as in $2 \times 15 \times 33 = 990$ out of 1000 or 99/100 or 99%. If you're allergic to multiplication, just ask yourself if driving, talking on a cell phone, and getting blown all at once seems like it's 10% dangerous or 99% dangerous. Oh . . . yes . . . YES . . . BOOM! **Answer: D.**

Logic Problems

Logic is a useful tool in your intellectual garden shed, so it's only logical that the BSAT focuses on this area.

Sample Logic Problem

While preparing an exam for her 4th graders, Miss Coppersmith (a.k.a. "Miss Potty Mouth") experiences a flare-up of her Tourette's syndrome. Below is the multiplication problem that got her fired from her job. Solve for "?"

$$\begin{array}{r} \text{I 9} \\ \times\, \text{4 2} \\ \hline \text{7 T} \\ \text{S 5 H} \\ \hline \text{?} \end{array}$$

A) S L U T
B) P I S S
C) S H H H
D) T I T S
E) S H I T

Answer: Doing the long multiplication, start with 2 × I 9. That means T = 8 and carry the 1. So (2 × I) + 1 = 7. Which means that I = 3. Moving to the tens place problem, we can now plug in 3 for I so 4 × 36 = S5H = 156. So now we know that S = 1, H = 6, T = 8, and I = 3 and substituting in the original problem:

$$
\begin{array}{r}
7\,8 \\
1\,5\,6 \\
\hline
1{,}6\,3\,8 = S\,H\,I\,T
\end{array}
$$

But taking the low road can save you a lot of work. It's easy to see that the answer has to end in T because the bottom part of the problem shows nothing to add to T. So the only possible answers are *A) SLUT* and *E) SHIT*. But SLUT can't be right since there's no way to evaluate L or U. The answer that uses only letters previously seen in the problem is SHIT. **Answer: E.**

Grid-Ins

Life is often multiple choice. Do I *A) go to class,* or *B) curl up in bed with a joint,* or *C) hang out at the Student Center wearing my cool beret?* But it's not always multiple choice. Sometimes you have to pluck the answer out of the air. That's why the BSAT occasionally presents you with math problems requiring "student-generated responses," a.k.a. grid-ins. On these you have to actually do the math and bubble in the answer, one digit at a time, on a grid as below:

Sample Grid-In

When are you likely to find a 7-11 store open for business?

Answer:

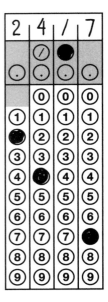

CHAPTER 9

ANALOGIES

What Are Analogies and How Do They Work?

In an analogy, you are given a pair of words or phrases that are related in some way. You are then asked to complete a second pair of words or phrases that bear the same relationship to one another as the first pair. It sounds more complicated than it is. Examples:

Mother is to daughter as father is to -------.

A) patriarch

B) daddy-o

C) son

D) Oedipus

E) prodigal

The answer, *C) son,* is intuitively obvious. A mother's offspring of the same sex is a daughter. A father's offspring of the same sex is a son. Duh.

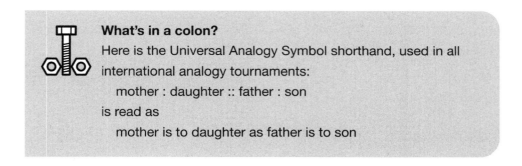

What's in a colon?
Here is the Universal Analogy Symbol shorthand, used in all international analogy tournaments:

mother : daughter :: father : son

is read as

mother is to daughter as father is to son

Analogies test our ability to make meaningful connections in the universe. (So do fraternity beer blasts, but those connections don't have a written component.) People construct analogies all day long without even realizing it.

For example, suppose you attend your school's spring musical, *Guys and Dolls,* and go out afterwards with your friends. As you sit around at Starbucks making snarky remarks, you might offer the opinion: "Whenever Sheila was on stage it was like the Reign of Terror." What you are really saying is:

Sheila's performance : *Guys and Dolls* :: The Reign of Terror : the French Revolution.

You are making the connection between what you've just witnessed and the low point of one of the ugliest episodes in all of human history. That is the awesome compressed power of the analogy.

Note that when you make this implicit analogy, you are trusting your buddies to know about the Reign of Terror, and thus to decode the brilliant comparison you've so cleverly constructed. Otherwise you might just as well have said, "Sheila sucked," which may be true but lacks elegance. In exactly the same way, we are trusting you to decode the insightful connections of the BSAT analogies.

They're not just bastards, they're idiots.
Several years ago the College Board, in its finite wisdom, decided that the analogy, that masterfully concise synthesis of logic and intuition, did not deserve to be on their lah-dee-dah examination. Schmucks!

How to Solve an Analogy

The way to solve an analogy is to construct a *test sentence* that embodies the relationship between the words or phrases in the complete pair. Then apply that sentence to the incomplete pair. If you've chosen the right test sentence, the answer will magically enter your brain. For example:

leg : *wood* :: *breast* : -------

A) turkey

B) marble

C) silicone

D) stabilizer

E) cul de sac

You might construct this test sentence: "*Wood* is a material that you could make an artificial *leg* out of." Applying that to the incomplete pair, you'd get:

"------- is a material that you could make an artificial *breast* out of." Then you'd scan the answers and, lo and behold! The word *silicone* is among them. Get the idea?

The Two-Blank Analogy

Now and then we'll throw you an analogy in the form:

Beatles : Beetles : : ------- : -------

A) Geese : Grease

B) Caterpillars : Larvae

C) Monkeys : Monkees

D) Cougars : Coogers

E) Camels : Dromedaries

In this case, each answer is a pair of words that embodies the same relationship as that of the given pair. The strategy for solving it is exactly the same as with one blank: Construct yourself a good test sentence and try all the possibilities. For instance, how about this:

The <u>Beatles</u> are a famous group whose name is a cute misspelling of <u>Beetles</u>.

Well, when you put it like that…

The <u>Monkees</u> are a famous group whose name is a cute misspelling of <u>Monkeys</u>.

Every other answer fails the Famous Group test.

 If you're stuck on an analogy, here's a little exercise. Look around and you'll notice everyone else working away like busy little beavers. Do they know something you don't? No. But they know enough not to let their attention wander. Get back to work!

Tune-Up Analogies

These analogies are in order of difficulty. You'll note that they can get pretty tricky. Sometimes you'll have to get creative with your test sentences. Good luck.

EX1 (pretty easy):

teeth : floss :: nostril : -------

A) plumbing snake
B) finger
C) snot
D) pipe cleaner
E) bowling ball

Answer: Form the sentence: "Floss is the perfect tool for getting gunk out of your teeth." So what's the perfect tool for getting gunk out of your nose? Yeah . . . right . . . get it waaayyy up in there. Mmmmm, work that . . . **Answer: B. finger.**

EX2 (medium):

pervert : chatroom :: lobbyist : -------

A) ethics
B) coat closet
C) playground
D) Minneapolis Airport men's room
E) Capitol Hill

Answer: "A *pervert* hangs around a *chatroom*. A *lobbyist* hangs around -------." It can only be *E) Capitol Hill*. Duh. (A lobbyist *can* hang around a playground or a men's room, but only if he's also a pervert.) **Answer: E. Capitol Hill.**

EX3 (medium hard):

assessment : you're an asshole :: ------- : go fuck yourself

A) innuendo
B) recommendation
C) observation
D) sing-along
E) epigram

Answer: "*Assessment* is an overly mild way to label the statement *you're an asshole.*" *A) innuendo* and *C) observation* are also overly mild, but neither applies to going and fucking yourself. *D) sing-along* is about the medium, not the message. This leaves *B) recommendation* and *E) epigram*. Since *go fuck yourself* probably doesn't qualify as an *epigram* (a concise, witty saying), the choice must be **Answer: B. recommendation.**

EX4 (hard):

supercomputer : arithmetic :: ------- : masturbation

A) onanism
B) intercourse
C) karaoke
D) hand
E) shop vac

Answer: "Only a jackass would use a *supercomputer* for *arithmetic*. Only a jackass would use a ------- for *masturbation*." Notice that all of these words relate to the subject at hand: *Onanism* is masturbation. *Intercourse* is an alternative to *masturbation*. *Karaoke* is a form of *masturbation*. The *hand* is the most common apparatus for *masturbation*. But the only jackass choice has to be **Answer: E. shop-vac.**

EX5 (ridiculously hard):

precedent : Eisenhower :: prostate : -------

A) Polident
B) wisenheimer
C) Coolidge
D) gland
E) prone

Answer: Imagine you're dumb. To dumb people, "precedent" sounds like "president," which is what Eisenhower was. Still imagining you're dumb, what word sounds like "prostate"? The answer is "prostrate" (in fact, dumb people make this mistake all the time), which is a synonym for *E) prone*, which means lying down. This problem is fiendish because you have to be smart enough to get inside the head of a dumb person and then get out just in time. (If you're *actually* dumb, you haven't got a chance, nor will you understand this explanation.) **Answer: E. prone.**

PART IV

FOUR BSAT PRACTICE TESTS— AM I SMART YET?

BSAT Test 1

BSAT Test 1

Answer Sheet

Answers on p. 134

Section 1

1 Ⓐ Ⓑ Ⓒ Ⓓ Ⓔ
2 Ⓐ Ⓑ Ⓒ Ⓓ Ⓔ
3 Ⓐ Ⓑ Ⓒ Ⓓ Ⓔ
4 Ⓐ Ⓑ Ⓒ Ⓓ Ⓔ
5 Ⓐ Ⓑ Ⓒ Ⓓ Ⓔ
6 Ⓐ Ⓑ Ⓒ Ⓓ Ⓔ

Section 2

1 Ⓐ Ⓑ Ⓒ Ⓓ Ⓔ
2 Ⓐ Ⓑ Ⓒ Ⓓ Ⓔ
3 Ⓐ Ⓑ Ⓒ Ⓓ Ⓔ
4 Ⓐ Ⓑ Ⓒ Ⓓ Ⓔ

Section 3

1

	Ⓐ	Ⓐ	
	⊘	⊘	
⊙	⊙	⊙	⊙
	⓪	⓪	⓪
①	①	①	①
②	②	②	②
③	③	③	③
④	④	④	④
⑤	⑤	⑤	⑤
⑥	⑥	⑥	⑥
⑦	⑦	⑦	⑦
⑧	⑧	⑧	⑧
⑨	⑨	⑨	⑨

2 Ⓐ Ⓑ Ⓒ Ⓓ Ⓔ
3 Ⓐ Ⓑ Ⓒ Ⓓ Ⓔ
4 Ⓐ Ⓑ Ⓒ Ⓓ Ⓔ
5 Ⓐ Ⓑ Ⓒ Ⓓ Ⓔ
6 Ⓐ Ⓑ Ⓒ Ⓓ Ⓔ
7 Ⓐ Ⓑ Ⓒ Ⓓ Ⓔ
8 Ⓐ Ⓑ Ⓒ Ⓓ Ⓔ
9 Ⓐ Ⓑ Ⓒ Ⓓ Ⓔ

Section 4

1 Ⓐ Ⓑ Ⓒ Ⓓ Ⓔ
2 Ⓐ Ⓑ Ⓒ Ⓓ Ⓔ
3 Ⓐ Ⓑ Ⓒ Ⓓ Ⓔ
4 Ⓐ Ⓑ Ⓒ Ⓓ Ⓔ
5 Ⓐ Ⓑ Ⓒ Ⓓ Ⓔ

Section 5

1 Ⓐ Ⓑ Ⓒ Ⓓ Ⓔ
2 Ⓐ Ⓑ Ⓒ Ⓓ Ⓔ
3 Ⓐ Ⓑ Ⓒ Ⓓ Ⓔ

Section 6

1 Ⓐ Ⓑ Ⓒ Ⓓ Ⓔ
2 Ⓐ Ⓑ Ⓒ Ⓓ Ⓔ
3 Ⓐ Ⓑ Ⓒ Ⓓ Ⓔ
4 Ⓐ Ⓑ Ⓒ Ⓓ Ⓔ
5 Ⓐ Ⓑ Ⓒ Ⓓ Ⓔ
6 Ⓐ Ⓑ Ⓒ Ⓓ Ⓔ

Section 7

1 Ⓐ Ⓑ Ⓒ Ⓓ Ⓔ
2 Ⓐ Ⓑ Ⓒ Ⓓ Ⓔ
3 Ⓐ Ⓑ Ⓒ Ⓓ Ⓔ
4 Ⓐ Ⓑ Ⓒ Ⓓ Ⓔ
5 Ⓐ Ⓑ Ⓒ Ⓓ Ⓔ
6 Ⓐ Ⓑ Ⓒ Ⓓ Ⓔ

Section 8

1 Ⓐ Ⓑ Ⓒ Ⓓ Ⓔ
2 Ⓐ Ⓑ Ⓒ Ⓓ Ⓔ
3 Ⓐ Ⓑ Ⓒ Ⓓ Ⓔ
4 Ⓐ Ⓑ Ⓒ Ⓓ Ⓔ
5 Ⓐ Ⓑ Ⓒ Ⓓ Ⓔ
6 Ⓐ Ⓑ Ⓒ Ⓓ Ⓔ
7 Ⓐ Ⓑ Ⓒ Ⓓ Ⓔ
8 Ⓐ Ⓑ Ⓒ Ⓓ Ⓔ

Section 9

1 Ⓐ Ⓑ Ⓒ Ⓓ Ⓔ
2 Ⓐ Ⓑ Ⓒ Ⓓ Ⓔ
3 Ⓐ Ⓑ Ⓒ Ⓓ Ⓔ
4 Ⓐ Ⓑ Ⓒ Ⓓ Ⓔ
5 Ⓐ Ⓑ Ⓒ Ⓓ Ⓔ
6 Ⓐ Ⓑ Ⓒ Ⓓ Ⓔ
7 Ⓐ Ⓑ Ⓒ Ⓓ Ⓔ
8 Ⓐ Ⓑ Ⓒ Ⓓ Ⓔ
9 Ⓐ Ⓑ Ⓒ Ⓓ Ⓔ

Section 10

1 Ⓐ Ⓑ Ⓒ Ⓓ Ⓔ
2 Ⓐ Ⓑ Ⓒ Ⓓ Ⓔ
3 Ⓐ Ⓑ Ⓒ Ⓓ Ⓔ
4 Ⓐ Ⓑ Ⓒ Ⓓ Ⓔ

NO TEST MATERIAL ON THIS PAGE

1   1   1

SECTION 1   Sentence Completions

DIRECTIONS: This section presents you with ------- that contain one or more -------. Below each ------- are five -------. Pick the ------- that seems the least -------.

---

1. Tommy was obsessed with his music teacher, Ms. Da Silva, not because of her ------- but because she seemed so -------.

   A) subtle beauty . . Portuguese
   B) ginormous boobs . . cryogenic
   C) piano technique . . desperate for sex
   D) clubfoot . . ready to snap
   E) any of the above

2. Don't make ------- out of -------.

   A) a mofo . . a mojo
   B) lemons . . lemonade
   C) fun of people who are . . their minds
   D) a mountain . . a molehill
   E) a tsimmis . . a kugel

3. The combination of the noise and the noxious odor finally convinced Bernadette that she needed a new -------.

   A) muffler
   B) diet
   C) boyfriend
   D) carton of *2000 Flushes*
   E) any of the above

4. His self-loathing became increasingly evident as Sid spent more and more time ------- in -------.

   A) smoking weed . . the basement
   B) playing World of Warcraft . . Azeroth
   C) drooling . . a bucket
   D) with a full-size inflatable doll . . the bathtub
   E) all of the above

5. After speaking at length with the transition counselor and the surgeon, Steve found himself wondering if ------- wasn't a whole lot easier than -------.

   A) Spanish . . Sanskrit
   B) being sick . . pretending to be a hypochondriac
   C) playing doctor . . actually going to medical school
   D) divorce . . suicide
   E) cross-dressing . . vaginoplasty

6. Children are affected by globalization every time a ------- dispatcher in Mumbai coordinates the nocturnal redemption of a molar in Cincinnati.

   A) taxicab
   B) turbaned
   C) canine
   D) tooth fairy
   E) take-out curry

GO TO NEXT PAGE

2   2   2

SECTION 2

Reading Passage Pair

DIRECTIONS: Read the two passages below and then answer the questions that follow. The correct response may be blatant or merely latent.

Passage 1

From "Gray's Anatomy."

Inside the aperture of the nostril is a slight dilatation, the vestibule, which extends as a small pouch, the ventricle, toward the point of the nose. The fossa, above and behind the

(5) vestibule, has been divided into two parts: an olfactory portion, consisting of the upper and central part of the septum and probably the superior turbinated bone, and a respiratory portion, which comprises the rest of the fossa.

Passage 2

From "Grey's Anatomy."

(10) SYNOPSIS: On hiatus from her on-again-off-again affair with McDreamy, Meredith Grey falls for a patient named Snafu, who is an inner-city crack dealer. She goes home with him for hot sex but afterwards a cockroach crawls up

(15) her nose and chews on her olfactory nerve, damaging her sense of smell so that everything reeks like rotten celery to her. The surgical repair is a rarely performed neural anastamosis that only McDreamy is qualified to do. But he

(20) is in physical rehab after tearing a rotator cuff in an arm wrestling match with McSteamy and doesn't trust himself to undertake the risky procedure. So Izzie performs the surgery, being talked through it by McDreamy over his cell

(25) phone with spotty reception while he has a reunion with his biological mother aboard the Vashon Island ferry in the rain. Afterward in the recovery room, Christina, the most self-centered bitch on the planet, asks Meredith's band-

(30) age-swabbed face why she, as Meredith's best friend, wasn't allowed to scrub in.

Meredith's Closing Monolog (V.O.):

Things happen for a reason. There's a reason that little girl was impaled on a merry-go-round

(35) horse.

(TRACKING SHOT of Trauma Team wheeling gurney through ER.)

We just don't know what the reason was. We all want answers . . .

(40) (CLOSE UP of a cockroach, perplexed, moving its antennae, crawling into a nose.)

. . . and we'll go strange places to get them. Maybe that's what I was doing in that filthy crack house with Snafu . . .

(45) (LONG SHOT of Watts Towers in South Central. CUT TO MEDIUM SHOT of half-naked Meredith on bare mattress in garbage-strewn room.)

. . . looking for a comforting substance to fill

(50) the answerless void. Just the way that roach was looking for the protective comfort of my nostril. Maybe that's enough of an answer. Everything happens for a reason.

(DISSOLVE into closing credits as ALT

(55) ROCK SONG "I'm Complex" swells.)

GO TO NEXT PAGE >

1. Passage 1 is from *Gray's Anatomy*, while Passage 2 is from *Grey's Anatomy*. Which of the following explains the widely dissimilar tone?

   A) Passage 1 is an ancient text that inspired Passage 2.
   B) Passages 1 and 2 are from the same novel, but 2 is from an earlier draft.
   C) Passages 1 and 2 are from one of those post-modern novels where you can include recipes, pop songs, whatever.
   D) Passage 1 is from the textbook; 2 is from the TV show.
   E) Passage 1 is from Wikipedia; 2 is from *Soap Opera Digest.*

2. In Passage 2 Meredith says, "Everything happens for a reason." If that is true, what is the reason for this pair of passages?

   A) to give you credit for hours spent in front of a TV
   B) to offer a sneak peek at next season
   C) to demonstrate that you cannot copyright a title
   D) to illustrate that everything DOES NOT, in fact, happen for a reason
   E) to mess you up with self-referential circles of nonsense

3. What is the relationship between McDreamy and McSteamy?

   A) McSteamy is McDreamy's landlord.
   B) McDreamy and McSteamy are identical twins, separated at birth to prove that surgeonhood is genetic.
   C) McDreamy and McSteamy are the same person at two different points in time.
   D) The two are soul mates, ripped apart by an unscrupulous warlord in the last days of the Tang Dynasty.
   E) They're former best friends, one whose wife slept with the other as a cry for more quality time.

4. The roach crawling into Meredith's nose is a dramatic device. Which one?

   A) plot complication
   B) poetic justice
   C) *deus ex terminix*
   D) Greek chorus
   E) greek kick line

GO TO NEXT PAGE

3   3   3

SECTION 3   Mathematics

DIRECTIONS: For each problem in this section there are y possible solutions offered, where y = the number of Golden Rings in the Twelve Days of Christmas. Choose the correct one. Use any blank space on the page for doodling.

Math Facts

Useful Conversions

- 1 cubic meter = 1,000 liters

- 1 score = 20

- 1262 decibels = the volume of Ruben Studdard

- 1 Imperial gallon = 4.54609188 liters

Poetic Conversions

A pint's a pound,

The whole world 'round.

A cc weighs a gram,

No matter where I am.

A mile, in klicks,

Is about 1.6.

- Volume of a cylinder = $\pi r^2 \times$ Height

- Value of π = approximately 3.14159

- Value of Entenmann's pie = $8.99

GO TO NEXT PAGE

---

1. Sid wants to play a joke on Suzy while she's crossing the street. He knows that the stopping distance of his car is proportional to the square of his speed at the time he hits the brakes. When Sid's car is going 25 miles per hour, its stopping distance is 25 feet. If he's driving 75 miles an hour, what is the minimum distance from Suzy that he has to apply the brakes in order to avoid killing her?

GRID-IN

---

2. Helga and Manfred, two geometry teachers, are into rough sex. Helga is excited to notice that the fingernail marks she has dug into Manfred's back are parallel. Manfred then begs Helga to use her whip to raise a straight welt that intersects with the lines.

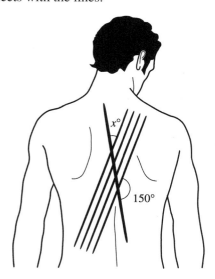

Based on the diagram above, find x, the angle of intersection of the welt and the claw marks.

A) 30 degrees and please don't stop, Helga!
B) 45 uncomfortable degrees
C) 50 deliciously painful degrees
D) 60 exquisitely anguished degrees
E) 90 blindingly excruciatingly agonizing degrees

---

3. Helga loves to have Manfred bite her vigorously on the butt. But she insists that he vary the location lest her skin become irritated. To keep track, she has had her behind tattooed with polar coordinates, as shown in the diagram below.

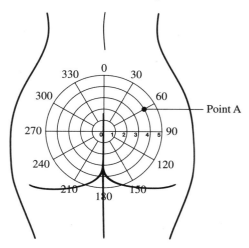

If Manfred starts on Night 1 at Point A (4, 60°) and each night rotates his love nibbles counterclockwise by 45 degrees, where on Helga's ass will Manfred be chewing on Night 12?

A) 0, 137°
B) 4, 60°
C) 4, 240°
D) 5, 145°
E) 3, 180° but don't go there!

---

4. At Miles' and Prudence's wedding feast there are four score and seven guests. The main dish is blackbird pie. If there are four and twenty blackbirds baked into each pie, how many whole pies must be served for each guest to have at least one half dozen blackbirds?

A) one score
B) one score and two
C) two score and two
D) three score and forty
E) a baker's dozen less two

GO TO NEXT PAGE ⇒

3   3   3

5. At the Mungertown Municipal Park, there's a kiddie pool measuring 5 meters × 5 meters × 1 meter that serves the town day camp. One hot July day, the pool opened at 10 a.m., and until 2 p.m. there was an average of 40 campers in the water at any given time. After 2 p.m. the pool population averaged 60 per hour. The average camper emits .2 liters of urine per hour in the water. At 5 p.m. the lifeguard noticed a yellow tinge to the water and closed the pool for health reasons. By the end of the day, how much total urine had been released into the pool?

A) 6.8 liters
B) 68 liters
C) 68 barrels
D) 680 liters
E) 6800 Imperial gallons

6. Assuming the water was pristine at 10 a.m., what was the concentration of urine at 5 p.m.?

A) 27%
B) 2.7%
C) .27%
D) .0027%
E) 2700 Imperial gallons

7. Just after 4 p.m., the concentration of urine had reached the critical point where it will react instantly with chlorine to turn blond hair green. If 35% of the campers are blond, how many campers came home with green hair?

A) 60
B) 40
C) 21
D) None: the blond kids are over at the Country Club.
E) 2.1

8. Bugs, a cartoon character, has an initial body volume of 450 cubic inches. Using a steamroller, Elmer, another cartoon character, flattens Bugs into a perfectly circular disk with a depth of 1 inch. What is Bugs' approximate diameter after Elmer's assault?

A) 1 inch
B) 12 inches
C) 24 inches
D) 144 inches
E) Impossible to know; according to Cartoon Physics, cartoon characters are infinitely elastic.

9. In the February Gland's End catalog, a Ding Dong costs $29.99 and the ElectroJammer Musical Vibrator costs $39.99. The sisters of sorority house ∑EX put together an order for a total of 18 assorted Ding Dongs and Electro-Jammers totaling exactly $661.82, including $12.00 for shipping and handling. How many Ding Dongs did they buy?

A) 7
B) 9
C) 11
D) None, they went with the special offer on Horse Power Hummers for $19.99 with free shipping.
E) I've tried three times and can't get this to come out to a round number!

GO TO NEXT PAGE

4   4   4

SECTION 4   Improving Sentences

> DIRECTIONS: The underlined portions of the sentences below may contain errors, from the piddling to the egregious. In some cases the entire sentence is underlined because the whole thing may be messed up. Figure out which of the five alternatives straightens things out the best. Choose answer A if you still prefer the original.

1. Hi, my name's Bob, it's Career Day and I'm here to get you as fired up as I am about the exciting field of suicide prevention.

   A) [awesome as is]
   B) share some funny stories from the
   C) tell ya, Wall Street may be dead but an equally lucrative future awaits you in the
   D) ... oh god, I'm so depressed ... (sob) I need help from someone in the
   E) act like I give a shit about the

2. Because the sex act of the stick insect takes six weeks, there's no such thing as a quickie.

   A) [exactly right]
   B) unfaithful stick insects never use the excuse "I was working late in the forest"
   C) busy stick insects often hurry though foreplay in under a month
   D) the most promiscuous stick insect in history got laid only 14 times
   E) all of the above

3. He looked at me like an idiot.

   A) [perfect]
   B) He looked at me like I was an idiot.
   C) He looked up to me as an idiot.
   D) He looked down on me as an idiot.
   E) He looked me up and down, one idiot to another.

4. When being interviewed by Oprah, wisdom dictates limiting your use of the term "butt plug."

   A) [It's pure gold.]
   B) the term "butt plug" is off-limits.
   C) your use of the term "butt plug" could make you famous.
   D) let her be the one to bring up the subject of butt plugs.
   E) we don't recommend using a butt plug.

5. At the Earth Day symposium, the faculty was given information on how to reduce the garbage it generates in the form of lectures, seminars, and articles.

   A) [If it ain't broke don't fix it!]
   B) in the form of garbage on how to reduce its lectures, seminars, and articles.
   C) on how to reduce its lectures, seminars, and articles to alternative forms of garbage.
   D) on how to misinform and inseminate its degenerate students by posing as articulate lecturers.
   E) in the form of lectures, seminars, and articles on how to reduce the garbage it generates.

GO TO NEXT PAGE ⟩

5   5   5

SECTION 5   Improving Paragraphs

DIRECTIONS: The passage below is an unedited draft that needs help. Read it carefully and try to improve it by answering the questions that follow.

Roman cavalry choirs
From Wikipedia, the free encyclopedia

[1] These informal singing groups became all the rage among Roman horse soldiers around 50 BCE, at about the time Julius Caesar was reaming out the land of Gaul. [2] With 20 to 60 singers each, these men-only ensembles usually had more tenors than basses, to avoid the muddy "barbarian" sound that was then popular among the Visigoths to the north. [3] The cavalry choirs' repertoire is thought to have consisted mainly of ancient mambos and boleros (Latin Music - Prehistoric). [4] The vocal arrangements, either *a capella* or accompanied by hydraulis (the Roman water organ), were created by off-duty centurians as they relaxed after the battle in their posing straps.

[5] References: The only known literary usage of "Roman cavalry choirs" is in Coldplay's song "Viva La Vida," where it doesn't seem to mean much of anything. [6] And what the hell are Jerusalem bells? [7] Like some sort of Middle Eastern veggie, you know, like a Jerusalem artichoke? [8] Or bell peppers. [9] Or maybe it's "Jerusalem belles"? [10] Like Jewish debutantes? [11] No clue.

GO TO NEXT PAGE

1. Which of the following would be the best way to restructure the entry?

    A)   [It doesn't need restructuring.]

    B)   Get rid of Sentences 6 through 11, all the off-topic stuff about Jerusalem bells.

    C)   Just make a quick reference to Jerusalem bells, then link it to its own entry.

    D)   Expand the Jerusalem bells discussion—for example, with a hyperlink to the AC/DC song "Hell's Bells."

    E)   Start the entry with Coldplay (the only reason anyone's reading it) and a discussion of how the title "Viva La Vida" makes even less sense than Jerusalem bells and Roman cavalry choirs.

2. Which of the following is the best improvement of the underlined portion of Sentence 1?

[1] These informal singing groups became all the rage among Roman horse soldiers around 50 BCE, about the time Julius Caesar was reaming out the land of Gaul.

    A)   [It's fine as is.]

    B)   which was a heck of a long time ago.

    C)   which was about 50 years before the Common Era.

    D)   back when most military vocal groups were still off-limits to horses.

    E)   a time when the barbarian horde was still in diapers.

3. This entry, so typical of Wikipedia, demonstrates -------.

    A)   nothing whatsoever.

    B)   that if it's on the web it must be true.

    C)   that you get what you pay for.

    D)   that history is written by the victors (in this case, Coldplay).

    E)   that the Visigoths' vocal sound sucked worse than the Jonas Brothers.

GO TO NEXT PAGE

6   6   6

SECTION 6   Reading Passages

DIRECTIONS: Read the passages below and then answer the questions that follow. The correct response may be overt or covert.

Short passage 1:
Excerpted from "YOU'RE GODDAMN RIGHT WE'RE ANGRY" by Moni Breisch, a right-wing radical feminist who died of apoplexy at the age of 34 in 1988.

All men are braggarts. While women are instinctively realistic about themselves, even the most modest statement out of a guy's mouth is some form of covert boast. When Einstein said,
(5) "$E=mc^2$," it was simply his passive-aggressive way of whipping out his massive intellectual cock and daring his physicist lifting buddies to do the same. And what about John F. Kennedy's infamous boast, "Ask not what your country can
(10) do for you; ask what you can do for your country?" Oh, please! He might just as well have been screaming, "Look at me! Look at me! I'm the President and you're not!" And spare me Martin Luther King. Text: "I have a dream."
(15) (like the rest of us don't?) Subtext: "How about if I ram my dream right down your goddamn throats!" And what about that typical alpha male who said, "Love your neighbor as you would yourself." Right, I'm supposed to love
(20) my neighbor just 'cause you're on this patriarchal power trip and need everybody else to do what you say. Yes, all men are braggarts without an ounce of reality in any statement they ever make. Thank the goddess I'm not like that.

1. Which of the following conclusions can be drawn from the passage?

   I. Men can be annoying, but they're cute.

   II. Women with massive intellectual cocks should keep them hidden.

   III. It's good to be the king.

   IV. The author is a militant lesbian.

   A) I
   B) I and II
   C) I, II and III
   D) I, II, III and IV
   E) only IV

2. Which of the following would NOT exemplify the author's idea of a "patriarchal power trip" (Line 20)?

   A) the 102nd Airborne Division
   B) the Skull and Bones Society at Yale
   C) Winnie the Pooh
   D) unisex bathrooms in college dorms
   E) an Eddie Murphy stand-up routine

3. Which of the following is NOT an example of a generalization?

   A) $E=mc^2$
   B) All Christians love their neighbors as they would themselves.
   C) I'm the President and you're not!
   D) All men are braggarts.
   E) The Beatles never made a bad record.

GO TO NEXT PAGE

Short passage 2:

This poem, an homage to the poet Walt Whitman, was anthologized in Brooklyn's Best High School Poets of 2009.

"Song of My Teen Self"

(25) A giant surge of love
looses my fecund energy,
like a puff of milkweed on the wind.
Can you catch my pods on all your yearning
surfaces,
(30) tickling your xy with my yyyyyyy
here in the summer of my terrifying ripeness?

No one else is me.
No one else can feel my sap rise skyward
through my core
(35) on this surge of love.
Why begrudge me my place
at the center of a self-centered universe,
brimful of me and ready to erupt?
No one else can feel my oats,
(40) my Wheaties,
my eclectic Kool-Aid,
the word of my body.
Inject yourself into my drunken dance? I don't
think so.

(45) I have a crush on myself.
I am so hot, so ample and so luscious.
O to smell myself in all my thick glory,
to touch my pliant bags of meal!
How do I do it? generate such unbuttoned ecstasy
(50) with nothing but my screaming parts?
I was not born to play a clarinet solo in the dark,
but to blare amidst the oom-pah band
from the town gazebo with the crickets
and the sticky children's dripping cones.

(55) My dream lovers exhaust me,
texting my body through the night,
rubbing up against my knees,
painting soft kisses on my pores,
g2g lol

(60) I am Teen Spirit,
the coursing liquid of life,
the fertilizing jungle of prom and date,
the random meandering vanity,
the peacock threads,
(65) the awesome lids
and the mad cool kicks.

I am in love with myself.
I award myself First Prize
and Runner-up
(70) and Honorable Mention.
I am the it, the all, the kisser and the kissee.

GO TO NEXT PAGE ⟩

4. Which of the following best describes the theme of the poem?

   A) coming out in the age of Viagra
   B) the hormone-driven narcissism of adolescence
   C) the difficulty of delivering effective social services during a hurricane
   D) the devastation of being pigeon-toed
   E) the poet's inability to find a soul mate in the cast of *High School Musical*

5. Select the best interpretation of the following lines:

   I was not born to play a clarinet solo in the dark, But to blare amidst the oom-pah band . . .

   A) The author is a horny little dooger who longs to reach out and touch someone.
   B) The author has dreams of a sextet at band camp.
   C) The author can't figure out which end of the horn to blow.
   D) The author is in love with his sister's Sousaphone.
   E) The author can't fall asleep without a nightlight.

6. Which of the following is the best evidence that the author is male?

   A) "tickling your xy with my yyyyyy"
   B) the metaphor of a clarinet solo
   C) "touch my pliant bags of meal"
   D) "my sap rising skyward through my core"
   E) This poem screams MALE.

GO TO NEXT PAGE

7

7

7

SECTION 7

Analogies

DIRECTIONS: In each question below you are given a pair of words, phrases, or whatevers that are somehow related. From the choices offered, complete the second pair so that they are related in the same way as the first pair.

---

1. urine : honey :: phlegm : -------

   A) moth
   B) sweetheart
   C) Splenda
   D) guacamole
   E) loogie

2. *Tristan und Isolde* : Music Video ::
   The Thinker : -------

   A) The Doer
   B) The Pietà
   C) Rodin
   D) Sculpture
   E) Garden Gnome

3. poodle : dog :: ------- : ballbuster

   A) wife
   B) teacher
   C) parent
   D) boss
   E) all of the above

4. sesor : der :: ------- : eulb

   A) trabajar
   B) steloiv
   C) seesaw
   D) light blub
   E) duh

5. Principle : Heisenberg :: Constant : -------

   A) Chinese water torture
   B) Penelope
   C) Planck
   D) unending
   E) h

6. roaring : twenties :: gay : -------

   A) teens
   B) sixties
   C) nineties
   D) party boys
   E) festive

GO TO NEXT PAGE

8   8   8

SECTION 8   Identifying Sentence Errors

DIRECTIONS: Each of the following sentences contains either a single error or no error at all. Select the underlined portion that contains the foozle or, if none, choose E) No error.

1. Just after impact but <u>still</u> sliding, Fritz felt not
                    A

   pain, but a <u>detached</u> fascination at the road-
             B

   level view of his iPod, his cell phone, and his

   skateboard bouncing along <u>behind</u> him in the
                      C

   <u>lengthening</u> red slick that had been the left side
      D

   of his face. <u>No error</u>
             E

2. In a <u>mad</u> sleepless rush to finish his <u>theses</u>,
       A   B

   Damian popped a handful of <u>Ritalins</u>, and at
                  C

   3:32 a.m. the ghost of <u>Hamlet's</u> father delivered
                   D

   Pericles' Funeral Oration. <u>No error</u>
               E

3. Everyone already knew that Grandma Ethel was

   <u>"tuned to her own podcast,"</u> so her <u>streaking</u>
             A   B

   the Town Council meeting generated more

   <u>haha</u> than <u>brouhaha</u>. <u>No error</u>
     C   D   E

4. Give a man a <u>fish</u> and you feed him for a <u>day,</u>
              A   B

   teach a man to <u>phish</u> and he'll <u>eat</u> at least until
            C   D

   the credit card is cancelled. <u>No error</u>
                E

5. Janet Jackson's <u>"wardrobe malfunction"</u> at
                A

   <u>Super Bowl XXII</u> was nothing <u>compared to</u>
       B   C

   Melissa's <u>"thong-a-palooza"</u> at the company
           D

   picnic. <u>No error</u>
         E

GO TO NEXT PAGE

6. Michaela is a gerbil <u>whisperer</u> who has had
                            A

   great success in <u>curing</u> treadmill phobias and
                     B

   <u>compulsive</u> burrowing, but she finds seed or
        C

   pellet bingeing <u>tractable</u>. <u>No error</u>
                 D   E

7. I've got so <u>many</u> different balls in <u>the</u> air, I'm
             A   B

   afraid <u>of</u> two of them <u>may</u> be my own.
        C   D

   <u>No error</u>
     E

8. Just as she was about to enter the <u>confessional,</u>
                              A

   Marie's dread and <u>guilt</u> vanished, replaced
                B

   <u>with</u> euphoria along with the <u>blessed</u> familiar
     C   D

   cramps, irritability, and urgent need for a

   bathroom. <u>No error</u>
          E

GO TO NEXT PAGE

9   9   9

SECTION 9   **Mathematics**

DIRECTIONS: For each problem in this section there are z possible solutions offered, where z is a positive integer and $6 > z > 4$. Choose the correct one. Use any blank space on the page for doodling.

Math Facts

- Probability of three-of-a-kind in poker: .021128

- Probability of Aliens landing in Stuttgart during Oktoberfest: .00392

- Probability of a U.S. Congressman acting on principle: .000179

- Example of base10 log: .4885507

- Example of natural log:

1. Helga and Manfred are playing a game. Helga places Manfred's testicles in a Craftsman 6″ Bench Vise ($74.99 at Sears), turning the handle just to the point of contact. Then she obtains a random number from 1 to 12 using a spinner from a child's board game and rotates the vise handle by the resulting number of degrees. Referring to the graph below, what is the probability that Manfred will be conscious after the first spin?

   A) $\frac{1}{12}$

   B) $\frac{1}{6}$

   C) $\frac{1}{2}$

   D) Manfred fainted just before the spin.

   E) $\frac{5}{6}$

[Graph: Pain (in KiloHurtz) on vertical axis from 0 to 500, "Blackout Threshold" line at 200, Degrees of vise handle rotation on horizontal axis from 1 to 12. Curve rising sharply after about 9.]

Pain (in KiloHurtz)

Blackout Threshold

Degrees of vise handle rotation

GO TO NEXT PAGE

2. Alphonse and Gaston are having a pissing contest. The score is calculated as duration multiplied by maximum distance. Gaston's distance is 50% greater than Alphonse's but his time is 50% less. Who wins?

   A) Gaston wins.
   B) Alphonse wins.
   C) It's a tie.
   D) By definition, no one wins a pissing contest.
   E) [This answer intentionally left blank.]

3. If it takes 10 aliens 2 hours to perform anal-probes on 6 abductees, how long would it take 5 aliens to do $\frac{1}{3}$ of the work?

   A) 20 minutes
   B) 40 minutes
   C) 1 hour
   D) 1 hour 20 minutes
   E) Cannot be determined because aliens operate outside the terrestrial time/space continuum, so their efforts cannot be judged by earthly standards.

4. State Senator Sam Smith, a candidate for Congress, is to deliver the keynote speech at his party's national convention. The chart below indicates the mix of important elements in the latest draft of his speech.

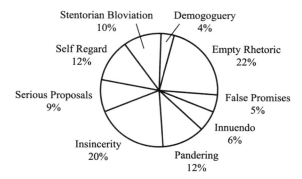

Sen. Smith's campaign manager has demanded changes to the speech, instructing the writers, "Dial back the Insincerity by a tenth, give me a third more Pandering, double the Demagoguery and put in three times as much Empty Rhetoric!" After the changes, what percentage of the speech is devoted to Serious Proposals?

   A) 9%
   B) 15%
   C) 6%
   D) There's no way to tell.
   E) Our campaign staff is reviewing this matter and we'll get right back to you.

GO TO NEXT PAGE

9   9   9

5. With the campaign in trouble, Sen. Smith has fired his campaign manager and now wants to take the high road and run a clean, positive race. He redirects his writers: "Cut out all Demagoguery, False Promises, Innuendo and Insincerity. Also, Serious Proposals are risky, so get rid of them. And make me more modest—one-third less Self Regard."

After the Senator's changes, as a ratio, how much more Empty Rhetoric is there than Serious Proposals?

A) twice as much
B) infinitely more
C) two-thirds more
D) I wasn't listening to the speech so I couldn't tell.
E) I was listening to the speech and I still can't tell.

6. The speech now consists of the following:

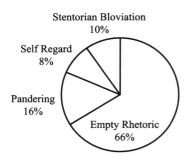

It's a triumph and Sen. Smith has jumped ten points in the polls. Buoyed by this success, he gathers his writers: "Boys and girls, here's the formula that's gonna take us over the top! Divide the Pandering by the Self Regard and subtract that from whatever's left after you get rid of all but twenty percent of the Stentorian Bloviation."

After those changes what is left?

A) 45% Pandering and 55% Self Regard
B) nothing but Empty Rhetoric
C) nothing but Pandering
D) Inflated Expectations leading to Dashed Hopes
E) Looming Disaster

GO TO NEXT PAGE

7. The strength of an earthquake is measured on the Richter scale, which is logarithmic: a 6.0 quake is 10 times more powerful than a 5.0 quake, which, in turn, is 10 times greater magnitude than a 4.0 quake.

When Eliza has good sex it feels to her like an earthquake, so she rates her boyfriends on the Richter scale. How much more powerfully does the earth move with Lance at 7.5 than with Seamus, at 4.1?

A) 1.83 times
B) 18.3 times
C) 340 times
D) 2,512 times
E) 34,000 times

8. Suppose Eliza were boinking Lance when an actual 7.5 earthquake struck. What would be the Richter Magnitude of Eliza's composite experience?

A) 7.5
B) 7.8
C) 15.0
D) 56.25
E) WHAT THE FUCK!???

9. Stacy told Jim that there's exactly a one-in-a-million chance that she'd ever sleep with him. His best friend Jack, a math major, suggests that by slamming his finger in a car door, Jim could generate enough sympathy that his chances with Stacy will improve by a factor of 5×10^5. Jim doesn't want to do it unless his odds are better than 50-50. What should Jim do?

A) Go for it!
B) Slam two fingers in two car doors.
C) He cannot decide.
D) Don't do it.
E) Do it, but only if you're sure that Stacy will sleep with you at least twice.

GO TO NEXT PAGE ⟩

10   10   10

SECTION 10   Reading Passage

DIRECTIONS: Read the passage below and then answer the questions that follow. The correct response may be circumlocuted rather than clearly locuted.

Excerpted from a classic public health reference work, 101 Exciting Epidemics.

The upstate New York town of Love Canal is a "cancer cluster," a place where the incidence of the disease is higher than statistics would predict. Cancer clusters are everywhere and by
(5) now we consider them no big deal. But Valdoshia, Pennsylvania, is different. This pokey little mining town south of Pittsburgh is the site of an "imbecility cluster." Residents of Valdoshia have less common sense than a bag of
(10) hammers and for decades no one knew why.

The mystery started in 1943, when a teacher at the junior high school noticed an uptick in her students' careless errors: forgetting to carry the 10s, spelling "people" as "poeple," tying
(15) their shoes incorrectly. Each succeeding class got goofier. And as these doofuses grew up and joined the workforce—mostly as night watchmen and valet parking attendants—an alert IRS agent noticed that every year more and more
(20) Valdoshia tax returns weren't even close. That triggered an investigation by the Centers for Disease Control, which came up with a surprising result. The pervasive Valdoshian dimness was not the result of any apparent disease,
(25) genetic mutation, or environmental factor. These people were simply morons.

By 1970 the general stupidity was evident the moment you entered town. Signage was an orthographic nightmare (Seers? The YCMA?).
(30) The idiotic planning board had created a one-way traffic pattern that resulted in whole sections of town with no way in. There were eight shoe repair shops on one block of Main Street. And it was easy to pick out the natives, dressed
(35) in striped-and-plaid ensembles or still in their pajamas. It was as if every resident was the village idiot.

Finally, with the declassification of government documents in the 1990s, the surprising eti-
(40) ology of this unique cluster was revealed: a 1934 secret government research program created to test the safety of a then-embryonic technology called television. Gullible Valdoshia residents were paid to watch three hours of
(45) primitive "live" TV each night. The declassified documents are cryptic about the content of the viewing experience. But notes hint that on several nights of each week the lab assistants held a singing contest, judged by three scientists, one
(50) of whom was notoriously hard to please. There are also references to a show called *60 Minutes,* during which someone read the *Valdoshia NewsPeeper* from cover to cover.

Ethical questions arose immediately. Did the
(55) researchers knowingly expose their subjects to harmful levels of TV? There are disturbing indications that this might have been the case, including the fact that the researchers themselves refused to watch the programming. As
(60) one scientist jotted in the margin of his notes, "When I want a lobotomy, I'll ask for it."

As the facts came to light in 1996, a civil liberties lawyer named Vincent Birdsong tried to make Valdoshians realize that their mistreat-
(65) ment was grounds for a potentially huge class-action lawsuit. But Valdoshians failed to grasp the concept, and nothing happened for years. However, Birdsong was finally able to convince a large group of the citizens' out-of-town rela-
(70) tives to get involved. In an unprecedented move, the whole town was declared mentally incompetent, and the next town over was declared their proxy.

GO TO NEXT PAGE >

A nine-figure settlement was quickly
(75) reached, almost all of it going to Birdsong and
grasping relatives. As Mayor Joseph Fliegel
said, "Hey, why not? We don't know nothin'
about that and they do." But Hizzoner had an
idea to use the town's pathetic share of the set-
(80) tlement to promote Valdoshia to tourists as The
World's Stupidest Town—a truly numbskull
idea on the face of it. Yet this is America, whose
good people are able to identify with a town
lobotomized by televised singing contests. So
(85) there is a measure of poetic justice in the fact
that Valdoshia's Annual Dolts and Dullards Festival, with its discounted Stupidity Junkets, has
become the biggest tourist attraction in the
region.

1. Which of the following "ethical questions" is
   NOT addressed by this passage?

   A) Is it ethical to subject humans to TV with-
      out their informed consent?
   B) When stupid people get tricked, whose
      fault is it?
   C) Is exploiting your own disability a cheesy
      way to make money?
   D) Is it OK to declare a whole town "mentally
      incompetent"?
   E) Should you be allowed to reproduce if you
      don't know the difference between Elvis
      Presley and Elvis Costello?

2. The author's primary goal in this passage is

   A) to prove that *American Idol* is not all that
      original.
   B) to point out the correct spelling of "poeple."
   C) to make fun of imbeciles.
   D) to tell a cautionary tale about secret gov-
      ernment programs.
   E) to warn everyone not to hire Vincent P.
      Birdsong as their lawyer.

3. Which of the following is cited as evidence of
   the epidemic?

   A) the use of poison ivy as a groundcover
   B) people eating their banana peels
   C) widespread splitting of infinitives
   D) an idiotic street grid
   E) a cult of Sarah Palin worshippers

4. Which of the following would be the LEAST
   likely booth or event at the Annual Dolts &
   Dullards Festival?

   A) 5 Dollars to Kiss My Ass
   B) Outrun the Thresher
   C) Spot the Tranny
   D) The Bottle Chew
   E) The Valdoshia County Math League

GO TO NEXT PAGE

11   11   11

SECTION 11   Essay

DIRECTIONS: Map out and write an essay in which you develop your views on the assigned issue. Support your position any way you choose. Make it AMAZING.

Think Box

Funerals serve many functions. They celebrate the life of the departed, they provide closure for relatives and friends, and they permit a community to come together in mutual support. They also affirm the turning of the great wheel of life itself.

ASSIGNMENT: At a funeral, is it OK to hit on members of the immediate family of the deceased? Even when it's open-casket?

GO TO NEXT PAGE

STOP
Don't even *think* of turning the page.

BSAT Test 1

Answer Key

Section 1

1 C
2 D
3 E
4 E
5 E
6 D

Section 2

1 D
2 E
3 E
4 A

Section 3

1 225
2 A
3 C
4 B
5 B
6 C
7 C
8 C
9 A

Section 4

1 A
2 E
3 B
4 D
5 E

Section 5

1 C
2 A
3 A

Section 6

1 E
2 D
3 C
4 B
5 A
6 E

Section 7

1 D
2 E
3 E
4 B
5 C
6 C

Section 8

1 E
2 B
3 B
4 B
5 B
6 D
7 C
8 D

Section 9

1 B
2 B
3 D
4 C
5 B
6 B
7 D
8 B
9 D

Section 10

1 E
2 D
3 D
4 E

Calculating Your Scores

Use the work sheet below to arrive at your "Raw Score" for each of the three sections of the test.

To discover your Real Scores and find out what they mean, turn to pages 39-40 and use the "Raw-to-Real Conversion Chart" and the "How-I-Did vs. How-I-Will-Do Chart."

Critical Reading:

Section 1:   Number Correct = _____ ; Number Incorrect = _____

Section 2:   Number Correct = _____ ; Number Incorrect = _____

Section 6:   Number Correct = _____ ; Number Incorrect = _____

Section 10:   Number Correct = _____ ; Number Incorrect = _____

Total Correct = _____ ;   Total Incorrect = _____

_____ − (_____ ÷ 4) = _____
Total Correct   Total Incorrect   RAW SCORE A

Writing Skills:

Section 4:   Number Correct = _____ ; Number Incorrect = _____

Section 5:   Number Correct = _____ ; Number Incorrect = _____

Section 8:   Number Correct = _____ ; Number Incorrect = _____

Section 11:   Essay Score × .4 = _____ ;

Total Correct + Essay = _____ ;   Total Incorrect = _____

_____ − (_____ ÷ 4) = _____
Total Correct + Essay   Total Incorrect   RAW SCORE B

Math & Reasoning:

Section 3:   Number Correct = _____ ; Number Incorrect = _____

Section 7:   Number Correct = _____ ; Number Incorrect = _____

Section 9:   Number Correct = _____ ; Number Incorrect = _____

Total Correct = _____ ;   Total Incorrect = _____

_____ − (_____ ÷ 4) = _____
Total Correct   Total Incorrect   RAW SCORE C

ANSWER EXPLANATIONS

SECTION 1: Sentence Completions

1. Why is Tommy is obsessed with his music teacher? The second half of each answer offers a possible quality of hers that might fuel his obsession. Which quality? The only logical answer is *C) desperate for sex*. Especially when he thinks about her great finger technique. **Answer: C.**

2. There's not much of a context clue here except that it feels like an old saying. We don't know what answer A means. You can't make *B) lemons out of lemonade*, or *E) a tsimmis*, which is broth-based, out of a *kugel*, which is noodle-based. And contrary to C, we see nothing wrong with making *fun of people who are* out of *their minds*. That leaves us with the old adage about not making *D) a mountain* out of *a molehill*." By the way, the first guy who figures out how to make an actual mountain out of a molehill will become very rich. **Answer: D.**

3. This is strictly Rocky Road. Something is causing the noise and the noxious odor problem for Bernadette. Is the problem in her garage, her kitchen, her bedroom, or her bathroom? It seems like it could be any of them. By the way, a *D) carton of 2000 Flushes* would only take care of the odor. For the noise, she'd need a plumber. **Answer: E.**

4. While far from complete, this is a very credible list of ways to express self-loathing. **Answer: E.**

5. The giveaways are transition counselor and surgeon. There's a major whiff of gender-reassignment going on here. And if you know that rhinoplasty is a nose job, then you'll easily figure out *vaginoplasty*. **Answer: E.**

6. Don't focus on globalization. The real context clues here are children and nocturnal redemption of a molar (a tooth). If that combo doesn't scream TOOTH FAIRY to you, then you probably have two sets of teeth. **Answer: D.**

SECTION 2: Reading Passage Pair

1. Even if you're clueless about Passage 1, you should immediately notice that Passage 2 is the script for a TV show. It is not *B) a novel*, even a *C) post-modern novel*. Nor is it from *E) Soap Opera Digest*, because their synopses don't include camera angles. Telltale words like ventricle and bone should help you realize that Passage 1 is a medical tract, not an ancient text. **Answer: D.**

2. This question, while maddeningly wise-ass and self-indulgent, does have an answer. Simplify the question to: Why did they combine these two passages? Rule out A and B, which deal only with the TV passage. C is trivial, while D is uselessly vague. However, the relationship between the anatomy of the nose (in Passage 1) and Meredith's nasal operation (in Passage 2) is a perfect example of *E) self-referential circles of nonsense*. **Answer: E.**

3. You may think this question requires that you've been following the series. But it doesn't. Using facts you picked up in Passage 2 itself (e.g., McDreamy is a surgeon, not a landlord) and the BSIQ you were born with, you should quickly eliminate all but the correct . . . **Answer: E.**

4. The far-reaching consequences of that roach crawling into Meredith's nose would suggest an *A) plot complication*. But let's check the other answers, just to make sure. (Pause.) Yep, it's a plot complication. **Answer: A.**

SECTION 3: Mathematics

1. Here at the BSAT, we don't much like grid-ins. For one thing, they're hard; with nothing to eliminate, the Low Road is blocked off and it's math, math, math. For another, figuring out how to enter the answer is more confusing than the rules to *Magic, the Gathering*. However, life hands you the occasional grid-in and, therefore, so do we.

   Generate the answer and enter it into the four-column grid for "student-produced responses."

   Set up the problem. As it says, distance is proportional to speed squared, so using K as the proportion of distance to speed:

   25 feet = K (25 mph)², and thus

   25 = K × 625, and, dividing both sides by 25,

   $\frac{1}{25}$ = K

   Now, by applying the constant K, we can find the stopping distance (D) for 75 mph:

   D = $\frac{1}{25}$ (75 mph)², and so

   D = 225 feet.

   It's interesting to note that from the time Sid slams on the brakes, Suzy will experience just about 2 full seconds of tire-screeching, deer-in-the-headlights terror before his car slides to a stop at her kneecaps. Sid's a funny guy. **Answer: 225 feet.**

2. Yes, we get it. Manfred is quivering in ecstasy. But unfortunately for him, the correct answer is the least enjoyable. It's simple geometry: the total of x and 150 must be 180, because the fingernail scratches are parallel. That's 30 degrees. **Answer: A.**

3. First, notice that Manfred stays at the same distance from the center each night, eliminating any answer that doesn't start with 4, leaving just B and C. Next, notice that each rotation is 45 degrees. 8 such rotations equals 360 degrees, or one full circle exactly. So 12 rotations is the same as just 4, and 4 × 45 degrees equals 180 degrees away from Point A, or the answer, 240 degrees. Manfred cleverly managed to avoid (3, 180°). **Answer: C.**

4. If you read the Math Facts at the beginning of this section, this is easy because you know that a "score" equals 20. If you didn't, you're in the ironic position of being an idiot forced to take the High Road, e.g. use algebra, and treat a "score" as a variable. So, letting S stand for one score:

   4S + 7 times 6 (the number of guests times the number of birds per guest), which equals . . . 24S + 42, or the total number of birds required. Divide that by the number of birds per pie (four and twenty) . . . $\frac{24S + 42}{24}$, to get . . . S + 1 remainder 18.

   This means that you need one score (S) plus almost 2 total pies (there will be six birds left over for Miles' hunting dogs). **Answer: B.**

5. This is a metric problem, so get rid of *C) 68 barrels* and *E) 6800 Imperial gallons* (which, by the way, would be around 31,000 liters of piss. Even if the kids were made of pure urine . . .). So, ballpark, how much urine are we talking about here? Since the remaining answers are hugely different, we don't have to calculate too carefully. Let's say that it's *around* 50 kids for 7 hours (10 a.m. to 5 p.m.) pissing out .2 liters per hour each. 50 × 7 × .2 = 70, which is very close to 68 liters. Once again, the Low Road's the way to go. **Answer: B.**

6. We're looking for concentration, which is the ratio of piss to pool water. We know how much piss there is (68 liters), so let's find the volume of the pool. The volume of the pool is 5m × 5m × 1m = 25m³, which equals 25,000 liters of water (see Math Facts). And the answer is $\frac{68 \text{ liters of piss}}{25,000 \text{ liters of water}}$ = .0027. Isn't that answer D? Not so fast, Sport! We're looking for a *percentage*!

Moving the decimal point two places brings us .27%. (Not that it's relevant, but if that were blood alcohol, you'd be unconscious.) **Answer: C.**

7. This problem is really easy if you don't let yourself get sidetracked by the bullshit science typical of the BSAT. (Remember: "Facts don't matter!") We know there are 60 kids in the pool at 4 p.m. and 35% of 60 is 21. **Answer: C.**

8. Cartoon Physics does not apply here, so don't be a smart-ass. The volume of a cylinder (which this is, albeit a very flat one), is $\pi r^2 \times$ depth. Since the depth is 1 inch, it's just πr^2, so:

$$450 \text{ in}^3 = \pi r^2$$

$$\frac{450}{\pi} = r^2, \text{ or approximately } 140$$

What's the square root of 140? 144 is a familiar square: 12×12. So r is approximately 12 inches, or answer B, right? WRONG. The question asks for the <u>diameter</u>, which is double the radius! Dumb bunny. **Answer: C.**

By the way, this volume would make Bugs about two feet tall.

9. When working with prices such as $19.99, you can often round up to the nearest dollar to avoid messy calculation. Set up the equations. Let D be the number of Ding Dongs and E the number of ElectroJammers. Remember that shipping and handling is NOT part of the total of the product cost, so subtract that:

$$\$30D + \$40E = \$662 - \$12 = \$650$$

We know that $D + E = 18$, and we're trying to find D, so put E in terms of D:

$$E = 18 - D$$

Substituting for E in the first formula and solving for D:

$$\$30D + \$40(18 - D) = \$650, \text{ leading to } \$30D + \$720 - \$40D = \$650, \text{ and } \$10D = \$70.$$

So the girls ordered 7 Ding Dongs. FYI, there are much cheaper devices on the market. Gland's End is the Neiman Marcus of personal pleasure probes. **Answer: A.**

SECTION 4: Improving Sentences

1. You're looking for a reality improvement here, rather than a grammatical or syntactical improvement (see Study Guide, Chapter 4). So D and E are nonstarters because neither approach would help Bob attract suicide prevention workers. C is wrong because no matter how dead Wall Street is, there's even less money in suicide prevention. As for B, no one goes into suicide prevention for the jokes. So stay with no change. **Answer: A.**

2. Again, a reality improvement is sought. You're being asked to think through the implications of a roll in the hay lasting 6 weeks. When you do, you'll realize that all the answers make sense, including D. But to prove D, try surreptitiously Googling "life span of a stick insect," which you'll find is about 3 years. That's roughly 150 weeks, which, at least theoretically, would leave time for 25 instances of rumpy-pumpy. But of course, there's more to life than rumpy-pumpy (sort of), so sure, 14 sex acts sounds about right. **Answer: E.**

3. In the original sentence, it's not clear who the idiot is, "he" or "me." Answers C, D, and E all make clear that "me" is the idiot, but also add other unnecessary elements like condescension, hero worship, and a sense of kinship. Only B cleanly nails down "me" as the idiot. **Answer: B.**

4. The original sentence includes a misplaced modifier that makes it appear that "wisdom" itself is being interviewed by Oprah. Oddly enough, D is the only grammatically correct advice being offered about butt plugs in relation to Oprah. **Answer: D.**

5. A misplaced modifier clause strongly suggests that the faculty's entire output—lectures, seminars, and articles—is garbage. While this may be true, it is probably not the writer's intent. Answers B, C and D only make matters worse. **Answer: E.**

SECTION 5: Improving Paragraphs

1. OK, it makes sense to mention Jerusalem Bells—I mean, it *was* in the Song of the Year in 2009. But the rant? Way over the top. What to do? We say C, give it its own link and its own fucked-up explanation. **Answer: C.**

2. While the phrasing of the original could be improved ("reaming out" a country is a questionable image), all of the remaining choices are either stupidly obvious or obviously stupid. Stick with what you've got. **Answer: A.**

3. Tough question. Let's use Process of Elimination. Cross off E: All Visigoth recordings have been lost, so the Visigoth sound is unknown (though we know the Jonas Brothers—the Visigoths could hardly have been more annoying). Cross off B: The most you can say is, "If it's on the web, it's on the web." Cross off C: Sometimes you pay $0 and yet you get even less. Cross off D: What history are we talking about? Roman history, obviously. The victors were the barbarians, not Coldplay. So, by POE, the answer is *A) nothing whatsoever.* **Answer: A.**

SECTION 6: Reading Passages

1. This is a global question where you must intuit Moni Breisch's coordinates at the heart of the Ruby-fruit Jungle. She's diesel-powered, and we say that with love and awe. **Answer: E.**

2. It's obvious that Mrs. Breisch would have flipped out over the male-dominant institutions in A, B, or E. But what would she have found wrong with *C) Winnie the Pooh?* It turns out Ms. Breisch wrote a pamphlet years ago specifically condemning the Hundred Acre Wood as "a disgusting old-boy network." **Answer: D.**

3. A) With E=mc² Einstein was generalizing about Relativity.

   B) *All Christians love their neighbors as they would themselves* generalizes about Christians, ignoring the ones whose neighbors play ABBA really loud on Sunday morning.

   C) *I'm the President and you're not!* is NOT a generalization, even if the president is also a general, like Washington or Grant.

   D) *All men are braggarts* generalizes about men, even those who aren't braggarts, like Forrest Gump or Mister Rogers.

   E) *The Beatles never made a bad record.* Oh really?? What do you call "Mr. Moonlight"?

   Answer: C.

4. If you happen to be an adolescent yourself, the answer may not be immediately obvious. So go back to the text. Do you see any mention of *Viagra, social services, pigeon-toes* or *High School Musical*? We didn't think so. **Answer: B.**

5. The image of *a clarinet solo in the dark* suggests the author's autoerotic isolation, which could be eased by some ensemble work under the town gazebo. In other words, he's *a horny little dooger.* **Answer: A.**

6. Submerge yourself in the universal genderhood of the entire joyful hymn, i.e. get global. Now, is the poem male or female? *Pliant bags of meal* could swing either way, but every other image in the poem is directly from Mars. **Answer: E.**

SECTION 7: Analogies

1. Test sentences:

   Urine is a semi-disgusting bodily emission that can easily be mistaken for honey.

   Phlegm is a semi-disgusting bodily emission that can easily be mistaken for ------.

   Answer *E) loogie* is an actual form of phlegm. The substance that is easily mistaken for phlegm would be . . . **Answer: D. guacamole.**

2. Test sentences:

   Tristan und Isolde (a great opera by Wagner) is High Art, whereas a music video is pop-culture schlock.

   The Thinker (a great sculpture by Rodin) is High Art, whereas a ------- is pop-culture schlock.

   The only available choice that is pure kitsch is **Answer: E. Garden Gnome.**

3. Test sentences:

   A poodle is a type of dog.

   A ------- is a type of ballbuster.

   Obviously wife, teacher, parent, and boss are all forms of ballbuster. **Answer: E. all of the above.**

4. Sometimes a test sentence doesn't help and you have to fall back on sheer brilliant insight. Do you see the answer yet? No? : .tnih a s'ereH. Get it? Still no? How's this: Sesor are red, steloiv are blue, and if that doesn't help, then what's wrong with you? **Answer: B. steloiv.**

5. Test sentences:

   Heisenberg had a Principle named after him.

   ------- had a Constant named after him.

   It's almost impossible to remember anything about Heisenberg's Uncertainty Principle or Planck's Constant. But they're famous, so be ready to mention them in case you're ever on Jeopardy. **Answer: C. Planck**

6. Test sentences:

   The adjective "roaring" is usually applied to the twenties.

   The adjective "gay" is usually applied to the -------.

   Answer: C. nineties

SECTION 8: Identifying Sentence Errors

1. This sentence contains no error, apart from the fact that it's longer than a speech by Fidel Castro. In fact, you could call it a run-on. But WE won't. We keep the Castro Reader in our bathroom. **Answer: E.**

2. Singular/plural problem. The sentence states that Damian was finishing multiple theses, not just a single thesis. No wonder he was so fried. **Answer: B.**

3. Offensive imagery. The image of Grandma Ethel <u>streaking</u> the Town Council meeting violates community standards of decency and, quite frankly, grosses us out. A better choice would be <u>falling off her chair during</u>. **Answer: B.**

4. Comma splice error. To join these two fiercely independent clauses together, you're going to need stronger glue than that little comma at B. We recommend a semi-colon**;** You could also use a period**.** **Answer: B.**

5. Factual error. Everyone knows that Super Bowl XXII was in 1988, a full 18 years before the Nipple Slip Seen 'Round the World. While we admit this isn't a grammatical error, we couldn't live with ourselves if we let that kind of sloppiness through. **Answer: B.**

6. Diction error. Michaela has had great success, <u>except</u> in curing the bingeing, right? So bingeing is not tractable (treatable), but <u>intractable</u>. (In fact, she can't even get the gerbils to admit they have a pellet problem.) **Answer: D.**

7. Faulty idiom. When you're <u>afraid of</u> something, it's usually a noun or a clause that functions like a noun ("I'm afraid of <u>the way you keep twirling that scimitar right by my head</u>.") But when you're <u>afraid that</u> something will happen, it leads to a subordinate clause with a nice active verb ("I'm afraid that <u>the boogey-man will rip my guts out</u>.") **Answer: C.**

8. Adverb vs. Adjective. The sentence suggests that Marie's cramps are both blessed and familiar. But the intention was that they are blessed<u>ly</u> familiar, as in "I never thought I'd get down on my knees and say, 'Thank you, God, for these menstrual cramps!'" **Answer: D.**

SECTION 9: Mathematics

1. We don't know why, but girls seem to have an easier time approaching this problem than guys. From the graph you can see that Manfred's blackout threshold is at 11 degrees. So 2 of the possible 12 outcomes (11 and 12) of the first spin will result in unconsciousness. 2 out of $12 = 1$ out of 6, or $\frac{1}{6}$. **Answer: B.**

2. It turns out that this kind of pissing contest <u>is</u> winnable. However, this problem is only winnable through algebra. (Sorry, morons.) The problem tells us that Score = duration × distance, so Alphonse's score (S_a) is:

$$S_a = D_a \times T_a$$

It also tells us that Gaston's distance is 50% greater than Alphonse's:

$$D_g = D_a \times 1.5$$

And Gaston's time is 50% less:

$$T_g = T_a \times .5$$

Now we can find Gaston's score (S_g) in terms of Alphonse's distance and time:

$$S_g = (D_a \times 1.5) \times (T_a \times .5)$$

$$S_g = D_a \times T_a \times .75$$

Since we already know Alphonse's score, $S_a = D_a \times T_a$, we now know:

$$S_g = S_a \times .75$$

Therefore, Gaston's score is only .75 of Alphonse's, and Alphonse wins the pissing contest! **Answer: B.**

3. Don't be intimidated by alien/anal probe problems. They can be solved just like zombie/chainsaw rate problems, by changing one variable at a time. We start with:

    10 aliens can probe 6 abductees in 2 hours.

Obviously just 5 aliens can do the same amount of work in twice as much time:

    5 aliens can probe 6 abductees in 4 hours.

Leaving the number of aliens the same, $\frac{1}{3}$ of the work would be just 2 abductees, and so $\frac{1}{3}$ of the time:

    5 aliens can probe 2 abductees in $\frac{4}{3}$ hours.

$\frac{4}{3}$ of an hour is 1 hour and 20 minutes. See? Aliens may be from another planet, but their problems are just like ours.

Answer: D.

4. Low Road method: If the answer were *A) 9%*, there would be no change in the percentage of Serious Proposals. *B) 15%* would be higher than the original, and *C) 6%* would be lower. Just glancing at all the changes to the speech shows a big overall increase in other elements but not in Serious Proposals. Therefore, Serious Proposals is diluted and its percentage goes down. So 6% is the answer and you barely had to think. Let's hear it for the Low Road! **Answer: C.**

    The High Road method involves the trick of ignoring the percentages in the pie chart and looking at the pieces as just numbers that happen to add up to 100. If you're actually good at math, you'll figure this all out for yourself. And if you're not, why try?

5. You're looking for a ratio here: Empty Rhetoric divided by Serious Proposals. Notice that whatever else has been cut, there's still reams of Empty Rhetoric. But it doesn't matter exactly how much, because you're going to divide it by Serious Proposals, which is now . . . zero. So the answer is a positive number divided by zero. And that, My Fellow Americans, is infinity . . . **Answer: B.**

6. While Sen. Smith may be facing *E) Looming Disaster,* and he's pretty likely to bring about *D) Inflated Expectations leading to Dashed Hopes,* we definitely know that 20% of 10% minus 16% / 8% equals zero. All the Pandering, Self Regard, and Stentorian Bloviation are gone, leaving just *B) nothing but Empty Rhetoric.* God Bless America! **Answer: B.**

7. Don't even think about taking the High Road for this one. Make yourself a little table of how much more Lance would rock Eliza's world than Seamus (who's a 4.1).

Lance's Richter value	How much more than Seamus
5.1	10 times
6.1	100 times
7.1	1,000 times
8.1	10,000 times

So at 7.5 Lance's comparative prowess is a number between 1,000 and 10,000. The only candidate is 2,512 times. **Answer: D.**

8. What happens when you pile two logarithms on top of each other? The most likely answer is "I haven't a clue," which may be honest, but not much help. Let's focus on *C) 15.0* for a moment. Ask yourself if Eliza's boinkfest could have felt like a 15 on the Richter scale. That would be 10^{10} (10 billion) times more powerful than Seamus' love tsunami. Not likely (though mind-boggling to imagine). A reading of *A) 7.5* would indicate no change, so the answer must be 7.8. **Answer: B.**

    Btw, *D) 56.25* would be an orgasm more explosive than all the energy contained in the entire universe. Pretty cool, huh?

9. A factor of 5×10^5 is 500,000. If Jim's chances improve from 1-in-1,000,000 to 500,000-in-1,000,000, then they are now $\frac{500,000}{1,000,000}$ or $\frac{1}{2}$, which is precisely 50-50. Jim wants better than 50-50, so he shouldn't do it. Answer B is interesting, but maybe Stacy would just think Jim's an idiot. E doesn't work because, at 50-50, we can't be sure enough of Stacy sleeping with Jim even once. **Answer: D.**

SECTION 10: Reading Passage

1. Scan the text and you'll discover that each "ethical question" is mentioned *except* whether ignoramuses should be allowed to reproduce. So the answer is E. Unfortunately, it's hard to stop ignoramuses from reproducing because they don't know how to do much else. **Answer: E.**

2. The author's goal is clearly larger than the trivial options offered by answers A, B, or E, none of which requires a 600 word essay to achieve. But how do we choose between the more global goals of C and D? To a limited degree the author manages *C) to make fun of imbeciles.* You he or she also portrays Valdoshians as innocent victims and give them the last laugh, with the triumph of the Dolts and Dullards Festival. So, by POE, the author is *D) trying to tell a cautionary tale about secret government programs.* **Answer: D.**

3. This question could be answered even by the average Valdoshian. Just reading the text (well, *that* wouldn't be easy for a Valdoshian), we note that any of these activities would be typically Valdoshian, but only *D) an idiotic street grid* is actually mentioned. **Answer: D.**

4. By the time you get to this question, you should be tuned in to the Valdoshian wavelength enough to realize that all of these would make great attractions EXCEPT *E) The Valdoshia County Math League.* In its place, they might substitute Tractor Jousting. **Answer: E.**

BSAT Test 2

BSAT Test 2   Answer Sheet

Answers on p. 168

Section 1

1 Ⓐ Ⓑ Ⓒ Ⓓ Ⓔ
2 Ⓐ Ⓑ Ⓒ Ⓓ Ⓔ
3 Ⓐ Ⓑ Ⓒ Ⓓ Ⓔ
4 Ⓐ Ⓑ Ⓒ Ⓓ Ⓔ
5 Ⓐ Ⓑ Ⓒ Ⓓ Ⓔ
6 Ⓐ Ⓑ Ⓒ Ⓓ Ⓔ

Section 2

1 Ⓐ Ⓑ Ⓒ Ⓓ Ⓔ
2 Ⓐ Ⓑ Ⓒ Ⓓ Ⓔ
3 Ⓐ Ⓑ Ⓒ Ⓓ Ⓔ
4 Ⓐ Ⓑ Ⓒ Ⓓ Ⓔ
5 Ⓐ Ⓑ Ⓒ Ⓓ Ⓔ
6 Ⓐ Ⓑ Ⓒ Ⓓ Ⓔ
7 Ⓐ Ⓑ Ⓒ Ⓓ Ⓔ

Section 3

1 Ⓐ Ⓑ Ⓒ Ⓓ Ⓔ
2 Ⓐ Ⓑ Ⓒ Ⓓ Ⓔ
3 Ⓐ Ⓑ Ⓒ Ⓓ Ⓔ
4 Ⓐ Ⓑ Ⓒ Ⓓ Ⓔ
5 Ⓐ Ⓑ Ⓒ Ⓓ Ⓔ
6 Ⓐ Ⓑ Ⓒ Ⓓ Ⓔ
7 Ⓐ Ⓑ Ⓒ Ⓓ Ⓔ
8 Ⓐ Ⓑ Ⓒ Ⓓ Ⓔ
9 Ⓐ Ⓑ Ⓒ Ⓓ Ⓔ

Section 4

1 Ⓐ Ⓑ Ⓒ Ⓓ Ⓔ
2 Ⓐ Ⓑ Ⓒ Ⓓ Ⓔ
3 Ⓐ Ⓑ Ⓒ Ⓓ Ⓔ
4 Ⓐ Ⓑ Ⓒ Ⓓ Ⓔ
5 Ⓐ Ⓑ Ⓒ Ⓓ Ⓔ

Section 5

1 Ⓐ Ⓑ Ⓒ Ⓓ Ⓔ
2 Ⓐ Ⓑ Ⓒ Ⓓ Ⓔ
3 Ⓐ Ⓑ Ⓒ Ⓓ Ⓔ

Section 6

1 Ⓐ Ⓑ Ⓒ Ⓓ Ⓔ
2 Ⓐ Ⓑ Ⓒ Ⓓ Ⓔ
3 Ⓐ Ⓑ Ⓒ Ⓓ Ⓔ

Section 7

1 Ⓐ Ⓑ Ⓒ Ⓓ Ⓔ
2 Ⓐ Ⓑ Ⓒ Ⓓ Ⓔ
3 Ⓐ Ⓑ Ⓒ Ⓓ Ⓔ
4 Ⓐ Ⓑ Ⓒ Ⓓ Ⓔ
5 Ⓐ Ⓑ Ⓒ Ⓓ Ⓔ
6 Ⓐ Ⓑ Ⓒ Ⓓ Ⓔ

Section 8

1 Ⓐ Ⓑ Ⓒ Ⓓ Ⓔ
2 Ⓐ Ⓑ Ⓒ Ⓓ Ⓔ
3 Ⓐ Ⓑ Ⓒ Ⓓ Ⓔ
4 Ⓐ Ⓑ Ⓒ Ⓓ Ⓔ
5 Ⓐ Ⓑ Ⓒ Ⓓ Ⓔ
6 Ⓐ Ⓑ Ⓒ Ⓓ Ⓔ
7 Ⓐ Ⓑ Ⓒ Ⓓ Ⓔ
8 Ⓐ Ⓑ Ⓒ Ⓓ Ⓔ

Section 9

1 Ⓐ Ⓑ Ⓒ Ⓓ Ⓔ
2 Ⓐ Ⓑ Ⓒ Ⓓ Ⓔ
3 Ⓐ Ⓑ Ⓒ Ⓓ Ⓔ
4 Ⓐ Ⓑ Ⓒ Ⓓ Ⓔ
5 Ⓐ Ⓑ Ⓒ Ⓓ Ⓔ
6 Ⓐ Ⓑ Ⓒ Ⓓ Ⓔ
7 Ⓐ Ⓑ Ⓒ Ⓓ Ⓔ
8 Ⓐ Ⓑ Ⓒ Ⓓ Ⓔ
9 Ⓐ Ⓑ Ⓒ Ⓓ Ⓔ

Section 10

1 Ⓐ Ⓑ Ⓒ Ⓓ Ⓔ
2 Ⓐ Ⓑ Ⓒ Ⓓ Ⓔ
3 Ⓐ Ⓑ Ⓒ Ⓓ Ⓔ
4 Ⓐ Ⓑ Ⓒ Ⓓ Ⓔ

NO TEST MATERIAL ON THIS PAGE

SECTION 1

Sentence Completions

DIRECTIONS: This ------ ------ you with ------- that ------ one or more ------. ------ each ------ are ------ ------. Pick ------ ------ that ------ the least ------.

1. It's time for *Mickey Mouse Club House* when Mickey's big hand is on ------- and Mickey's little hand is on -------.

   A) Minnie's left tit . . her right one
   B) the 12 . . the 7
   C) the blow torch . . the fire extinguisher
   D) his crotch . . the potted geranium
   E) the third rail . . the cold water pipe

2. Proving that a great soul can also be disturbingly eccentric, Mahatma Gandhi ------- every day of his adult life.

   A) played a game of Hungry Hungry Hippos
   B) wore a beanie
   C) repaired a toaster
   D) drank a cup of his own urine
   E) kissed a water buffalo

3. Charlotte, always fussy, developed full-blown ------- in college, carefully ------- every surface, hidden or visible, with -------.

   A) Cubism . . rendering . . charcoal
   B) OCD . . swabbing . . rubbing alcohol
   C) nymphomania . . licking . . glee
   D) syphilis . . covering . . rubber
   E) pyromania . . drenching . . lighter fluid

4. They snickered and called him a pervert but he kept on playing with ------- anyway.

   A) less than a full deck
   B) the Anaheim Ducks
   C) himself
   D) little Suzy
   E) green plastic army men

5. Billy, a -------, saw his profession as -------.

   A) circus clown . . in need of government regulation
   B) pimp . . endangered by globalization
   C) software pirate . . swashbuckling and exciting until the feds closed in
   D) high school math teacher . . lacking glory and recognition
   E) pathological liar . . different from what he told people

6. It was a perfect example of her ------- that she accidentally speed-dialed her parole officer while buying a bag of Cambodian red.

   A) alternative lifestyle
   B) haplessness
   C) haberdashery
   D) exemplariness
   E) deft touch

GO TO NEXT PAGE ⟩

2   2   2

SECTION 2   Reading Passage

> DIRECTIONS: Read the long passage below and then answer the questions that follow. The correct response may be either intimated or exclamated.

June 14: At the interview, Mr. Slocum wasn't sure I had enough experience for a flock this large. Uncle Mel's farm in the Berkshires didn't impress him. At first he said 200 head of sheep
(5) for 3 months is too much responsibility for one (not quite) college freshman. I guess my enthusiasm finally convinced him.

June 16: Just arrived at the foot of Sacagawea Peak. Wow, it's big. We leave at dawn, 6
(10) rams, 157 ewes, 33 lambs. The trick will be to keep the sucklings away from the coyotes. I know I can do it, I hope.

June 20: It rained all night. The tent leaked. Note to self: The air mattress goes smack in the
(15) middle of the ground cloth. A big ol' ram I've named Philip has been bullying some of the younger males. I poked him with a stick. He just stared at me.

June 24: Big scare last night. Two lambs I
(20) named Harold and Kumar wandered off. I didn't notice till dinnertime headcount. After an hour I found them stranded on a rock formation on the other side of what I call the No Fly Zone. Carried them one at a time back up what I call
(25) the Yellow Meadow. Harold's dam, who I've named Nancy, seemed pretty relieved. I'll definitely have some stories to tell at Dartmouth this fall.

June 25: Nancy looked worried all day. Does
(30) she blame me for the close call or is she grateful for my saving little Harold? Sheep are even harder to read than people.

June 28: I'm adapting pretty well to shepherd life. But I didn't know it would be so
(35) lonely. I wish I'd brought my accordion or a GameBoy or something.

June 30: Cassandra got eaten by a wolf last night. I feel terrible. I've documented the inci-

dent, as Mr. Slocum instructed. She was only a
(40) yearling. I'll just have to sleep during the day and stand guard all night. These sheep are counting on me.

July 4: Independence Day! In the far distance—outskirts of Bozeman?—I saw eerie lit-
(45) tle sparkles of fireworks. My dad is barbecuing back in Massachusetts. I'm missing my friends pretty bad—even though I hardly have any. It's lonely up here. Nancy wandered over to the campfire and nuzzled me. She's one fine look-
(50) ing ewe.

July 7: Last night I crossed a boundary. I'm not proud of it but surprisingly not ashamed either. Philip has been looking at me strangely. I hope there aren't going to be any hard feelings.

(55) *July 14:* A magical week. I feel new self-esteem and competence. We try to be discreet. Harold is off playing with the other little ones, which leaves Nancy and me more time. In a week or two Harold will be weaned. I can't
(60) wait.

July 15: Uh oh. I knew it—Philip is going to make trouble. I awoke this afternoon to find his nose in my tent. He lowered his head and glared. Those horns look hard.

(65) *July18:* Our last time together was breathtakingly beautiful. There amid the buttercups and lupine, the smell of glacier lily mingling with her distinctive aroma, I came closer to true happiness than any time since my friend Skip
(70) scored us a bottle of poppers off his piano teacher. The whole world lay at our feet. It broke my heart to tell her it was over. I feel sad but also relieved. Maybe I was in over my head.

August 1: Chloe is incredible! She's a more
(75) active participant than Nancy ever was. I get a feeling I'm not her first shepherd and she seems

GO TO NEXT PAGE ▷

pretty popular among the flock. I'm leery of Beavis and Butthead in particular, so we've found a little thicket out beyond the No Fly
(80) Zone. Our personal Xanadu.

August 4: I really think Philip must have a screw loose. He's become completely irrational, following me around night and day, snorting menacingly. Last night he tried to eat my bur-
(85) rito. This has to stop.

August 5: I think I'm falling in love with Chloe. I obsess about her. Her insouciantly matted coat, the cute little "BAPCO" brand just in front of her udder. I find myself dreaming up
(90) ways to see her after the summer pasturing ends. Maybe I could pose as a Dept. of Agriculture inspector?

August 12: My fantasies are running away with me. I've been ruminating on how to
(95) remove the last obstacle to our happiness. Maybe I've crossed another line but I'm too upset and confused and in love to be sure. Dartmouth's a million miles away tonight.

August 24: I've just slaughtered Philip. I feel
(100) like we got off on the wrong foot. But there was no other solution.

August 30: Chloe has been strangely cool to me all week. Doesn't she realize I did it for her, for us? She's beautiful, but God, she can be
(105) dense. Well, what's done is done. She has to get used to it.

August 31: Nancy strolled by my tent this morning. Subtle, but I get it. Philip was extremely controlling, but now that he's out of
(110) the picture, it's suddenly clear to me that she is jealous of Chloe! I don't know what she's comfortable with but my mind toys with unconventional arrangements . . . No, STOP! I can't go there. I'm just too old-fashioned. Tomorrow we
(115) start down to the valley. The heart is so complex!

September 4: The Labor Day barbecue was fun. Dad was surprised by my change of plans, but he's OK with the University of New Hamp-
(120) shire. Mr. Slocum has promised to write me a

recommendation. They have a fine hands-on animal husbandry program. It's a field that excites me. It's my bliss. They always say to follow your bliss.

1. This excerpt is in the form of

  A) a dialogue
  B) a diatribe
  C) a diuretic
  D) a diary
  E) an epistolary bestiary

2. Which of the following sources may have influenced the author?

  A) *Brokeback Mountain*
  B) *Charlotte's Web*
  C) *Dr. Strangelove*
  D) *Ewes Gone Wild: Mating Season!*
  E) A, B, and C, but not D

3. What feelings does the June 30th death of Cassandra evoke in the narrator?

  A) He feels guilt for not keeping better watch.
  B) He's annoyed about all the paperwork.
  C) He fears widespread wolf panic in the flock.
  D) He feels satisfied that Cassandra got what she deserved.
  E) He feels sheepish, just in general.

4. On July 4th the narrator tells us he hardly has any friends. Try to infer the reason.

  A) He plays the accordion.
  B) He's not a good listener.
  C) He has poor people skills.
  D) He's a raving, sheep-butchering wingnut.
  E) It's impossible to say.

GO TO NEXT PAGE

5. On July 7th the narrator says, "Last night I crossed a boundary." What exactly does he mean?

    A) He crosses the Idaho-Montana state line.
    B) He becomes spiritually attuned to his flock.
    C) He puts on guyliner.
    D) He engages in unprotected sex.
    E) He fucks a sheep.

6. On August 1st the narrator writes that he's leery of Beavis and Butthead. Why?

    A) He finds their humor dated.
    B) They want to eat his burrito.
    C) He suspects that they're gay.
    D) They are rivals for Chloe's affections.
    E) They are from the Department of Agriculture.

7. What moral might be drawn from this passage?

    A) Sheep-to-shepherd ratios should be state-mandated.
    B) Interspecies dating is the next big thing.
    C) Follow your bliss except in the 37 states where it's illegal.
    D) There is a flock for even the weirdest shepherd.
    E) No moral can be drawn.

GO TO NEXT PAGE

3   3   3

SECTION 3   **Mathematics**

DIRECTIONS: For each problem in this section there are c possible solutions offered, where c is the length of the hypotenuse of the right triangle pictured below. Choose the correct one. Use any blank space on the page for doodling.

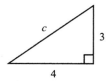

Math Facts

- Transitive property: If a > b and b > c, then a > c

- Distributive property: a(b + c) = ab + ac

- Commutative property: a + b = b + a

- Community property: (income of husband) + (income of wife) – (income of attorney)

- Volume of a sphere: $\dfrac{4}{3}\pi r^3$

1. Let operation "A 🖕 B" be defined as "A tells B to go fuck himself." Which of the following statements are true?

    I. A 🖕 B is Commutative

    II. A 🖕 B is Transitive

    III. A 🖕 B is Transgressive

A) only I
B) I and II
C) I and III
D) II and III
E) only III

GO TO NEXT PAGE ⇨

3   3   3

In the following five questions match each Law with its definition below.

2. The Distributive Law: A (B and C)

3. The Communicative Law: A (B 👆 C)

4. The Reflexive Law: A 👆 A

5. The CircleJerkative Law

6. The ClusterFuckative Law

A) A tells B to tell C to go fuck himself.
B) A tells B to go fuck himself; B tells C to go fuck himself; C tells A to go fuck himself.
C) A tells both B and C to go fuck themselves.
D) A tells himself to go fuck himself.
E) Everybody tells everybody to go fuck himself.

7. 76 trombones led the big parade, with 110 cornets right behind. If trombones and cornets constitute 62% of the marching band, and double belled euphoniums are 2%, what term best describes the euphonium section of the band?

A) a trio of double-belled euphoniums
B) quartet of double-belled euphoniums
C) a sextet of double-belled euphoniums
D) a sex orgy of double-belled euphoniums
E) a flock of duck-billed euphoniums

8. During a Wimbledon match being watched live online by 100,000 internet viewers, Maria Sharapova loses a contact lens. Afraid it might get stepped on, she refuses to let anyone help her look for it. On her hands and knees, Maria can examine 52 square feet of grass per minute. The tournament webmaster notices that for every 3 minutes that Maria's search continues, the number of viewers doubles. Basing your calculation on the diagram below, if Maria has to search her entire side of the court without finding the lens, how many people will be watching by the end?

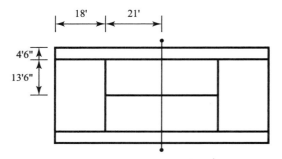

A) 256,000
B) 5,120,000
C) 51,200,000
D) 26,214,400,000
E) Not as many as would for Anna Kournikova.

GO TO NEXT PAGE

9. Suzy has an STD. There is a one-third chance of her spreading it to any particular partner and another one-third chance of that partner passing it further. Suzy sleeps with Tom and Umberto (both previously clear), but one of them definitely doesn't catch the bug. Later, both of them sleep with Valerie (also clear). What are Valerie's chances of picking up "a dose"?

A) $\dfrac{1}{9}$

B) $\dfrac{2}{9}$

C) $\dfrac{17}{81}$

D) $\dfrac{2}{3}$

E) Cannot be determined. I'd need to know if Tom and Umberto do Valerie sequentially or in a 3-way.

GO TO NEXT PAGE

4   4   4

SECTION 4   **Improving Sentences**

DIRECTIONS: The underlined portions of the sentences below may contain errors, from the piddling to the egregious. In some cases the entire sentence is underlined because the whole thing may be messed up. Figure out which of the five alternatives straightens things out the best. Choose answer A if you still prefer the original.

1. Suddenly Jillian came face to face with a big scary man with a mustache weighing over 275 pounds.

    A) [no change]
    B) an average-sized man with a big scary 275-pound mustache
    C) a big scary mustache on a 275-pound man
    D) 275 pounds of big, hairy, scary man
    E) a big scary, 275-pound man with a mustache

2. One of composer Felix Mendelssohn's greatest joys was playing duets with his sister, Fanny.

    A) [very nice]
    B) playing "duets" with his sister's Fanny
    D) playing trios with his sisters, Fanny and Muffie
    C) playing fanny duets with his sister Muffie
    E) playing Parcheesi in the fuck-hutches of Tangier

3. Nothing could stem the tide of his verbal diarrhea, which eventually carried his career into the dumper.

    A) [no change]
    B) hold back the flow of
    C) hold a candle to
    D) corral the floating chunks of
    E) close the deal like

4. Passing the time after school at www.assbook.com and then waking to his Mom calling him downstairs for dinner, Stu's laptop and blanket might best be described as crusty.

    A) [Looks good to me.]
    B) Stu mused that his laptop and blanket
    C) Stu's 57-year-old IM buddy, Stanlislas
    D) Stu was overcome with a kind of remorse that
    E) she

5. A tuna sandwich can go bad quick.

    A) [How fresh!]
    B) A tuna sandwich can go bad real quick.
    C) A tuna sandwich can go bad quickly.
    D) A tuna sandwich can go bad quick if not refrigerated.
    E) Even a good tuna can go bad if not quickly reeducated.

GO TO NEXT PAGE

5   5   5

SECTION 5   Improving Paragraphs

DIRECTIONS: The passage below is an unedited draft that needs help. Read it carefully and try to improve it by answering the questions that follow.

Editorial

[1] For years, environmentalists have made a whipping boy of bovine flatulence. [2] Only now are they beginning to realize the equally horrible effects of human air biscuits on our atmosphere. [3] But all stinkers are not created equal. [4] Originally the sudden, explosive fart, known to some as a "deal-breaker," got most of the attention. [5] But lately the spotlight is on the "crop-duster"—the pooter who drops a string of "silent-but-deadlies" into a room and then moves on, leaving others to deal with the fallout. [6] There is nothing courteous about such a "courtesy stroll." [7] Inflicting a relentless stream of environmental damage, slicing the Muenster in this irresponsible fashion should perhaps more properly be called "methane dumping" and prosecuted no differently than, say, an oil spill off Santa Monica—with stiff fines and public humiliation. [8] High volume greenhouse gas blasters should be required to plant oxygen-restorative trees or pay a "ripper tax." [9] We can't permit the hole in someone's ass to enlarge the hole in the ozone.

1. What is the best version of the underlined portion of Sentence 1?

   For years, environmentalists have made <u>a whipping boy</u> of bovine flatulence.

   A) [no change]
   B) a big huge hairy deal
   C) a kinky sex slave
   D) a baked bean banquet
   E) a scrapegoat

2. What is the most glaring omission from this editorial?

   A) [There is no glaring omission.]
   B) There is an omission but it doesn't glare.
   C) There's no mention of cap-and-trade for trouser gasses.
   D) Humans account for only 5% of planetary wind breakage.
   E) Ooh, ooh! Tell me more about the whipping boy.

3. All of the following are acceptable substitutes for "slicing the Muenster" EXCEPT:

   A) playing the colonic calliope
   B) firing the retro-rockets
   C) stepping on the toad
   D) doing the Lord's work
   E) floating a great brown cloud

GO TO NEXT PAGE >

6   6   6

SECTION 6   Reading Passage

> DIRECTIONS: Read the short passage below and then answer the questions that follow. The correct response may be glaring at you or just winking.

Excerpted from Bill Toohey's Plastic Maverick, *a biography of the pioneering toy inventor Herman Smill.*

Boys don't play with girls' toys and vice versa. At least that was the thinking until Herman Smill came along with his revolutionary PopPets. PopPets are really two toys in one,
(5) crossing that almost unbridgeable gender divide. For $9.95 a little girl can buy one Pop-Pet complete with attached birth certificate tag. When she's done playing with it, her brother can pop it into the microwave for 30 seconds on
(10) high power. When the bell rings—ding—there it is, magically transformed: eyes bulging, head split open, brains in a puddle, guts oozing from its bottom. What's more, a special temperature-sensitive ink has changed the birth certificate
(15) into a <u>death</u> certificate! Now called a Cadaver Pal, what used to be a cute and girly PopPet has become . . . a boy's toy!

The inventor's breakthrough insight was to harness the inherent sadism of little boys and
(20) thereby create a marketing phenomenon. Once that PopPet entered the house, little brother would not rest until he somehow maneuvered it into the microwave. As soon as sister saw what had become of her beloved doll, she became
(25) inconsolable and simply had to have a new one. It's hard to manufacture that kind of built-in obsolescence. The factories couldn't keep up with the orders.

Naturally there were lawsuits from folks
(30) whose family pets were put through the PopPets play pattern, but they were quietly settled and never slowed the double-gendered PopPet juggernaut. For the inventor, Herman Smill, Pop-Pets meant yet another fortune and the Toy
(35) Industry Hall-of-Fame.

1. In line 26, what does the writer mean by "built-in obsolescence"?

   A) It's like obsolete but with more "essence."
   B) It's the age when you grow hair under your arms.
   C) It's another name for the stuff that oozes out of the toy's butt when you heat it up.
   D) It's when some cynical bastard designs a product to intentionally fall apart.
   E) It's the plaintive sound of a little girl wailing at the wrenching loss of a beloved toy.

2. In line 18, what was Smill's "breakthrough insight"?

   A) Brains can form a puddle.
   B) Juggernauts are often double-gendered.
   C) The depravity of little boys can be exploited to generate repeat sales.
   D) Parents are looking for ways to educate young children about death and loss.
   E) Reincarnation is a viable play pattern.

3. Herman Smill displays all of the following EXCEPT:

   A) a delight in brutally dashing the dreams of little girls
   B) a willingness to exploit inter-sibling conflict
   C) a celebration of gruesomeness and death
   D) a deep belief in wholesome collaborative play
   E) a lust for profit by whatever means necessary

GO TO NEXT PAGE

7   7   7

SECTION 7   Analogies

> DIRECTIONS: In each question below you are given a pair of words, phrases, or whatevers that are somehow related. From the choices offered, complete the second pair so that they are related in the same way as the first pair.

1. boogers : snotrag :: jism : -------

   A) scumbag
   B) douchebag
   C) condom
   D) toilet
   E) dumper

2. scientist : Scientologist :: cosmologist : -------

   A) *Cosmo*girl
   B) cosmetologist
   C) cosmonaut
   D) cosmopolitan
   E) episcotistor

3. 32 : 212 :: 0 : -------

   A) 98.6
   B) 451
   C) -273
   D) 100
   E) 213

4. girls : math :: fish : -------

   A) swimming and it's NOT FUNNY
   B) bicycle
   C) non-linear algebra
   D) grill
   E) this is SOOO hard!

5. laced : decal :: radar : -------

   A) Adidas
   B) sneaker
   C) reverse
   D) radar
   E) radio

6. Facebook : privacy :: ------- : -------

   A) *Dancing with the Stars* : hernia
   B) xkcd : nerd heaven
   C) *Deal or No Deal* : tax bracket
   D) *The Biggest Loser* : dignity
   E) TRESemme Hair Salon : Tim Gunn

GO TO NEXT PAGE

8   8   8

SECTION 8   Identifying Sentence Errors

DIRECTIONS: Each of the following sentences contains either a single error or no error at all. Select the underlined portion that contains the foozle or, if none, choose E) No error.

1. A hairless albino dwarf, Stimson made an

   unlikely UPS man, until you notice the size of
      A   B   C   D

   his package. No error
              E

2. Caution demanded that Igor collect body parts
             A

   from as few graves as possible in order that it
         B   C D

   not draw attention to himself. No error
                       E

3. One of the most mind-numbing memoirs ever
                   E

   written, *Late Bloomer: The Early Years*

   exemplify the narcissistic outpourings of
      B   C

   recent offerings like *A Blivot of Prose, Editing*

   Is for Wimps, and the breathtakingly candid *If I*
                  D

   Wrote It, It Must Be Brilliant. No error
                     E

4. Without Nurse Betty, Grandpa could never of
      A   B   C

   licked his Viagra dependancy. No error
                D   E

5. In just two weeks, "Suzy's Night with the
         A

   Rugby Team" got 758,221 hits on YouTube,

   but the first that she learned of it was her

   boyfriend's text message: "i c u r a team
                         B C D

   player." No error
           E

6. As her ankle swelled from the rattler's bite,
              A

   Uma Thurman calmly produced her holistic
                    B

   first-aid kit, with its herbs, crystals, and

   pyramids, and then channels her shaman from
                 C   D

   two lives ago. No error
                 E

GO TO NEXT PAGE

7. We never <u>used to</u> lose much sleep <u>toward</u>
            A   B

pollution until we noticed mercury <u>among</u> the
                                C

listed ingredients on that can of

<u>Bumblebee tuna</u>. <u>No error</u>
      D   E

8. Not <u>until</u> he <u>had</u> died alone in his cluttered
      A   B

apartment <u>all by himself</u> did anyone suspect
             C

that the moyel <u>had</u> collected such a ghastly
             D

stash in the crisper of his refrigerator. <u>No error</u>
                      E

GO TO NEXT PAGE

9   *9*   *9*

SECTION 9   **Mathematics**

DIRECTIONS: For each problem in this section there are *k* possible solutions offered, where *k* is the number of sides of a polygon with internal angles totaling 540°. Choose the correct one. Use any blank space on the page for doodling.

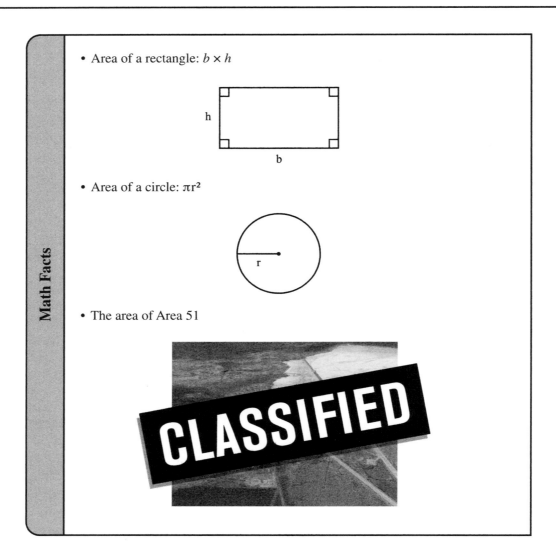

Math Facts

- Area of a rectangle: $b \times h$

- Area of a circle: πr^2

- The area of Area 51

CLASSIFIED

GO TO NEXT PAGE

1. Steve is a Las Vegas businessman who employs four transgendered personal entertainers. Their earnings in dollars across four successive nights are shown in the table below.

	Friday	Saturday	Sunday	Monday
Bianca	1,000	11,500	2,000	1,500
Coyote	500	1,500	600	1,400
Destiny	1,000	1,000	1,000	1,000
Ethel	100	150	50	100

Which employee's productivity seems to be substandard among the group?

A) Ethel
B) Bianca
C) Coyote
D) Destiny
E) Steve

2. One of them spent Saturday night entertaining the Dallas Cowboys. Which one?

A) Ethel
B) Bianca
C) Coyote
D) Destiny
E) Steve

3. Coyote and Destiny look sort of alike. Twins can charge 50% more if they work together. If Steve's commission is 50%, how much more would he have earned with Coyote and Destiny working as "twins"?

A) $4,000
B) $2,000
C) $1,000
D) $8,000
E) $10

4. The student boosters at Butkus Regional High School are trying for the world's record bus moon, the greatest amount of ass skin ever pressed against the windows of one side of a school bus (driver's window included). If 45 kids managed to cover 75% of the glass area of the bus shown below, what is the area of the average single butt cheek?

All windows 24" × 36"

B.R.H.S.

A) .6 ft²
B) 1.2 ft²
C) 1.2π ft²
D) 6π ft²
E) just above the back of the visible thigh

GO TO NEXT PAGE

9   9   9

5. A blivot is the standard unit of "overstuffed-ness." One blivot is traditionally defined as twenty pounds of shit in a ten-pound bag. Noting that zero blivots equals ten pounds of shit in a ten-pound bag, how many blivots is eleven pounds of shit in a ten-pound bag?

A) 1.1 blivots
B) 0.1 blivots
C) $\sqrt{11}$ blivots
D) It cannot be determined.
E) It can be determined, but I cannot determine it.

6. Just so we're clear, a blivot is the ratio of excess stuff to its container. Any units—pounds, imperial gallons, whatever—may be used as long as they're the same for both container and contents. With this in mind, how many blivots is a size-24 opera singer in a size-16 dress?

A) 1 mega-blivot
B) 1.5 blivots
C) 0.5 blivots
D) It should not be determined.
E) –0.5 blivots

7. Dave, a 75-year-old embezzler, is making a prison break chained at the ankle to Phil, a 27-year-old pedophile. For the first five minutes they're able to run at six miles per hour, but then Dave has a heart attack, passes out, and has to be dragged at three miles per hour for one-and-a-half miles until they meet Phil's pickup truck driven by his 12-year-old girlfriend Lucy.

How far do Dave and Phil go before reaching Lucy?

A) 2 miles

B) $3\frac{1}{2}$ miles

C) 4 miles

D) only to first base

E) all the way to the pickup truck

8. If Dave doesn't receive medical care within forty minutes after losing consciousness, he won't recover. Assuming Lucy is not a doctor, what are Dave's chances?

A) 50-50
B) If the truck has jumper cables, he'll be fine.
C) 1 out of 3
D) None—he's dead.
E) It cannot be determined.

9. If Lucy is 12 years old now, how old was she when Phil entered prison?

A) 11
B) 10
C) 9
D) You people are sick.
E) It cannot be determined.

GO TO NEXT PAGE

> DIRECTIONS: Read the two passages below and then answer the questions that follow. The correct response may be skittering on the surface or semi-submerged.

Passage 1:

Memo

TO: Customer Service Associates
FROM: Verizon Wireless Retail HQ
SUBJECT: New types of fraudulent warranty claims

The company is seeing a clear upsurge in replacement claims for phone instruments that have been mistreated in ways that void the warranty. Recently, some customers have presented the company with creative forms of product abuse that are difficult to detect.

Be on the lookout for the following abuses:

(5)
- The instrument has spent time submerged in a toilet. Telltale signs: The instrument may seem unnaturally clean or display an unusual tint. There may be evidence of attempted blow-drying.
- The instrument has been involved in gay hamstering ("Richard Gere-ing"). Telltale signs: The instrument will be on vibrate and will smell funny.

(10)
- The instrument has been used to detonate a bomb. Telltale signs: Parts of the phone are either mangled or absent. Low-cost models more popular for jihad usage.

When you have reason to suspect that a phone failure is due to one of these reasons, do not confront the customer. Simply explain that before the claim can be honored, the instrument must be sent to Warranty Forensics for analysis. Before shipment, please seal it in one

(15) of the provided sterilized hazmat bags.

You can further assist Warranty Forensics by noting suspicious behavior or appearance on the part of a claimant, e.g., the customer is wearing sequined short-shorts or displays evident powder burns on the stumps of missing fingers.

Our fast-growing business brings constant challenges. Thank you for helping us meet

(20) them with commitment and vigilance.

Alberta Myrmidon
Warranty Claims Dept.

GO TO NEXT PAGE ⟶

10   10   10

Passage 2:

COOKE COUNTY

FROM: Sheriff's Department
TO: All Deputies
SUBJECT: Policy Change

Dear Deputies:

For several years now, local anti-profiling guidelines have prohibited stop-and-search on the basis of skin color. Our department's compliance record has been exemplary. Congratulations.

As you know, we have achieved this record by finding creative alternative criteria to establish blackness. This has allowed us to continue our crime preemption program uninterrupted, but with-

(25) out reference to skin color. Current stop-and-search criteria include:

- suspicious bling flash
- wheels that continue to spin after the vehicle has come to a full stop
- exterior hip-hop sound levels in excess of 125 decibels
- Cadillac Escalades in convoys of three or more

(30) But today we face a new challenge. Many non-black teens are now acting black, causing widespread confusion, with their "rep-Ra-ZEN-tin" and jean crotches down at ankle level.

Unfortunately, this has resulted in white kids being pulled over for "driving while black," which has caused our department embarrassment and loss of credibility. In seeking to prevent recurrences of these regrettable blunders, the Department has been forced to adopt a new policy:

(35) From now on, we will arrest only persons who have actually committed a crime.

Sadly, this means that the "pre-apprehension" method is out, replaced by the much less effective "presumption of innocence" method. Let's hope that this step backwards is only temporary and that a compromise will soon be reached that allows our proud department to get back to the work of stopping bad guys before they do what we all know they're going to do anyway.

Sincerely,
Constable Elroy Barnes
Cooke County Sheriff's Department

GO TO NEXT PAGE →

1. In Passage 1, the concept of "fraudulent warranty claims" is most analogous to what concept in Passage 2?

   A) flashing your bling
   B) merengue dancing after curfew
   C) a diamond inset in your tooth
   D) crime the bad guys haven't done yet (but
      we all know they're going to)
   E) tuberculosis screening

2. Which definition below fits the use of the adjective "creative" in both Passage 1 (line 3) and
   Passage 2 (line 23)?

   A) unlawful
   B) anti-Darwinian
   C) deeply offensive
   D) warranty-voiding
   E) saxophone-playing

3. The writer of the first passage differs most from
   the writer of the second in that the latter is more

   A) careful in his personal grooming.
   B) likely to break someone's nose just for fun.
   C) afraid of losing his credibility.
   D) able to identify with illegal immigrants.
   E) likely to sing "The Lonely Goatherd" from
      The Sound of Music.

4. Passage 1 and Passage 2 share a general tone
   of -------.

   A) B-flat minor
   B) suicidal pessimism
   C) bureaucratic euphemism
   D) religious ecstasy
   E) Sarah Silverman on ecstasy

GO TO NEXT PAGE

11   11   11

SECTION 11   Essay

DIRECTIONS: Map out and write an essay in which you develop your views on this issue. Support your position any way you choose. Make it AMAZING.

Think Box

Some people say that video games are too violent. But in an age of global terrorism and an over-extended military, maybe the real question ought to be, are video games violent enough to produce the soldiers we'll need for the army of tomorrow?

ASSIGNMENT: What are some good ideas for making *Halo* more violent? Can you think of a way to weaponize *Dance Dance Revolution*?

GO TO NEXT PAGE

STOP
Don't even *think* of turning the page.

BSAT Test 2

Answer Key

Section 1

1 B
2 D
3 B
4 C
5 D
6 B

Section 2

1 D
2 E
3 A
4 D
5 E
6 D
7 D

Section 3

1 E
2 C
3 A
4 D
5 B
6 E
7 C
8 C
9 A

Section 4

1 E
2 A
3 B
4 B
5 C

Section 5

1 A
2 D
3 D

Section 6

1 D
2 C
3 D

Section 7

1 A
2 B
3 D
4 A
5 D
6 D

Section 8

1 C
2 D
3 B
4 C
5 E
6 D
7 B
8 C

Section 9

1 A
2 B
3 B
4 A
5 B
6 C
7 A
8 E
9 E

Section 10

1 D
2 C
3 C
4 C

Calculating Your Scores

Use the work sheet below to arrive at your "Raw Score" for each of the three sections of the test.

To discover your Real Scores and find out what they mean, turn to pages 39-40 and use the "Raw-to-Real Conversion Chart" and the "How-I-Did vs. How-I-Will-Do Chart."

Critical Reading:

Section 1:   Number Correct = _____ ; Number Incorrect = _____

Section 2:   Number Correct = _____ ; Number Incorrect = _____

Section 6:   Number Correct = _____ ; Number Incorrect = _____

Section 10:   Number Correct = _____ ; Number Incorrect = _____

Total Correct = _____ ;   Total Incorrect = _____

_____ − (_____ ÷ 4) = _____
Total Correct   Total Incorrect   RAW SCORE A

Writing Skills:

Section 4:   Number Correct = _____ ; Number Incorrect = _____

Section 5:   Number Correct = _____ ; Number Incorrect = _____

Section 8:   Number Correct = _____ ; Number Incorrect = _____

Section 11:   Essay Score × .4 = _____ ;

Total Correct + Essay = _____ ;   Total Incorrect = _____

_____ − (_____ ÷ 4) = _____
Total Correct + Essay   Total Incorrect   RAW SCORE B

Math & Reasoning:

Section 3:   Number Correct = _____ ; Number Incorrect = _____

Section 7:   Number Correct = _____ ; Number Incorrect = _____

Section 9:   Number Correct = _____ ; Number Incorrect = _____

Total Correct = _____ ;   Total Incorrect = _____

_____ − (_____ ÷ 4) = _____
Total Correct   Total Incorrect   RAW SCORE C

ANSWER EXPLANATIONS

SECTION 1: Sentence Completions

1. This entire sentence is one big context clue. Ask yourself, "In what situation would Mickey Mouse have a big hand and a little hand?" (No, not a Toontown symposium on birth defects.) That's right—we are obviously talking about a Mickey Mouse watch! Btw, in the Central Time Zone, Mickey's little hand would be on the 6 when the show begins. **Answer: B.**

2. The best context clue is <u>disturbingly eccentric</u>. While eccentric behavior could easily include compulsively A) *playing Hungry Hungry Hippos*, C) *repairing toasters*, or E) *kissing water buffaloes*, only D) *drinking a cup of his own urine* would qualify as disturbing. **Answer: D.**

3. Let's be logical. Charlotte's being <u>fussy</u> develops into something full-blown. But what? Certainly not A) *Cubism*, whose main warning sign is Impressionism, not fussiness. Nor does fussiness lead (necessarily) to E) *pyromania*, C) *nymphomania*, or D) *syphilis*. But it does lead to B) *OCD*, (obsessive-compulsive disorder). **Answer: B.**

4. The big context clue: <u>They . . . called him a pervert</u>, but he kept doing it. Doing what? Rule out A and B, since neither is especially perverted. Same for E, unless he was putting the green plastic army men in icky places. If he'd been playing with D) *little Suzy*, they wouldn't let him keep on doing that. So, by POE, it's clear that he was "the object of his own affections," not that there's anything wrong with that. Except on the cross-town bus. **Answer: C.**

5. No matter what Billy's profession, the only pairs of blanks that make any sense whatsoever are D and E. But since, apart from politicians, no one gets paid for being a pathological liar, we'll go with an under-appreciated D) *high school math teacher*. **Answer: D.**

6. What personal quality would be displayed by someone's <u>accidentally speed-dialing her parole officer</u> while scoring drugs? Skipping the birdbrain choices A, C, and D, is it B) *haplessness* (constant dumb bad luck) or is it E) *deft touch*? **Answer: B.**

SECTION 2: Reading Passage Pair

1. Don't be seduced by E) *an epistolary bestiary.* Yes, the passage is somewhat epistolary, but it's not quite a bestiary. At your age, you should know that this passage is a diary without us having to write "Dear Diary" before each entry. Even if you've never kept one of your own, you must have at least read your sister's. **Answer: D.**

2. This one's tough because all the answers look good: A) *Brokeback Mountain*—a tale of forbidden passion under the big sky, B) *Charlotte's Web*—a moving interweaving of animal and human destinies, C) *Dr. Strangelove*—love and strange knotted together, and D) *Ewes Gone Wild: Mating Season!*—which would really be a lot of fun, if only it existed. Oh well. **Answer: E.**

3. Read the entry for June 30. When Cassandra is killed by a wolf, the author writes, "I feel terrible . . . these sheep are counting on me." He thinks it was his fault. For you sociopaths, that's what the rest of us call *guilt*. **Answer: A.**

4. Answers A, B, and C are ways one might describe a normal person who is slightly maladjusted. This kid, however, is not normal. He's a whack-job, a head-case, a psycho. He has no friends and it's easy to see why: D) *he's a raving sheep-butchering wingnut.* **Answer: D.**

5. For this question you must marshal all your powers of textual analysis. The answer is: E) *he fucks a sheep.* **Answer: E.**

6. In this passage Beavis and Butthead are obviously sheep, which eliminates A and E. And they weren't threatening to *B) eat his burrito*—that was Phillip. And although Beavis and Butthead may actually be *C) gay*, it's not supported by the text. This leaves D, which makes sense, since Chloe sounds like quite the party girl. **Answer: D.**

7. The passage contains no references whatsoever to either *A) Sheep-to-shepherd ratios* or *C) 37 states where it's illegal*. While the writer's activities could be seen as *B) Interspecies dating*, these are actually deeper relationships. As for D, it's perfect. In fact, we like to call this passage "The Parable of the Weird Shepherd." **Answer: D.**

SECTION 3: Mathematics

1. If you can dredge from your memory the definitions of "commutative," etc., this problem is a trivial snap of a piece of cake. If not, don't beat yourself up. Just look at the Math Facts at the top of the section.

   FYI, the operation of telling someone to go fuck himself is *not* commutative (I) because "A tells B to go fuck himself" is not the same thing as "B tells A to go fuck himself." Nor is the operation transitive (II), which would mean that A telling B to go fuck himself and then B telling C to go fuck himself amounts to the same thing as A telling C to go fuck himself, which is obviously not true. Therefore, A ⚙ B must be transgressive (III) because E is the only answer choice that doesn't involve I or II, which are both false. (Also because transgressive happens to mean socially unacceptable, which it kind of is.) **Answer: E.**

2–6. The answers to these five problems don't require anything but common knowledge, for instance the difference between a clusterfuck and a circle jerk. You *do* know the difference, don't you?

   Answers: 2. C 3. A 4. D 5. B 6. E

7. The good news is, you can solve this problem without knowing what a double-belled euphonium is. (Even we're not sure—but we think it's like a mini-French horn.)

   Start by figuring our how big the whole marching band is: If 76 t-bone players and 110 cornet players are 62% of the band, then the whole band is

   $$\frac{76 + 110}{.62} = 300 \text{ players}$$

   So the double-belled euphonium section is 2% of $300 = 6$ db-euph players.

   Now it becomes a word problem (that is *so* BSAT). Which answer phrase means "6"? Maybe you don't know what "sextet" means (if, for instance, you come from Mars). But you know that none of the other answers means "6," so the answer has to be sextet. **Answer: C.**

8. We want to know how many times the number of viewers of Maria's gear doubles. And that's based on how many minutes she has to search, divided by 3, because the viewers double every 3 minutes. Take a look at the answers. Those numbers are *so* far apart that exactness is not needed. We can estimate. The area of her side of the court is *around* $40 \times 35 = 1400$ sq ft. At *around* 50 sq ft / min searching speed, Maria needs *around* 28 minutes for her search. Dividing by 3 we get *around* 9. That's 9 doublings of 100,000 viewers. Just count the doublings on your fingers (100,000, 200,000, 400,000 etc.) to get answer *C) 51,200,000.* By the way, that's almost 1% of the planet's population. Which is why Maria has been called the Russian Rump Roast and presented with the keys to the Western Hemisphere. **Answer: C.**

9. Tom and Umberto each have a one-third chance of infection, but only one of them has caught the drip. So Valerie is in danger from just one of the boys, but not both. So she has a one-third <u>of</u> one-third chance of picking it up. That's $\frac{1}{9}$. **Answer: A.**

SECTION 4: Improving Sentences

1. Because of a misplaced modifier, Jillian is a facing a man whose mustache weighs over 275 pounds. Both C and E more reasonably suggest that it's the man, not the mustache, that's so heavy. However, C still unnecessarily emphasizes the mustache over the man. **Answer: E.**

2. Mendelssohn did indeed have a sister named Fanny, with whom he played duets. But there is no evidence of another sister, Muffie. If you didn't know any of this, you might have been tempted by B. But we can't quite imagine this duet, unless Fanny could fart *La Marseillaise* like the famous 19th-century French virtuoso flatulator, Le Pétomane. **Answer: A.**

3. "Stem the tide" is a metaphor. "Verbal diarrhea" is a different metaphor. When you mix them, things get messy. Forget C, which introduces yet another metaphor, while D has us up to our necks in diarrhetic detail that even *we* find disgusting. Go with the straightforward (and correct) "hold back the flow of." **Answer: B.**

4. Stu should be the subject of the adverbial clause, rather than his blanket or laptop. B or D fill that requirement. Rule out D, however, since remorse can't be crusty. **Answer: B.**

5. How does a sandwich go bad: "quick" or "quickly"? You want the adverbial form "quickly," which appears in answers C and E. The only problem with E is that it's complete drivel. **Answer: C.**

SECTION 5: Improving Paragraphs

1. It helps to know what things mean. "Whipping boy" means "the one who takes all the punishment," but in the sense of "a scapegoat," as opposed to *C) a kinky sex slave*. Note, however, that *E) a scapegoat* is different from "a scapegoat," in the minor sense that the former is a ridiculous malapropism, i.e., it doesn't actually exist. **Answer: A.**

2. Answers B and E are easy to rule out, being so stupid. But what about C and D? Regarding *C) cap-and-trade* solutions: they won't work in this case because measuring human greenhouse gas emissions is impossible, short of inserting a hose in every . . . well, you know. However, the contribution by humans to the overall planetary load of fartrogen dioxide is indeed highly relevant. **Answer: D.**

3. Here's a typical tasteless BSAT slang blitz. Use common sense and the memories of your shit-faced uncles making fart jokes while bass fishing to find the stinker in this pile. Obviously *D) doing the Lord's work* has nothing to do with flatulo-turbulence. By the way, pulling your own figure actually works! **Answer: D.**

SECTION 6: Reading Passage

1. Examples of obsolescence: your parents or any book by Ayn Rand. "Built-in obsolescence" is where something *is designed* to wear out. You can argue about whether that's a cynical thing to do, but not about the . . . **Answer: D.**

2. The answer is staring at you in line 19. It was to harness "the inherent sadism of little boys," which is pretty similar to *C) the depravity of little boys*, or, as King Lear famously noted: "As flies to wanton boys are we to the gods. They kill us for their sport." Little bastards. **Answer: C.**

3. The fun of this global question is that you get to tote up Herman Smill's personal failings. He is a sadistic (as in A), exploitative (as in B), ghoulish (as in C) money-grubber (as in E). However, he wouldn't know *D) wholesome collaborative play* if it ran up his nightshirt. **Answer: D.**

SECTION 7: Analogies

1. Test sentences:

     A <u>snotrag</u> is normally used to hold <u>boogers</u>.

     A ------- is normally used to hold <u>jism</u>.

   Assuming you know what jism is, the correct answer is obviously either *A) scumbag* or *C) condom*, both of which hold jism. But notice that booger, snotrag, and jism are all slang terms, just like . . . **Answer: A. scumbag.**

2. Test sentences:

     <u>Scientist</u> is a serious occupation, but when you add just a few letters, it turns into <u>scientologist</u>, which is a joke.

     <u>Cosmologist</u> is a serious occupation, but when you add just a few letters, it turns into -------, which is a joke.

   Answer: B. cosmetologist.

3. One for you nerds. The giveaway should be answer *A) 98.6*. That's a famous number—normal human body temperature. And once you notice that we're talking about degrees on a thermometer, you can make a little story that, while not precisely a test sentence pair, should help you to a certain degree.

     <u>32</u> and <u>212</u> are the freezing and boiling points of water in Fahrenheit.

     <u>0</u> and ------- are the freezing and boiling points of water in Centigrade.

   "This belongs on the Physics BSAT," you whine? Sorry, that doesn't exist yet. Get over it. **Answer: D. 100.**

4. Test sentences:

     <u>Girls</u> are completely at home with <u>math</u>.

     <u>Fish</u> are completely at home with _____.

   Answer: A. swimming and it's NOT FUNNY.

5. This analogy is evil. The relationship between "laced" and "decal" is simply that one is the other spelled backward. And "radar," spelled backward, is . . . **Answer: D. radar.**

6. This analogy's format is a little different. You're given one related pair of words and asked to choose a word pair that is similarly related. The solution still depends on coming up with the right test sentence:

     The moment you enter <u>Facebook</u>, you abandon every last shred of <u>privacy</u>.

     The winner by a mile: The moment you enter <u>The Biggest Loser</u>, you abandon every last shred of <u>dignity</u>.

   Answer: D. *The Biggest Loser.*

SECTION 8: Identifying Sentence Errors

1. Verb tense error. The first verb, "made," is in the past tense. What starts in the past tense stays in the past tense. You don't <u>notice</u>, but rather, you <u>noticed</u> Stimson's package. Hard to miss. **Answer: C.**

2. Pronoun confusion. Igor is not an <u>it</u> (or so we must assume). Igor is a <u>he</u> who shouldn't draw attention to himself. He shouldn't be robbing graves, either. **Answer: D.**

3. Subject-verb agreement problem. The subject here is a book *Late Bloomer: The Early Years*. It's singular. So the verb's number must also be singular. Accordingly, it exemplifies. **Answer: B.**

4. Diction blunder. Grandpa "could never have licked," not "could never of licked." The talented Nurse Betty, however, could probably lick anything. **Answer: C.**

5. No error, except maybe Suzy's original decision to ride with the team. **Answer: E.**

6. Parallelism/verb tense error. What idiot used swelled and produced in the past tense and then tried to stick us with channels in the present tense? (Actually we know the idiot. He works for us. He's one of our best writers.) **Answer: D.**

7. Idiotic idiom. If you have to lose sleep, do it right. You lose sleep over poisoned tuna fish, not toward it. **Answer: B.**

8. Redundancy. As his wife said on her way out the door, "It's either me or those foreskins!" So it's not surprising that this moyel died alone. But it's redundant to say that he died both alone and also all by himself. In case you don't know, a moyel is the guy who performs Jewish circumcisions. **Answer: C.**

SECTION 9: Mathematics

1. This one's a gift. You don't even need math. Just look at the numbers. Ethel, whatchoo been up to, bitch? You really askin for it. **Answer: A.**

2. The Dallas Cowboys are a bunch of regular guys but they're also highly paid professional athletes who party hearty. OK—they got Bianca's phone number by accident. But they made a lot of memories and they don't regret a minute of it. They were also very generous in their appreciation. **Answer: B.**

3. Don't guess on this one—you actually have to do the math. Together Coyote and Destiny earned a total of $8,000 but *could* have earned 50% more ($12,000) as twins. Steve's commission could have been $6,000 instead of $4,000 or an extra *B) $2,000* that he didn't have to do a thing for. No wonder he is generously considering treating them to matching boob-jobs, which he figures should close the sale for the most twin-fetishists. **Answer: B.**

4. First find the total window area available for mooning. The window dimensions are easily converted into feet: 2 ft × 3 ft = 6 ft² per window. 12 windows × 6 ft² = 72 ft² total window area. We're told that 75% of that glass is covered with ass:

   75% of 72 ft² = 54 ft² total ass on glass

   Divide that by 45 kids:

   $\dfrac{54 \text{ ft}^2}{45} = 1.2$ ft² per full butt

Remember, we're looking for the average individual cheek. And that's just half the full butt, or .6 ft². **Answer: A.**

5. This question is really an introduction to the concept of the blivot. Nerds will see right away that a blivot is the ratio $\dfrac{(x-y)}{y}$ where x is the amount of shit and y is the size of the bag. The rest of us just need to know that one blivot is when a container holds 100% more stuff than it was designed for. The answer is clearly B because 11 pounds is only $\dfrac{1}{10}$ of the way from zero blivots to a full classic 20-pound blivot. **Answer: B.**

6. Answer *A) 1 mega-blivot*, is tempting because of the sheer enormity of the fashion choice, but it would be wrong, because that dress is holding only 50% more opera singer than it was designed for. By definition that's just half a blivot. A full blivot, in this case, would have been that size-24 opera singer blossoming out of a size-12 outfit, a situation almost beyond contemplation. Interestingly, *E) –0.5 blivots* would have had our diva in a size-48 dress (possibly available at a sailing outfitter) and would actually have been loose-fitting! **Answer: C.**

The blivot is also a useful measure of dorm room garbage cans, politicians, and Speedos.

7. This is a normal sort of rate problem, if your idea of normal includes pedophilia. Note that because the two guys are chained together, you can treat them as one floppy awkward object, an "FAO." At first they go 6 mph for just 5 minutes, which is $\frac{1}{12}$ of an hour. That's $\frac{1}{12}$ of 6 miles or $\frac{1}{2}$ mile. For the second part of the trip, with Phil dragging the unconscious Dave, the speed doesn't matter, because the problem tells you they went $1\frac{1}{2}$ miles. So there you have it: $1\frac{1}{2} + \frac{1}{2}$ = answer *A) 2 miles*. Incidentally, answer E, though literally true, is too dumb to count. **Answer: A.**

8. Dave passed out and the FAO then traveled $1\frac{1}{2}$ miles at 3 mph, which clearly took $\frac{1}{2}$ hour, or 30 minutes. What are their chances of getting Dave to a doctor in the remaining 10 minutes? Since they don't know where to find a doctor, the answer must be that it cannot be determined. But it doesn't look good for Dave. **Answer: E.**

9. We have no idea how long ago Phil entered prison, so there's no other answer possible but it cannot be determined. **Answer: E.**

SECTION 10: Reading Passage Pair

1. Both memos deal with crime prevention. Passage 1 deals with insurance fraud, while Passage 2 deals with what crime? There's only one choice that even mentions actual crime. That's *D) crime the bad guys haven't done yet (but we all know they're going to)*. **Answer: D.**

2. OK, you're trying to narrow in on a peculiar definition of "creative." In Passage 1, "creative forms of product abuse" turns out to mean things like hamstering and terrorism, which are both "warranty-voiding" and "deeply offensive" (to some), though maybe not "unlawful" (at least the hamstering). In Passage 2, "creative alternative criteria to establish blackness" refers to ways to ignore anti-discrimination laws, which *is* unlawful, as well as "deeply offensive," though not "warranty-voiding." So the two passages share "deeply offensive." **Answer: C.**

3. We know nothing about either author's *A) personal grooming* or taste in music (as in E). We may infer that the sheriff of Passage 2 is the kind of public servant who is *B) likely to break someone's nose* and probably not *D) able to identify with illegal immigrants* but, frankly, we don't know how to compare him with the author of Passage 1. However, in line 33, the sheriff confides that false arrests have eroded the department's credibility. Close enough. **Answer: C.**

4. Three idiotic answers! Another gift from the Wizards of Bellows Falls. Your real choices are between B and C. But if you've read your Sylvia Plath or Virginia Woolf, you know that neither of these passages contains two shits worth of suicidal pessimism. **Answer: C.**

BSAT Test 3

BSAT Test 3

Answer Sheet

Answers on p. 202

Section 1

1 (A) (B) (C) (D) (E)
2 (A) (B) (C) (D) (E)
3 (A) (B) (C) (D) (E)
4 (A) (B) (C) (D) (E)
5 (A) (B) (C) (D) (E)
6 (A) (B) (C) (D) (E)

Section 2

1 (A) (B) (C) (D) (E)
2 (A) (B) (C) (D) (E)
3 (A) (B) (C) (D) (E)
4 (A) (B) (C) (D) (E)
5 (A) (B) (C) (D) (E)

Section 3

1 (A) (B) (C) (D) (E)
2 (A) (B) (C) (D) (E)
3 (A) (B) (C) (D) (E)
4 (A) (B) (C) (D) (E)

5

	/	/	
.	.	.	.
	0	0	0
1	1	1	1
2	2	2	2
3	3	3	3
4	4	4	4
5	5	5	5
6	6	6	6
7	7	7	7
8	8	8	8
9	9	9	9

6

	/	/	
.	.	.	.
	0	0	0
1	1	1	1
2	2	2	2
3	3	3	3
4	4	4	4
5	5	5	5
6	6	6	6
7	7	7	7
8	8	8	8
9	9	9	9

7 (A) (B) (C) (D) (E)
8 (A) (B) (C) (D) (E)

Section 4

1 (A) (B) (C) (D) (E)
2 (A) (B) (C) (D) (E)
3 (A) (B) (C) (D) (E)
4 (A) (B) (C) (D) (E)
5 (A) (B) (C) (D) (E)

Section 5

1 (A) (B) (C) (D) (E)
2 (A) (B) (C) (D) (E)
3 (A) (B) (C) (D) (E)

Section 6

1 (A) (B) (C) (D) (E)
2 (A) (B) (C) (D) (E)
3 (A) (B) (C) (D) (E)
4 (A) (B) (C) (D) (E)
5 (A) (B) (C) (D) (E)

Section 7

1 (A) (B) (C) (D) (E)
2 (A) (B) (C) (D) (E)
3 (A) (B) (C) (D) (E)
4 (A) (B) (C) (D) (E)
5 (A) (B) (C) (D) (E)
6 (A) (B) (C) (D) (E)

Section 8

1 (A) (B) (C) (D) (E)
2 (A) (B) (C) (D) (E)
3 (A) (B) (C) (D) (E)
4 (A) (B) (C) (D) (E)
5 (A) (B) (C) (D) (E)
6 (A) (B) (C) (D) (E)
7 (A) (B) (C) (D) (E)
8 (A) (B) (C) (D) (E)

Section 9

1 (A) (B) (C) (D) (E)
2 (A) (B) (C) (D) (E)
3 (A) (B) (C) (D) (E)
4 (A) (B) (C) (D) (E)
5 (A) (B) (C) (D) (E)
6 (A) (B) (C) (D) (E)
7 (A) (B) (C) (D) (E)
8 (A) (B) (C) (D) (E)
9 (A) (B) (C) (D) (E)
10 (A) (B) (C) (D) (E)

Section 10

1 (A) (B) (C) (D) (E)
2 (A) (B) (C) (D) (E)
3 (A) (B) (C) (D) (E)
4 (A) (B) (C) (D) (E)

NO TEST MATERIAL ON THIS PAGE

1   1   1

SECTION 1

Sentence Completions

DIRECTIONS: This ------- screwed up.

1. "Everyone's me trying to make fail!" declared the -------.

   A) dyslexic paranoid
   B) guy in the Yoda suit
   C) subject line of a Viagra eblast
   D) online translation program
   E) Gibberator™

2. The weird thing about the TV show *24* is -------.

   A) that Jack Bauer never has to eat, sleep, or piss
   B) that the technology always works
   C) that it makes us realize how cool torture really is
   D) its high ratings
   E) all of the above

3. Learning how to play ------- requires patience, practice, and, above all, a baritone kazoo.

   A) left tackle
   B) pinochle
   C) Grimaldi's *Concerto for Orchestra and Baritone Kazoo*
   D) both ends against the middle
   E) well with others

4. As if punctuating the difficult landing, Orville came to a stop with -------.

   A) aplomb
   B) a plum
   C) his nuts in his throat
   D) a sickening thud
   E) his fuselage intact

5. Ethan and Karl, ------- after both getting dumped again by their girlfriends, realized they were actually quite -------, so they drove through the night to ------- and got -------.

   A) plastered . . compatible . . Boston . . married
   B) despondent . . handsome . . Madame Chloe's . . laid
   C) initially puzzled . . relieved . . Funkytown . . jiggy wit it
   D) preparing to litigate . . without a leg to stand on . . Tijuana . . matching Glocks
   E) any of the above

6. I thought we all looked pretty good, considering we were up till 4 a.m. doing -------.

   A) the Macarena
   B) tequila shots
   C) flu shots
   D) unto others as they were doing unto us
   E) it

GO TO NEXT PAGE >

2   2   2

SECTION 2   Reading Passage Pair

DIRECTIONS: Read the two passages below and then answer the questions that follow. The correct response may be dropped like a bombshell or floating like a hint.

Below are two emails, received 5 weeks apart at the offices of the BSAT. We reproduced them unedited.

Passage 1:

```
From Mis Jane Aboje
Côte d'Argent
AFRICA


HELLO DEAR CHOSEN ONE,
```

Please I was given your name by a TRUSTED SOURCE who vouches for your spot-less repute. I know you will be kind when I expose my predicaments, which I write with an orphan's tears.

(5) I am Miss Jane Aboje, legitimate daughter of Col. Samson Aboje who was head of the Secret Police of the African dictocracy of Côte d'Argent before being elevated to High Commissioner of Ethics after a truce in our bloody civil war. By the Grace of God my father was able to divert a sum of £19,000,000 Pounds Sterling intended for purchase of yellowcake uranium into a SECRET FUND domi-ciled at a GOOD BANK in our capital of Ubuville.

(10) But the truce did not last and my father was dragged from inside his bed by rebels and heartlessly boiled in motor oil. These same rebels subsequently ran over our capital, establishing a parliamentary democracy that everyone in Côte d'Argent throws their shoes at.

Although I am under house arrest I have advised the bank to verify about the (15) SECRET FUND of £19,000,000 which is still there but the MANAGER said I am not up to the age that they reach in agreement with my father, stating that I must have a guardian to help me receive what is rightfully mine as NEXT OF KIN.

I want to transfer this money to a US account to pursue BLUE CHIP INVESTMENT opportunities. If I could transfer the money to your a/c I would gladly pay (20) you 20% of the total sum. It has to be a FOREIGN Account. This is ABSOLUTELY LEGAL but please don't tell the authorities in my country because it would mean humiliations for me, including Death.

Also could you set up BLUE CHIP INVESTMENT opportunities and could you find a place for me to stay that is safe for a beautiful young girl. Do you have a (25) spare bedroom in your house where I could sleep?

Please if you don't want to help me delete this email but I beg you in God's merciful name not to be mean and surly to an orphan who has already suffered so much trials. I have the right to freedom and happiness, too, not just you.

I feel a bond already with you and know that God will help us form a mutu-
(30) ally beneficial and loving relationship.

Write to me soon with your name, address, phone number and the a/c number of
your principal checking account. For easier verification purposes please
include your social security number and mothers maiden NAME.

Yours in Gods love,
Miss Jane Aboje

Passage 2:

From Miss Jane Aboje
Côte d'Argent
AFRICA

Hello Again, Dear Chosen One,

(35)   I write with joyous news! My father Col. Samson Aboje is not dead after all
and I am not an orphan! Instead he has been working with the REBELS to establish normalised Weapons Procurement methods for the new army from vendors in
Chad and Boca Raton. In this capacity he has been fortunate to secrete funds
worth USD 27,000,000 into a personal account while working for the good of all
(40) LONG SUFFERING Côte d'Argent peoples. I pray that you will do your part to
relieve our national sorrows.

My father lives under threat of discovery on his mission of mercy. It is
imperative that the USD 27,000,000 be expatriated to a safe FOREIGN a/c in a
FOREIGN bank. Even though YOU AND I did not do business last time I still
(45) trust you and beseech you to help me in my deepest dilemmas and bothers for
the same 20% share of funds as before.

And now I will tell you a secret. My father and I hope to relocate to
Newark, N. Jersey, USA to pursue BLUE CHIP INVESTMENT strategies and schemas
and we need to find a N. Jersey, USA CITIZEN to help us, granting him 35% of
(50) all profits free and clear and 100% ABSOLUTELY LEGAL and ABOVE BOARD. This
will benefit us mutually and also help the LONG SUFFERING people of heart-
grievanced Côte d'Argent.

Please send to me, a young and beautiful girl who has only admiration, trust
and love for you, your NAME, address, Principal Checking A/C # and PIN. The
(55) fate of the peoples of my country lie within your gentle power.

Only yours in God's Bounty and Goodness,
Miss Jane Aboje

GO TO NEXT PAGE

2   2   2

1. In the two passages the author tries to ingratiate herself by all of the following strategies EXCEPT:

   A) by promising easy money (and lots of it)
   B) by dangling the prospect of sick sex with a pretty young girl
   C) by evoking sympathy for an orphan
   D) by guaranteeing the scheme is ABSOLUTELY LEGAL and ABOVE BOARD
   E) by offering to tattoo a wildebeest on a body part of the reader's choosing

2. How are the passages related?

   A) Passage 1 is the sequel to 2.
   B) Passage 2 is the prequel to 1.
   C) Passages 1 and 2 are both part of a government bailout.
   D) Passage 2 is the bastard son of 1.
   E) Both 1 and 2 are examples of traditional Nigerian handicraft.

3. What prompted the writer to send the second email?

   A) Miss Jane Aboje became even more desperate for WARM and LOVING companionship.
   B) There was a total eclipse of the moon.
   C) The recipient failed to take advantage of the first offer.
   D) The rebels were at the door.
   E) Joyous news! Col. Aboje came back from the dead.

4. How much does the reader stand to make by posing as Miss Aboje's "legal guardian?"

   A) £38,000.00
   B) £3,800,000.00
   C) £380,000,000,000,000,000.00
   D) £38,000,000,000,000,000,000,000,000,000,000,000,000,000,000,000,000,000,000,000,000,000,000,000,000,000,000,000,000,000,000,000,000,000,000,000,000,000,000,000,000,000,000,000,000,000,000,000,000,000,000,000,000,000,000,000,000.00
   E) £0.00

5. What kind of people would fall for a transparent scam like this?

   A) people with an orphan fixation
   B) old folks who are losing their marbles
   C) horny greedy gimme boys
   D) N. Jersey USA citizens with BLUE CHIP INVESTMENT opportunities
   E) God only knows.

GO TO NEXT PAGE

3   3   3

SECTION 1   Mathematics

DIRECTIONS: For each problem in this section there are m possible solutions offered, where m is given by the volume integral

$$\iiint_E 2x\,dV,$$

$$\text{where } E = \{(x,y,z) \mid 0 \le y \le 2,\ 0 \le x \le \sqrt{\tfrac{9}{2}-y^2},\ 0 \le z \le y\}$$

Choose the correct one. Use any blank space on the page for doodling.

Math Facts

- The area of a right triangle: $\dfrac{\text{Side} \times \text{Side}}{2}$
- The total degrees in a circle: $360°$
- The sum of the internal angles of a triangle: $180°$
- The sum of the internal angles of Ruben Studdard: ∞
- The sum of the internal layers of a Reuben sandwich: 4 (corned beef, sauerkraut, Swiss cheese, Russian dressing)

---

1. Roxanne is very smart but she has trouble getting dates, so she joins the Geometry Club. At the first meeting everyone is supposed to bring in a challenging problem. Here's Rox's:

   Assume the following line pairs are parallel: DR and SU, DI and SO, OR and IU.

   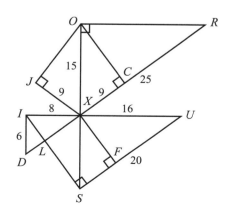

   Which of the following triangles is the biggest in terms of area?

   A) COX
   B) DIX
   C) Kind of SUX
   D) Definitely SUX
   E) Size doesn't matter.

GO TO NEXT PAGE

3   3   3

2. Which pair of triangles has the same ratio of areas as ROX : SUX?

   A) SIX : DIX
   B) JOX : COX
   C) SIX : JOX
   D) JOX : DIX
   E) None of the above

3. Which set of triangles is listed in descending order of area?

   A) ROX LIX SIX COX
   B) ROX SUX SIX DIX
   C) ROX SUX JOX COX
   D) ROX FUX SIX JOX
   E) ROX LIX JOX DIX

4. Inflation in Zimbabwe runs at 100,000% per year. A wheelbarrow holds 2,000,000 Zimbabwean Dollars (ZWD). On September 1, a chicken cost 650,000 ZWD. How many wheelbarrows full of ZWD will it take to buy a chicken on the following September 1?

   A) 325 wheelbarrows
   B) 3,250 wheelbarrows
   C) 32,500 wheelbarrows
   D) 325,000,000 wheelbarrows
   E) Chickens are no longer available in Zimbabwe due to a shortage of wheelbarrows.

GO TO NEXT PAGE

5. Four zombies can eat three victims in two hours. How many zombies does it take to eat nine victims in three hours?

   GRID-IN

6. The only way to stop zombies is with chainsaws. If three defenders can chainsaw twelve zombies per hour, how many zombies are dismembered by seven defenders in two and a half hours?

   GRID-IN

7. Starting with 2,400 zombies, if their number grows by 20% per day, how many chainsaws are needed to keep the zombie population from increasing and eventually taking over the world.

   A) None; zombies cannot take over the world because they can't get through airport security without photo ID.
   B) 400 chainsaws
   C) 5 chainsaws
   D) 96 chainsaws
   E) It's hopeless; the zombies cannot be stopped.

8. It's hard for Vitruvio to hide his feelings about women (see diagram below).

   He perfectly illustrates the axiom, "The angle of the dangle is proportional to the heat of the meat," or $A_D = K(H_M)$, where K is the Peter Meter Coefficient.

   Vitruvio thinks that Sarah is hot at 120 degrees. He finds Tammy half as hot as Sarah but still twice as hot as Uma. Valerie turns Vetruvio off—she's negative hot, in fact, precisely as *not* hot as Uma is hot. Xandra, on the other hand, is as hot as Sarah plus one-and-a-half Tammy's, one Uma, and three Valerie's put together. How hot is Xandra?

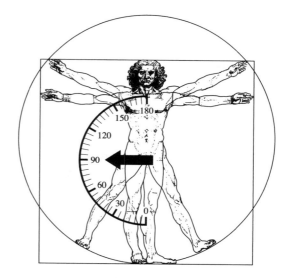

   A) 32 degrees ("the Dicksicle")
   B) 90 degrees ("Polly's Perch")
   C) 150 degrees ("the Scud")
   D) 180 degrees ("the Washington Monument")
   E) 212 degrees ("the Red-Alert")

GO TO NEXT PAGE

4   4   4

SECTION 4   Improving Sentences

DIRECTIONS: The underlined portions of the sentences below may contain errors, from the piddling to the egregious. In some cases the entire sentence is underlined because the whole thing may be messed up. Figure out which of the five alternatives straightens things out the best. Choose answer A if you still prefer the original.

1. The toilet was reported clogged by the visiting dietician.

   A) [Leave it alone!]
   B) The visiting dietician reported that the toilet was clogged.
   C) The visiting dietician was reported to have clogged the toilet.
   D) The toilet was reportedly visited by the clogged dietician.
   E) The toilet was reportedly clogged with a visiting dietician.

2. His dangling modifier hanging out of his pants, this sentence needs a lot of work.

   A) [as is]
   B) his main clause nowhere to be found
   C) his limp diction stuck in his zipper
   D) but his girlfriend stuffed it back in
   E) he went trick-or-treating dressed as a grammatical error

3. The boys of Camp Lumpybunk decided to delay their panty raid on Camp Ukantutchett until the moon had rose over Lake Kickapoopoo.

   A) [love it]
   B) had a rose over Lake Kickapoopoo
   C) had arosen over Lake Kickapoopoo
   D) had aroused over Lake Kickapoopoo
   E) had risen over Lake Kickapoopoo

4. On the seventh count of murder in the first degree, the jury finds the defendant guilty as charged and recommends that he be hung by the neck until dead.

   A) [beautiful in its present form]
   B) that he be hanged by the neck until dead
   C) that he be hanged by the neck (but not until dead)
   D) that he be harangued by his wife until dead
   E) that he be let off with a warning

5. Our "fearless leader" is sailing the ship of state down the road to ruin.

   A) [Do not touch.]
   B) driving the ship of state down the road to ruin
   C) driving the RV of state down the road to ruin
   D) piloting the spaceship of state a long time ago, in a galaxy far, far away
   E) sailing the ship of state onto the rocky shoals of ruin

GO TO NEXT PAGE

5   5   5

SECTION 5

Improving Paragraphs

DIRECTIONS: The passage below is an unedited draft that needs help. Read it carefully and try to improve it by answering the questions that follow.

Colonel Samson Aboje
Cote d'Argent
AFRICA

[1] Dear Trusted Friend

[2] I write to you with humiliated concern because I found your name among address books of my daughter Jane Aboje, with whom you have relations. [3] Now I must inform you that my daughter is not a well lady and has not told you the truth of her situation or mine. [4] Did she tell you I was Minister of Reconciliation? [5] I am not. [6] Did she say I infiltered the dastard rebels? [7] I have not.

[8] Instead I am a successful private person like yourself, who only wants happiness and peace for his little girl, who is not stable and might have made to you promises and propostitions she will never bring about. [9] She intends well but her mind is adrift.

[10] How can I ever make restitution for the pain and heartache you've experienced on behalf of my naughty daughter? [11] Would money be of any interest to you? [12] I am a wealthy man, thanks to providence and an uncle in the government. [13] I would like to transfer a gift of 14.000 USD directly to your account by electronic wire. [14] This is completely AND 100% LEGAL AND ABOVE BOARD.

[15] Please accept this insufficient token of my gratitude and emoluments. [16] If you would be so kind as to provide your acct # as well as your name and phone number and SS#, I will consider the debt I owe you discharged and sleep with an easy mind.

[17] Your faithful servant,
Colonel Aboje

[18] PS. I have recently come into possession of 3 pieces of artwork looted during Wrld War 2 by the german high command. [19] One of the paintings alone is called "Blue Dog, Red Rug and Green Countess" by M. Pblo Picaso and has been appraised at worth of £ 21.000.000.

[20] Because of the sensitive past of the art it must be disposed of with utmost speed. [21] You can honor me to become my FULL PARTNER in this venture. [22] Why not apply my little gift to you of 14.000 USD, on condition that you send another 66.000 USD to me by tomorrow afternoon. [23] This urgent opportunity is 100% ABSOLUTLELY LEGAL AND ABOVE BOARD. —Col S.A.

GO TO NEXT PAGE >

5   5   5

1. Which would be the best revision of the underlined portion of Sentence 6?

   [6] Did she say I infiltered the dastard rebels?

   A) the dastard rebels [no change]
   B) the dastardly rebels
   C) the bastard rebels
   D) the bastardly rebels
   E) the rebels

2. Which of the following would most improve
   the effectiveness of Col. Aboje's email?

   A) Get right to the point by beginning with
       sentence [18].
   B) Omit sentence [14], a dead giveaway that
       the Colonel and his daughter are the same
       person.
   C) Double the gift offered in [13] to 28.000
       USD.
   D) Spell Pablo Picasso's name correctly in
       [19].
   E) This is a top-quality Nigerian scam letter—
       don't change a thing.

3. Taking the author at his word, which of the following best describes his purpose in adding the
   post-script that begins with Sentence 18?

   A) to generously offer the recipient a no-
       brainer slam-dunk payday
   B) to show off his intimate knowledge of "the
       german high command"
   C) to get another chance to use the phrase
       "100% ABSOLUTELY LEGAL AND
       ABOVE BOARD"
   D) to pick up a quick sixty-six grand
   E) to ease his conscience about his daughter's
       naughty antics

GO TO NEXT PAGE

SECTION 6

Reading Passages

DIRECTIONS: Read the passages below and then answer the questions that follow. The correct response may be a screaming headline or the gentlest whisper.

Passage 1:

On our home planet, Earth, a full body cavity search is uncomfortable and demeaning, but, with terrorist bombs on the rise, we take it in stride, thinking, "it could be worse." And it
(5) could. Consider the planet 3ß-Carinae, where spaceport security is so tight that the pat-down of choice is the "Möbius strip search," where they literally turn you inside out so that anything ingested or "orificed" falls clattering to
(10) the Carinaean tarmac.

a Möbius Strip

Unlike the traditional Möbius Strip, which short-circuits a 2-dimensional object through the 3rd dimension, this draconian procedure bends your 3-dimensional innards around the
(15) 4th dimension. Although this is but a minor inconvenience to the highly elastic and multi-dimensional 3ß-Carinaeans, Earthlings have a hard time pulling themselves together after such treatment.

1. In what time period was this passage most likely written?

A) 1492
B) 1860–1890
C) 1891–1945
D) 1946–2018
E) 2031–2279

2. What is meant in line 13 by "this Draconian procedure"?

A) going through spaceport security
B) the "Möbius strip search"
C) being "orificed"
D) "a minor inconvenience"
E) taking the BSAT

GO TO NEXT PAGE

6   **6**   **6**
___

Passage 2:

The following sonnet recently came to light in the Bodleian Library at Oxford. An academic debate currently rages as to whether it might be a Shakespearean first draft.

"Untitled Sonnet"

(20) Shall I compare thee to a pile of poo?
Thou smellest sweeter than the noxious turd.
Whilst flies buzz round the horrid heap of doo
You host the butterfly and hummingbird.

Betimes with gaze toward lofty heaven cast
(25) I've trod by chance upon a coiled heap
And not remarked until th' event was past
The residue of doo-doo dark and deep.

But thou, my love, art never to be found
Squeezed out in foul malignant stinking mass.
(30) Thine essence is no squat and steaming mound
That late resided up some canine ass.

So long as thou adherest not to my shoe
I'll ne'er compare thee to a pile of poo.

3. The rhyme scheme of this poem is:

   A) ABAB BCBC CDCD EE
   B) ABAB CDCD EFEF AA
   C) BABA CACA DADA OO
   D) CACA POOP OOPS AH
   E) ABCD EFGH IJKL BB

4. In this context, what is meant in line 13 by "adherest"?

   A) stickest fast
   B) takest umbrage
   C) speakest without couth
   D) frotheth from the mouth
   E) bringeth thuccor

5. It has been proposed that the subject of the poem is not, in fact, the poet's lover. If true, which of the following is instead the most likely subject of the poem?

   A) the poet's 7-week-old son
   B) his beagle
   C) Lord Bunbury, Chancellor of Sewers
   D) the poet himself
   E) there's no way to tell

GO TO NEXT PAGE

7   7   7

SECTION 7

Analogies

DIRECTIONS: In each question below you are given a pair of words, phrases, or whatevers that are somehow related. From the choices offered, complete the second pair so that they are related in the same way as the first pair.

1. barfing : calling Ralph on the big white phone :: jerking off : -------

   A) going on a date with Pamela Handerson
   B) stamping your own passport
   C) giving yourself a low-five
   D) beating the piss out of your best friend
   E) any of the above

2. touchy feely : hippy dippy :: wishy washy : -------

   A) namby pamby
   B) Walla Walla
   C) hunky dory
   D) sticky wicket
   E) picky picky

3. retard : drool :: intellectual : -------

   A) swamp gas
   B) reason
   C) drivel
   D) prevaricate
   E) Nietzsche

4. twelve : gross :: thirteen : -------

   A) grosser
   B) one hundred ninety-six
   C) baker's gross
   D) bad luck
   E) $(dozen + 1)^2$

5. jockeys : boxers :: leotards : -------

   A) bun-warmers
   B) rebellion
   C) muumuus
   D) circus big top
   E) wrestlers

6. fellatio : buggery :: tablet : -------

   A) suppository
   B) laptop
   C) lap dance
   D) Moses
   E) migraine

GO TO NEXT PAGE

8   8   8

SECTION 8   Identifying Sentence Errors

DIRECTIONS: Each of the following sentences contains either a single error or no error at all. Select the underlined portion that contains the foozle or, if none, choose E) No error.

1. A woman of <u>large</u> <u>appetites,</u> Kate described
           A   B

   herself <u>on</u> her <u>luvnut.com</u> dating profile as
        C   D

   Massively Multiplayer. <u>No error</u>
               E

2. Michael's career as a speech therapist <u>for</u>
                         A

   parrots didn't take <u>off</u> until he moved <u>in</u> an
             B   C

   area thick <u>with</u> pirates. <u>No error</u>
          D   E

3. When Louis heard that <u>sex</u> offenders were to
                 A

   be <u>legally</u> registered, he called the office
       B

   <u>wanted</u> to find out how he <u>could</u> sign up.
     C   D

   <u>No error</u>
     E

4. Fastidiously <u>working</u> from 2,000-year-old
             A

   Roman patterns, Louise was convinced that

   her sewing <u>would</u> finally win her friends and
           B

   make for the <u>most awesomest</u> toga party ever,
             C

   but nobody gave a <u>shit</u>. <u>No error</u>
             D   E

5. Aunt Ella's <u>pussy</u> has often been treated
            A

   <u>harshly</u>, but somehow <u>it</u> always lands on <u>her</u>
      B   C   D

   feet. <u>No error</u>
       E

GO TO NEXT PAGE

6. It <u>can't</u> have been easy for Johnny to tell his
      A

   father, <u>who</u> even his mom called The Colonel,
            B

   that he <u>had</u> dropped out of West Point and
           C

   enrolled <u>in</u> Barnum & Bailey Clown College.
            D

   <u>No error</u>
      E

7. To determine the size of the financial settle-

   ment, the archbishop <u>sought</u> the help of the
                         E
   Sisters of the Infinite Host, a mathematical

   <u>order</u> of nuns who <u>has</u> taken a <u>vow</u> of
    B   C   D
   calculus. <u>No error</u>
              E

8. When Louis learned in biology class that the

   <u>growth</u> of many living things <u>is</u> limited only by
    A   B
   the size of their <u>enclosure</u>, he bought <u>himself</u>
                      C   D
   looser underpants. <u>No error</u>
                      E

GO TO NEXT PAGE

9   9   9

SECTION 9   **Mathematics**

DIRECTIONS: For each problem in this section there are h possible solutions offered, where h is the determinant of the 3×3 matrix A

$$A = \begin{bmatrix} \dfrac{1}{\pi} \sum\limits_{n=1}^{\infty} \dfrac{1}{n^2} & \oint_c (2x\cos y - y\cos x, \, -x^2\sin y - \sin x, \, 0) \cdot d\vec{r} & e^{i\pi} + 0! \\[2ex] 6.02 \times 10^{23} & \sqrt{1 + 2\sqrt{1 + 3\sqrt{1 + \ldots}}} + 2 & \nabla \cdot \left(\nabla x \left(4xye^{zy}, \, x^2 \ln(y), \, \dfrac{z}{xy} \right) \right) \\[2ex] 42 & \lim\limits_{n \to \infty} \left(1 + \dfrac{1}{n} \right)^n & 3\left[1 - \sum\limits_{n=1}^{\infty} \left[(4n+1)(-1)^n \left(\prod\limits_{k=1}^{n} \dfrac{2k-1}{2k} \right)^3 \right] \right] \end{bmatrix}$$

Choose the correct one. Use any blank space on the page for doodling.

Math Facts

- Formula for a parabola: $ax^2 + bx + c = y$
- Formula for an hyperbola: $\dfrac{x^2}{a^2} - \dfrac{y^2}{b^2} = 1$
- Formula for hyperbole: $\dfrac{x^2}{a^2} - \dfrac{y^2}{b^2} =$ **The best 1 ever!**

1–4. The graph below plots a standard Bifurcated Boobaloid function represented by the formula:

For $-12 \le x \le 0$, $y = x^2 + x + 5$ AND

for $0 \le x \le 12$, $y = x^2 - x + 5$ AND

For $-7 \le x \le -3$, $y = x^2 - x - 1$ AND

for $3 \le x \le 7$, $y = -x^2 + x - 1$

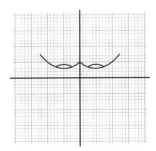

In the each of the following four questions, a change in coefficients is made from the original Boobaloid function above. Match each change with the corresponding resulting curves below.

1. Which graph shows the effect as x^2 goes to $4x^2$?

2. The effect as x goes to $2x$?

3. The effect as x goes to $0x$?

4. As x^2 goes to $2x^2$ and x goes to $3x$?

GO TO NEXT PAGE ⟹

A) Uniboobaloid

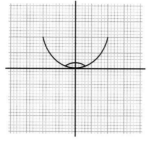

B) Triboobaloid

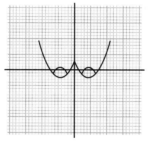

C) Geriatric Droopaloid

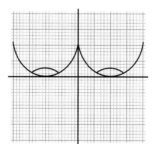

D) Jessicasimpsaloid

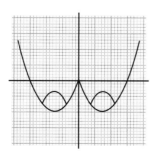

E) Bigmamaloid

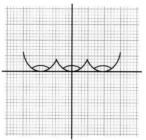

5. There are 99 bottles of beer on the wall, 99 bottles of beer. If three frat boys take $\frac{1}{3}$ of them down and pass them around, and then smash $\frac{3}{11}$ of the rest in the parking lot, and then play Intramural Beer Pong with $\frac{1}{2}$ of the remainder, that leaves how many bottles of beer on the wall?

A) Twennnyfoooour
B) zzzzzzzzzzzzzzzz
C) Youknowwutt??? I lovvvyouman!
D) Thurrrysixxx
E) Sevendee . . .***BLURRRRGHHH***
    . . . sorry

6. Kent has the runs. When he enters the stall, there is a fresh roll of toilet paper consisting of 1,000 sheets and with dimensions as indicated in the figure below.

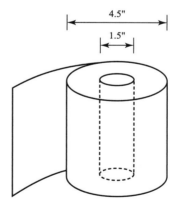

When he is finished wiping, the roll is down to a diameter of 3 inches. How many sheets of bum wad has he used?

A) 333 sheets
B   500 sheets
C) 625 sheets
D) 667 sheets
E) a shit load

GO TO NEXT PAGE

9   9   9

7. Kathy is a booty babe. Lucy is a double booty babe. Marcy is even more of a booty babe than Lucy but not quite a triple booty babe. If Nancy is as much of a booty babe as Kathy and Lucy put together, who's more of a booty babe, Kathy, Marcy, Lucy, or Nancy?

   A) Kathy
   B) Lucy
   C) Marcy
   D) Nancy
   E) They're equal. You're either a booty babe or you're not.

8. Having wasted her first semester on drink and debauchery, Roxanne has repented and wants to deliver the message of virtue to her fellow sinners on campus. Accordingly, she has begun to monitor and catalog depraved conduct. Of the 410 students in her class, Rox has determined that 215 are binge-drinkers, 273 are promiscuous, and 53 are neither. How many are promiscuous binge-drinkers?

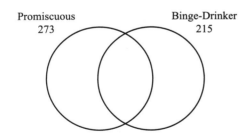

Promiscuous 273   Binge-Drinker 215

   A)   357
   B) 142
   C) 131
   D) 84
   E) not as many as would like to be

9. Roxanne has expanded her crusade to include Plagiarists and Grade-Grubbers. Noting that some students indulge in more than one of the four iniquities at a time, how many combinations of two or more are possible? Refer to the diagram below.

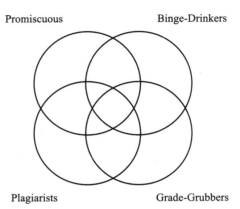

Promiscuous   Binge-Drinkers

Plagiarists   Grade-Grubbers

   A) 4
   B) 6
   C) 9
   D) 12
   E) I have no idea—there are so very many ways to combine just sex and alcohol alone.

GO TO NEXT PAGE

10. Inspired by her study of Dante's *Inferno*, Roxanne has developed a system of categorization and punishment in the world-to-come for practitioners of various college peccadilloes.

Roxanne's Taxonomy of College Iniquities

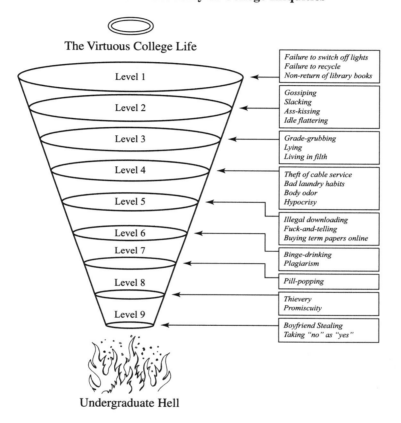

The Virtuous College Life

Level 1	Failure to switch off lights / Failure to recycle / Non-return of library books
Level 2	Gossiping / Slacking / Ass-kissing / Idle flattering
Level 3	Grade-grubbing / Lying / Living in filth
Level 4	Theft of cable service / Bad laundry habits / Body odor / Hypocrisy
Level 5	Illegal downloading / Fuck-and-telling / Buying term papers online
Level 6	Binge-drinking / Plagiarism
Level 7	Pill-popping
Level 8	Thievery / Promiscuity
Level 9	Boyfriend Stealing / Taking "no" as "yes"

Undergraduate Hell

Roxanne is satisfied with her system for condemning sinners to suitable levels of Undergraduate Hell. But she is now grappling with the problem of multiple sins. For instance, what should be the fate of a Grade-Grubber (Level 3) who also fails to return a library book (Level 1)? So Roxanne has devised a formula to determine the level to which you descend for combinations of offenses. L stands for the total of the levels of your various sins. Desiring to be merciful as well as thorough, she has made an allowance for youthful error in the square-root term.

$$\text{Damnation number} = L^2 - \sqrt{\frac{\text{Age}}{18} + 3}$$

If their average number of offenses is 3 and their average level is also 3, what is the likely fate of the average 18-year-old freshman?

A) Level 2
B) Level 5
C) Level 8
D) They're all going to the deepest uncharted reaches of hell.
E) They have to date Roxanne.

GO TO NEXT PAGE

10   10   10

SECTION 10   Reading Passage

DIRECTIONS: Read the long passage below and then answer the questions that follow. The correct response may be crushingly obvious or bewilderingly esoteric.

Excerpted from the short story "After The Bombs" by the Peruvian master of pornographic magical realism, Manuel Garcia-Infante. The protagonist's village has become a battleground between "los narcotraficantes" and government soldiers.

On the morning of June 3rd, Juan Roberto crawled out of his tent and walked a few meters up the steep Northern Path to relieve himself. He noted yet again the eerie calm, devoid of
(5) school children's squeals, buzzing motorbikes, or bleating goats. The previous Sunday, during high mass, half of the village houses and the entire guava crop had been torched by El Guapo and his thugs. Privation herself pressed down on
(10) everyone's shoulders.

When he opened his fly he noticed that he had two dicks. *This should be interesting*, he thought, as he pulled them both out. *Which will the piss come out of?* The answer was immedi-
(15) ate—both.

Juan Roberto was not a naturally curious man. By sundown he had grown to accept his new physique. "Perhaps I have been blessed," he shrugged. "Or cursed. What's the differ-
(20) ence?" Out of habit he joined his fellow soldiers at the local cantina. The moment he entered he noticed a tall, wiry woman of sad eyes and indeterminate age sitting by herself in the corner, nursing what could be either tea or
(25) absinthe. Juan Roberto made a joke, and soon they were laughing and touching. *If this goes where I think it's going*, he thought, *I'll soon have a decision to make. Right or left?*

When she sat on his lap he noted that both
(30) boys were equally enthusiastic. He wondered whether La Estrella (for that was what she called herself) would be repulsed or intrigued when she beheld his arrangement. It could go either way. And did these fellows have inde-
(35) pendent appetites? Would Señor Derecho's adventure satisfy Señor Izquierda, or would he insist upon his own moment of glory?

[The protagonist takes his new friend to the other cantina in the village, where he meets his
(40) *sergeant, who owes him money but is too drunk to find his wallet. Juan Roberto begins to think he is in love with La Estrella and that his future happiness depends on the outcome of their encounter tonight. They duck into a utility*
(45) *closet.]*

As he unbuttoned La Estrella's dress he felt a wave of paralysis, as if caught in a crossfire and unsure which way to run. Was it his fate to always be the innocent victim, now of his par-
(50) ents squabbling over money, now of the incessant battle between the drug cartel and the government and, any minute, of macho discord in his trousers? As she reached for his belt his anxiety caused his knees to shake.

(55) He need not have worried. La Estrella had three cunts, an extra asshole, and a dick of her own, for good measure. This night was like no other. Hushed, careful exploration gave way to giddy bouts of romping and frolicking, only to
(60) be interrupted by the realization of some new, never-imagined configuration.

[Ten pages of details follow.]

The next morning the bomb craters were gone, the children were back in school, a jas-
(65) mine-scented breeze rolled off the sunny mountain, and Juan Roberto had only one dick.

GO TO NEXT PAGE ⟶

1. What evidence does the author give that La Estrella is, in some sense, magical?

    A) She says "Presto Change-O" a lot.
    B) She has no last name.
    C) She can drink absinthe without throwing up.
    D) She has an extra asshole.
    E) His night with her healed the whole town.

2. Within the anatomical givens of the passage, how many different ways are there for the narrator and La Estrella to do it?

    A) 2
    B) fewer than 9
    C) more than 16
    D) an infinite number of ways
    E) do what?

3. In line 9 the sentence "Privation herself pressed down on everyone's shoulders . . ." is an example of which rhetorical device?

    A) miasma
    B) appendectomy
    C) synecdoche
    D) personification
    E) metamucil

4. What is the LEAST apt title for the passage?

    A) Juan Roberto Gets Lucky
    B) Two Dicks Diverged in a Yellow Wood
    C) The Duality of Life in Time of War
    D) My Night of Pretentious Pornographic Bullshit
    E) Pippi Longstocking Goes to Rehab

GO TO NEXT PAGE

11   11   11

SECTION 11   Essay

DIRECTIONS: Map out and write an essay in which you develop your views on the assigned issue. Support your position any way you choose. Make it AMAZING.

Think Box

There seems to be a universal impulse toward a belief in the transcendental. It's hard to think of a culture that doesn't exhibit religious tendencies, whether expressed through concrete symbols in the world, or through more abstract, even psychological belief systems. As varied as they may be, all societies share a profound yearning for a power greater than the individual.

ASSIGNMENT: What is the stupidest religion you can think of? Compare and contrast it with other incredibly stupid belief systems.

GO TO NEXT PAGE

11   11   11

_____
_____
_____
_____
_____
_____
_____
_____
_____
_____
_____
_____
_____
_____
_____
_____
_____
_____
_____

STOP
Don't even *think* of turning the page.

BSAT Test 3

Answer Key

Section 1

1 A
2 E
3 C
4 D
5 E
6 B

Section 2

1 E
2 E
3 C
4 E
5 E

Section 3

1 D
2 E
3 B
4 A
5 8
6 70
7 C
8 C

Section 4

1 B
2 E
3 E
4 B
5 E

Section 5

1 B
2 E
3 A

Section 6

1 D
2 B
3 B
4 A
5 E

Section 7

1 E
2 A
3 C
4 E
5 C
6 A

Section 8

1 E
2 E
3 C
4 C
5 D
6 B
7 C
8 C

Section 9

1 C
2 D
3 A
4 E
5 A
6 C
7 D
8 C
9 C
10 D

Section 10

1 E
2 C
3 D
4 E

Calculating Your Scores

Use the work sheet below to arrive at your "Raw Score" for each of the three sections of the test.

To discover your Real Scores and find out what they mean, turn to pages 39-40 and use the Raw-to-Real Conversion Chart and the How-I-Did vs. How-I-Will-Do Chart.

Critical Reading:

Section 1: Number Correct = _____ ; Number Incorrect = _____

Section 2: Number Correct = _____ ; Number Incorrect = _____

Section 6: Number Correct = _____ ; Number Incorrect = _____

Section 10: Number Correct = _____ ; Number Incorrect = _____

Total Correct = _____ ; Total Incorrect = _____

_____ − (_____ ÷ 4) = _____

Total Correct · · · Total Incorrect · · · RAW SCORE A

Writing Skills:

Section 4: Number Correct = _____ ; Number Incorrect = _____

Section 5: Number Correct = _____ ; Number Incorrect = _____

Section 8: Number Correct = _____ ; Number Incorrect = _____

Section 11: Essay Score × .4 = _____ ;

Total Correct + Essay = _____ ; Total Incorrect = _____

_____ − (_____ ÷ 4) = _____

Total Correct + Essay · · · Total Incorrect · · · RAW SCORE B

Math & Reasoning:

Section 3: Number Correct = _____ ; Number Incorrect = _____

Section 7: Number Correct = _____ ; Number Incorrect = _____

Section 9: Number Correct = _____ ; Number Incorrect = _____

Total Correct = _____ ; Total Incorrect = _____

_____ − (_____ ÷ 4) = _____

Total Correct · · · Total Incorrect · · · RAW SCORE C

ANSWER EXPLANATIONS

SECTION 1: Sentence Completions

1. Any of these answers could conceivably account for the weird word order of the sentence. The best answer, though, would explain both the content of the message and the fucked-up syntax (word order). That would be *A) dyslexic paranoid*. **Answer: A.**

2. This one is very Rocky Road. More than just completing a sentence, you're asked to draw certain conclusions from the twenty-four hours you spend every season fretting over traitors within CTU, compromised security codes, impossible roof-top SWAT team raids, etc. If you have no idea who Jack Bauer is, you need to pick up a couple of seasons from Netflix and start syncing up with the rest of us. NOW!! **Answer: E.**

3. To solve this elegant logic puzzle, try focusing on the baritone kazoo and the special circumstances that might call for its use. Like a *C) Concerto for Orchestra and Baritone Kazoo*. **Answer: C.**

4. The giveaway here is that he is punctuating a landing, probably with a sudden bump. Neither *A) aplomb* (unflustered ease) nor *B) a plum,* (a pointless play on "aplomb") includes a bump. In fact, the only bump within sight would be *D) a sickening thud*. **Answer: D.**

5. If you've ever been dumped repeatedly, then you know the astonishingly wide array of emotions and behaviors that can occur when you're on the rebound, as Ethan and Karl are in this heroic four-blanker. The despondency, the bewilderment, the anger, etc., it's all here, in a rich, true-to-life human tapestry. If, on the other hand, you're just a smug little hottie who's never been dumped, fuck you! **Answer: E.**

6. Here's a case where the context clue is the whole sentence. Whatever they were doing until 4 a.m., it was something that would usually make you look like hell. Answers C and D are daft space shots, while E would actually give you a healthy glow (unless it's with whips and chains). So the choice is between A and B. As bad as *A) the Macarena* obviously is, it's less damaging than an all-nighter of *B) tequila shots*. **Answer: B.**

SECTION 2: Reading Passage Pair

1. Close inspection of both passages reveals a total lack of wildebeest references. **Answer: E.**

2. If you have an email account, you'll quickly realize that these passages are Nigerian "419" scam letters, named after the section of that country's legal code that outlaws them. Nigeria's fraud email industry is so dynamic that it contributes over 10% of the country's GDP. **Answer: E.**

3. Try not to get personally involved in Miss Aboje's life narrative, fascinating though it may be. If you stay objective, you'll see that "she" is a salesman, pursuing a wary prospect. **Answer: C.**

4. As mathy as this question looks, it involves no computation. All it requires is street sense. **Answer: E.**

5. We know what you're thinking: "This is one of the most perplexing philosophical debates of our time, and yet you expect me to solve it right here on your stupid multiple choice test?" Actually, we don't. **Answer: E.**

SECTION 3: Mathematics

1. You can do this problem by math—the long way—or by "inspection," which is probably what Roxanne had in mind. Ignoring C and E, examine COX and DIX and also SUX. Which *looks* biggest? Definitely SUX, right? That's the correct answer, D. Nerds would have noticed that these are all 3-4-5 right triangles and used the Pythagorean theorem to get the same result. That's the hard way and definitely sucks. **Answer: D.**

2. BSAT drawings, like SAT drawings, are to scale unless you're told otherwise. Knowing this can save a lot of time. ROX is obviously bigger than SUX by roughly 50%. You can eliminate both B and C since SIX, COX, and JOX are all pretty close in size. Neither A nor D seems right because DIX is much smaller than either SIX or JOX. That leaves *E) None of the above,* the correct answer. This problem can also be done with formal geometry, but fuck it. **Answer: E.**

3. To get the most out of this problem, read each answer aloud to your friends over a pitcher of beer.

   Of course ROX is the largest triangle, so she is listed first in every answer. Answers A and E cannot be right, because LIX, being least, should be listed last. As to the remaining three: C can get tossed because the last two, JOX and COX are equal. B looks good since SUX, SIX, and DIX are clearly in descending order.

   What about answer D? SUX is a 3-4-5 triangle, so line segment SX is 12. JOX is equal to COX, so line segment JO is also 12. SIX is therefore smaller than JOX, ruling out D. Of course, from Roxanne's point of view, there are no wrong answers and now she's president of the Geometry Club. **Answer: B.**

4. How many wheelbarrows does it take to buy a chicken this September 1? Answer: about $\frac{1}{3}$. And next September 1, it's going to cost 1000 times that (100,000% = a factor of 1000). Multiply $\frac{1}{3}$ times 1000 and you get approximately 333, which is very close to 325. **Answer: A.**

5. Solve this one just like a typical alien and anal-probe rate problem, by changing two elements at a time instead of all three. To start:

   > 4 zombies can eat 3 victims in 2 hours

   We're looking for how many zombies can eat 9 victims in 3 hours. So let's increase both victims and zombies proportionally, but leave the hours alone. To eat 9 victims in the same amount of time requires 3 times as many zombies:

   > 12 zombies can eat 9 victims in 2 hours

   Next, we want the feast to last for 3 hours instead of 2. For the same number of victims, more eating time means fewer zombies. So we multiply hours and divide zombies—both by $\frac{3}{2}$ (dividing by $\frac{3}{2}$ is the same as multiplying by $\frac{2}{3}$):

   > 8 zombies can eat 9 victims in 3 hours

   9 victims split up among 8 zombies? Hmm. That last victim is family style. Sweet. **Answer: 8 zombies.**

6. If you're a fan of movies like 28 Days Later, you may be tempted to assume that the splatter from a chainsawed zombie will zombify the splatteree. Don't! Keep it simple. Once again, let's change just two variables at a time:

   > 3 defenders can chainsaw 12 zombies in 1 hour

   Change hours and zombies first:

   > 3 defenders can chainsaw 30 zombies in $2\frac{1}{2}$ hours

Now defenders and zombies (we have to multiply by $\frac{7}{3}$):

7 defenders can chainsaw 70 zombies in $\frac{1}{2}$ hours

Answer: 70 zombies.

7. Keep in mind that the task is not to eliminate zombies but merely to keep the zombie population in check. Starting with 2,400 of them and a 20% growth rate, we have to dismember 480 of them per day to stay even (20% × 2400 = 480).

From the previous problem, we know that 3 defenders can chainsaw 12 zombies per hour, resulting in a rate of 4 zombies per hour for each chainsaw. But we've got a full day, 24 hours, to mutilate 480. Now just eliminate wrong answers. Clearly 400 chainsaws is too many (that would be 1,600 chopped zombies per *hour*!) and so is 96 (that number would maim nearly 400 in a single hour). So skip the math! The answer is obviously *C) 5*. If you want to proove it to yourself: $\frac{480}{20} = 20$ zombies per hour, which would take exactly 5 chainsaws slashing zombies full time. **Answer: C.**

8. Start by calculating everyone's temperature. Take them one at a time:

Sarah = 120 degrees

$\text{Tammy} = \frac{\text{Sarah}}{2} = 60$ degrees, which equals Uma × 2, so . . .

Uma = 30 degrees

Valerie = negative Uma = −30 degrees

Using that list, Xandra is the total of:

Sarah 120

$1\frac{1}{2}$ Tammy's 90

1 Uma 30

3 Valeries −90
_____

Xandra total: 150

At 150 degrees, Xandra's a Scud—that's <u>really</u> hot. For you virgins, rest assured that these temperatures are metaphorical. **Answer: C.**

SECTION 4: Improving Sentences

1. Because of a misplaced modifier, this sentence appears to accuse the visiting dietician of clogging the toilet herself, rather than just reporting the problem. (Talk about shooting the messenger!) Which alternative cleans up the mess? Neither C nor D offers any improvement, while E is just gruesome. Fortunately, B fixes both the misplaced modifier *and* the toilet. **Answer: B.**

2. Here is a modifier that is fated to dangle until it hooks up with the correct main clause, which A is not. B and C are so pathetic, they're not even complete sentences. D is a full sentence, but has the defect of being gibberish. However, in E everything comes together: modifier, main clause, and meaning. And they live happily ever after. **Answer: E.**

3. As we've pointed out elsewhere, the past participle gets no respect anymore (See Study Guide, Chapter 4). Here are four exciting new ways to mangle this poor part of speech, as the moon rises over Lake Kickapoopoo. Only E gets it right, but that's probably just dumb luck. **Answer: E.**

4. Even some professional executioners don't know this, but coats are *hung*; people must be *hanged*. The two "hanged" possibilities are B and C. Go with B because hanging someone by the neck but *not* until dead is cruel and unusual. **Answer: B.**

5. A horror show: mixed metaphor meets faulty idiom. Sure, a "ship of state" can sail, but please—not down "the road to ruin." An RV can drive down the road, but "the RV of state" and "space ship of state" are just ridiculous imagery. Answer E, while a little over-the-top, is OK because it parlays two nautical metaphors into one big extended shipwreck. **Answer: E.**

SECTION 5: Improving Paragraphs

1. Don't you wish you could use a lifeline to find out exactly what "dastard" means? Never mind—we'll tell you: a dastard is a coward who commits a brutal act without giving his victim a chance. That makes it a better term for the rebels than "bastard." However, you need the adjectival form, which is "dastardly," not "dastard." **Answer: B.**

2. Frankly, the rules of these scam letters are different from those of everyday letter writing. And since this one is the work of a tribal professional at the top of his game, we recommend trusting his expertise and going with E. **Answer: E.**

3. This one is tricky. You must decide if the question is about the author's purpose *within* the fictional universe of Colonel Aboje or, on a meta-level, his purpose in real life. Hmm. Answer A would describe Col. Aboje's purpose, while D would describe the scammer's evil intent. But wait! The phrase "taking the author at his word" limits us to the fictional world of the email. That nails it. **Answer: A.**

SECTION 6: Reading Passages

1. Don't overthink this problem. Just because the passage seems to deal with future-ish things, it couldn't possibly have been written in the future. How could we have received it? So cross off E. However, the passage's modern references like "spaceport security" and "tarmac" make *D) 1946–2018* a time period we can all feel comfortable with. **Answer: D**

2. "Draconian" means really, really, really harsh. It refers to an ancient Greek judge who punished pretty much every infraction with death, including loitering and public belching. In the passage, "this draconian procedure" refers specifically to being turned inside-out, the "Möbius strip search." **Answer: B.**

3. A refresher on rhyme scheme notation: Any line-ending words that rhyme get the same capital letter. For example, the rhyme scheme for limericks is: AABBA. The Gettysburg Address rhyme scheme is: ABCDEFGHIJKLMNOPQRF. Anyway, the classic sonnet of Shakespeare's time has the rhyme scheme: ABAB CDCD EFEF AA. **Answer: B.**

4. The verb "to adhere" means to cling, to stay attached—in short, to *stick* fast. Don't get thrown off by the old-timey second-person singular verb form, "stickest." It's just more Shakespearean blather. **Answer: A.**

5. In line 28, the poet addresses the subject as "my love," which would likely rule out *C) Lord Bunbury, Chancellor of Sewers*. As for D, it seems a little kinky to call yourself "my love," while comparing yourself to dog shit. That leaves two other possibilities: *A) the poet's 7-week-old* son or *B) his beagle*, but no criteria for choosing between them. **Answer: E.**

SECTION 7: Analogies

1. Test sentences:

    Calling Ralph on the big white phone is a polite term for barfing.

    ------- is a polite term for jerking off.

This problem is like masturbation itself—there is no wrong way to do it. That is to say . . . **Answer: E. any of the above.**

2. Test sentences:

> Touchy feely is pretty much the same thing as hippy dippy.

> Wishy washy is pretty much the same thing as -------.

If you don't know these useful terms, you need to spend more time at *www.urbandictionary.com*. **Answer: A. namby pamby.**

3. Test sentences:

> A retard involuntarily emits drool.

> An intellectual involuntarily emits -------.

If you're at all tempted by answer *B) reason*, you've obviously never met an intellectual, many of whom are French. **Answer: C. drivel.**

4. This analogy demonstrates that setting up test sentences doesn't *always* provide a solution. For example, you may have set up something like this:

> If twelve is gross, then thirteen is -------.

And maybe you thought the answer was *A) grosser*. Sorry. Remember, a gross is a dozen dozens, aka 12×12 or 12^2 or 144. So you're looking for something that's like that for 13×13. If you're really clever you know that a "baker's dozen" is 13, so maybe you think there's something called a baker's gross! Sorry, there isn't. Then how about *B) 196*? That must be 13×13. Nope. Sorry again. 13×13 is 169. There's only one good . . . **Answer: E. (dozen + 1)^2.**

5. Test sentences:

> Jockeys fit snugly, whereas boxers fit loosely.

> Leotards fit snugly, whereas ------- fit loosely.

While you may know them by the less formal *tent dress*, their real Hawaiian name is . . . **Answer: C. muumuus.**

6. Test sentences:

> Fellatio is administered orally, while buggery is administered anally.

> Tablet is administered oral, while ------- is administered anally.

Answer: A. suppository.

SECTION 8: Identifying Sentence Errors

1. No error. Not to digress, but we highly recommend lovenut.com, which is soon to become part of BSAT World Enterprises LLC. **Answer: E.**

2. Faulty idiom. Arrrgh. It *is* possible to move in a neighborhood, but only if you're already there. Michael, however, moved into the pirate neighborhood from his previous low-crime area. **Answer: E.**

3. Verb tense misdemeanor. Maybe grammar offenders should be legally registered, like sex offenders. Then we'd haul in this author for writing wanted instead of wanting, which is correct. **Answer: C.**

4. Adjective error. Louise's toga party could be either the most awesome or, more colloquially, the awesomest. Not both. (And probably neither.) **Answer: C.**

5. Wrong pronoun, with serious consequences. We trust you understand that this sentence is talking about a mistreated <u>cat</u> of indeterminate gender. Thus, <u>it</u> will always land on <u>its</u> feet, not <u>her</u> feet. **Answer: D.**

6. Pronoun malfunction—who vs. whom. Johnny's father was the one <u>whom</u> even Johnny's mom called The Colonel. Object, not subject. But Johnny was the one <u>who</u> preferred big floppy shoes to combat boots. **Answer: B.**

7. Subject verb agreement error, but a subtle one. It is not the religious order who <u>has</u> taken the vow of calculus, but rather the nuns who are members of that order who <u>have</u> done so. Lord only knows why. **Answer: C.**

8. Singular/plural problem. The "many living things" are limited by the size of their <u>enclosures</u>, in the plural. They're not all stuffed into the same box. **Answer: C.**

SECTION 9: Mathematics

1. To solve this problem you must grasp the Boobaloid in all its variations and have a good feel for the curves. Basically, the top formulas define the two boobs and the bottom ones (with $-x^2$) define the nipples, which we can pretty much ignore (but we'll get to them later).

   As x^2 goes to $4x^2$, a general stretching downward can be expected. This effect can be seen only in the Geriatric Droopaloid. **Answer: C.**

2. As x goes to $2x$, a widening, swelling effect can be expected, filling out the graph voluptuously, like the Jessicasimpsaloid. **Answer: D.**

3. As x goes to $0x$, what were two distinct equations become one, and the quasi-mythical Uniboobaloid results. **Answer: A.**

4. Finally, as x^2 goes to $2x^2$ and x goes to $3x$, a pair of curves balloons into view, both stretching *and* widening, engulfing almost all the graph space, leaving little room for other equations or even your own opinions—this can only be the Bigmamaloid. **Answer: E.**

5. Assuming we can interpret the brew-sodden mumblings of a bunch of drunks, this problem is pretty easy. $\frac{1}{3}$ of 99 is obviously 33, leaving 66 bottles of beer on the wall. Because 66 is a clean multiple of 11, the fraction $\frac{3}{11}$ of that is clearly 18, leaving 48 bottles of beer on the wall. Half of that is 24 ("Twennnyfoooour") unopened, unsmashed bottles of beer on the wall. (Please excuse the guy in answer E. He didn't mean to do that.) **Answer: A.**

6. Instead of counting sheets, look at this as a volume problem, or even simpler, as an area problem. The diagram shows one end of the toilet paper roll.

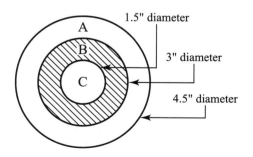

Low Road approach: A and B together comprise the whole roll of 1,000 sheets. Area A is what Kent uses, and B is what's left at the end. Right off, we can eliminate 2 answers. A is obviously much bigger than B as a proportion of the total of 1,000 sheets, so Kent used much more than half, which flushes A and B down the crapper. Answer *E) a shit load* is poetically correct, but not quantitative enough for us. The Low Road got us pretty far! Now it's either a 50-50 guess between C and D, or if you're not a gambler . . . math.

Are you ready for the High Road? We're looking for what part of 1,000 is represented by area A as a proportion of A + B. Turning that into a formula:

$$\frac{x}{1000} = \frac{A}{(A + B)}$$

Boot up your calculator; let's calculate A and B. Don't forget to subtract the hole, area C. The area of a circle is πr^2 and π is about 3.14. (Note that the drawing shows <u>diameters</u>, not radii.) Rounding to tenths:

$$A + B + C = 3.14 \left(\frac{4.5}{2}\right)^2 = 15.9 = \text{the whole circle}$$

$$B + C = 3.14 \left(\frac{3.0}{2}\right)^2 = 7.1 = \text{everything inside B}$$

$$C = 3.14 \left(\frac{1.5}{2}\right)^2 = 1.8 = \text{C alone}$$

So A is 15.9 – 7.1 = 8.8 and B = 7.1 – 1.8 = 5.3.

So: $\frac{x}{1000} = \frac{8.8}{8.8 + 5.3}$, and solving for x, we get 624, which is close enough to answer *C) 625*.

Remember, we rounded to tenths, which accounts for the difference. **Answer: C.**

7. We can eliminate answer E because the problem itself clearly supports the idea of booty babe-ness occurring in variable amounts. How to solve? Set up a booty babe number line:

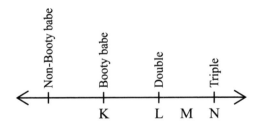

Kathy (K) is a basic booty babe. Lucy, being double, is located just to the right. Marcy is clearly between double and triple, and Nancy, being the sum of K + L, is a triple. **Answer: D.**

8. We're looking for the overlap between the circles, or area B.

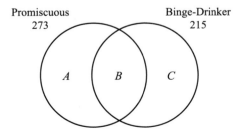

Out of the total of 410 students in the class, take out 53, who are neither promiscuous nor binge-drinkers:

410 – 53 = 357, which is the total of Promiscuous and/or Binge-Drinkers, areas A + B + C.

Subtract from that the total Promiscuous:

$$(A + B + C) - (A + B)$$
$$357 - 273 = 84$$

which is the total of Binge-Drinkers who are not also Promiscuous, which is area C.

Now subtract C from the total number of Binge-Drinkers (which is B + C):

$$(B + C) - C$$
$$215 - 84 = 131$$

which is the total number of Binge-Drinkers who are also Promiscuous, area B, and precisely the number of degenerates that we're looking for! It's problems like this that stand between Roxanne and the popularity she craves. **Answer: C.**

9. You're looking for combinations of two or more vices at a time. Each combination is seen in overlapping sections of the circles in the Venn diagram. Where each depravity overlaps with just one other (e.g. Promiscuous and Plagiarists), we can count a total of four. Where three overlap (the small triangle-ish sections near the center), we get another four. Finally, the very center shows a single group at the very heart of wickedness—Promiscuous, Binge-drinking, Plagiarizing Grade-grubbers. That's a total of 9. You may disregard answer E, which shows a nasty creativity but misses the point. **Answer: C.**

10. If the average number of freshman sins is 3 and their level also 3, then L is typically 9 and so L squared = 81! That's reduced by Roxanne's pretty stingy idea of mercy, which comes to a measly 2. Bottom line is 79, which puts you well beyond even the deepest reaches of Roxanne's righteous fury. The answer is D, unless you want *E) to date her* (Trust us, you don't). **Answer: D.**

SECTION 10: Reading Passage

1. Magicians *A) say "Presto-Change-o"* all the time. That doesn't make them magical. In fact, the world is full of non-magical people who use *B) no last name*, people who successfully *C) drink absinthe without throwing up*, and people who have *D) an extra asshole* (though these are, admittedly, rarer). However, healing a whole town? **Answer: E.**

2. This question involves a little math and a lot of imagination. Simply add up all the available genitalia, throw in other favorite orifices, and it's apparent that, although not infinite, there are many more than 16 ways for these characters to play hide-the-baloney. **Answer: C.**

3. The non-ludicrous answers are *C) synecdoche* and *D) personification*. Synecdoche is a figure of speech in which a part stands for the whole, as in "Give us this day our daily bread" or "Get your ass out of here." On the other hand, *D) personification* is when something abstract is treated like a person, in this case, a masseuse, who is somehow able to give the whole town a back rub ("Privation herself pressed down on everyone's shoulders.") **Answer: D.**

4. Since Pippi Longstocking is not mentioned (at least, by name—she could be a serving wench in the cantina), it's safe to say she doesn't belong in the title. **Answer: E.**

BSAT Test 4

BSAT Test 4 — Answer Sheet

Answers on p. 238

Section 1

1 Ⓐ Ⓑ Ⓒ Ⓓ Ⓔ
2 Ⓐ Ⓑ Ⓒ Ⓓ Ⓔ
3 Ⓐ Ⓑ Ⓒ Ⓓ Ⓔ
4 Ⓐ Ⓑ Ⓒ Ⓓ Ⓔ
5 Ⓐ Ⓑ Ⓒ Ⓓ Ⓔ
6 Ⓐ Ⓑ Ⓒ Ⓓ Ⓔ

Section 2

1 Ⓐ Ⓑ Ⓒ Ⓓ Ⓔ
2 Ⓐ Ⓑ Ⓒ Ⓓ Ⓔ
3 Ⓐ Ⓑ Ⓒ Ⓓ Ⓔ
4 Ⓐ Ⓑ Ⓒ Ⓓ Ⓔ

Section 3

1 Ⓐ Ⓑ Ⓒ Ⓓ Ⓔ
2 Ⓐ Ⓑ Ⓒ Ⓓ Ⓔ
3 Ⓐ Ⓑ Ⓒ Ⓓ Ⓔ
4 Ⓐ Ⓑ Ⓒ Ⓓ Ⓔ
5 Ⓐ Ⓑ Ⓒ Ⓓ Ⓔ

6 (grid-in answer box)

7 Ⓐ Ⓑ Ⓒ Ⓓ Ⓔ
8 Ⓐ Ⓑ Ⓒ Ⓓ Ⓔ
9 Ⓐ Ⓑ Ⓒ Ⓓ Ⓔ
10 Ⓐ Ⓑ Ⓒ Ⓓ Ⓔ

Section 4

1 Ⓐ Ⓑ Ⓒ Ⓓ Ⓔ
2 Ⓐ Ⓑ Ⓒ Ⓓ Ⓔ
3 Ⓐ Ⓑ Ⓒ Ⓓ Ⓔ
4 Ⓐ Ⓑ Ⓒ Ⓓ Ⓔ
5 Ⓐ Ⓑ Ⓒ Ⓓ Ⓔ

Section 5

1 Ⓐ Ⓑ Ⓒ Ⓓ Ⓔ
2 Ⓐ Ⓑ Ⓒ Ⓓ Ⓔ
3 Ⓐ Ⓑ Ⓒ Ⓓ Ⓔ

Section 6

1 Ⓐ Ⓑ Ⓒ Ⓓ Ⓔ
2 Ⓐ Ⓑ Ⓒ Ⓓ Ⓔ
3 Ⓐ Ⓑ Ⓒ Ⓓ Ⓔ
4 Ⓐ Ⓑ Ⓒ Ⓓ Ⓔ
5 Ⓐ Ⓑ Ⓒ Ⓓ Ⓔ
6 Ⓐ Ⓑ Ⓒ Ⓓ Ⓔ
7 Ⓐ Ⓑ Ⓒ Ⓓ Ⓔ

Section 7

1 Ⓐ Ⓑ Ⓒ Ⓓ Ⓔ
2 Ⓐ Ⓑ Ⓒ Ⓓ Ⓔ
3 Ⓐ Ⓑ Ⓒ Ⓓ Ⓔ
4 Ⓐ Ⓑ Ⓒ Ⓓ Ⓔ
5 Ⓐ Ⓑ Ⓒ Ⓓ Ⓔ
6 Ⓐ Ⓑ Ⓒ Ⓓ Ⓔ

Section 8

1 Ⓐ Ⓑ Ⓒ Ⓓ Ⓔ
2 Ⓐ Ⓑ Ⓒ Ⓓ Ⓔ
3 Ⓐ Ⓑ Ⓒ Ⓓ Ⓔ
4 Ⓐ Ⓑ Ⓒ Ⓓ Ⓔ
5 Ⓐ Ⓑ Ⓒ Ⓓ Ⓔ
6 Ⓐ Ⓑ Ⓒ Ⓓ Ⓔ
7 Ⓐ Ⓑ Ⓒ Ⓓ Ⓔ
8 Ⓐ Ⓑ Ⓒ Ⓓ Ⓔ

Section 9

1 Ⓐ Ⓑ Ⓒ Ⓓ Ⓔ
2 Ⓐ Ⓑ Ⓒ Ⓓ Ⓔ
3 Ⓐ Ⓑ Ⓒ Ⓓ Ⓔ
4 Ⓐ Ⓑ Ⓒ Ⓓ Ⓔ
5 Ⓐ Ⓑ Ⓒ Ⓓ Ⓔ
6 Ⓐ Ⓑ Ⓒ Ⓓ Ⓔ
7 Ⓐ Ⓑ Ⓒ Ⓓ Ⓔ
8 Ⓐ Ⓑ Ⓒ Ⓓ Ⓔ

Section 10

1 Ⓐ Ⓑ Ⓒ Ⓓ Ⓔ
2 Ⓐ Ⓑ Ⓒ Ⓓ Ⓔ
3 Ⓐ Ⓑ Ⓒ Ⓓ Ⓔ

NO TEST MATERIAL ON THIS PAGE

1   1   1

SECTION 1   Sentence Completions

> DIRECTIONS: The following sentences contain blanks. Replace the blanks with live ammo.

1. Only upon arriving at the competition itself did the boys discover that ------- had nothing do with drinking excessive quantities of beer.

   A) beer pong
   B) hurling
   C) vomiting
   D) tiddlywinks
   E) Anheuser Busch

2. Between the rejection of the ------- tissue and the mismatched -------, Stanley's transplant didn't go as well as the doctors had predicted.

   A) packing . . moving vans
   B) replacement . . blood types
   C) scrotum . . testicles
   D) toilet . . curtains
   E) beef . . buns

3. His brilliance notwithstanding, Wilbur's stubborn and relentless pursuit of a flawed thesis proved that he had ------- in his head.

   A) an embolism
   B) a pair of Jacks
   C) shit-for-brains
   D) an *idée fixe*
   E) an airfoil lodged

4. Help, I've ------- and I -------!

   A) fallen . . can't get up
   B) got erectile dysfunction . . can't get it up
   C) bitten off more than I can chew . . can't chew it
   D) started watching YouTube . . can't stop
   E) Got Rhythm . . 've Got Music

5. Mr. Zimmerman, the idealistic new teacher at notoriously troubled PS 76, resolved to begin the school year by ------- in order to -------.

   A) quietly reading e. e. cummings aloud . . set the proper tone
   B) identifying the toughest kid in the class and beating the shit out of him . . gain street cred
   C) flashing wads of $100 bills . . buy drugs
   D) giving the principal an apple . . get into her pants
   E) dissecting a student . . get his watch back

6. Herman, an inventor, decided to ------- and then ------- when the government issued a Class III Toy Safety recall of his latest creation, Baby Nunchuk.

   A) have dinner . . dessert
   B) swallow gasoline . . have a smoke
   C) appeal the decision . . stalk the commissioners
   D) go for broke . . actually went there
   E) B, C, or D

GO TO NEXT PAGE

2   2   2

SECTION 2   Reading Passage

DIRECTIONS: Read the passage below and then answer the questions that follow. The correct response may be an inescapable stench or just the slightest whiff.

"Xanaxa's Emotikon" appeared as an article in the Journal of Very Old Ideas, Volume LXI (2009), pp. 45–48.

Introduction:

150 years before Aristotle showed up at Plato's Academy in Athens, a self-taught philosopher-shepherdess named Xanaxa laid the foundation for modern psychology with her trea-
(5) tise *Emotikon*, which survives only in fragments. Uncannily, Xanaxa's *Emotikon* codifies the full range of human emotions 2,500 years before the invention of the QWERTY keyboard. Here is a modern translation of the 5 surviving papyrus
(10) fragments (which were originally entrusted to Xalamander the Elder, who refused to read them because they were written by a girl).

Fragment 1: The Humors

The mental humors are four in number. They
(15) are *sanguinity* :-) *melancholia* :- (*choler* >:-o and *phlegm* :-o~ The humor of *apathy* :-I is an illusion as it is normally found to be either a case of *melancholia lite* :'-[or a simple matter of *fatigue* @v@ The proof is that a one-hour
(20) nap (-.-)z brings refreshment OvO and a full night of slumber (L___L)~zzzzz completes the conversion to sanguinity :-) as evidenced by the broadest of smiles upon waking ^_____^

Fragment 2: The Psyche and Strong Waters

(25) The humors are not fixed . . . highly volatile. For example, three stiff chalices YYY of unmixed Thracian wine will transmute even the most bilious choler]:-@ into something much more convivial :*-] or even ecstatic *L*
(30) However, later there may be a price to pay for this cheeriness (' <======{

Fragment 3: The Warrior

The young Spartan warrior has a mind that is often either confused %-l or depressed %-(
(35) What he needs is a hug {{{young Spartan warrior}}} or some long-stemmed flowers @>--;--- or a long walk by the wine-dark sea ~~~~ But alas, such are the rigors of the Spartan regimen that he can't always get what he
(40) wants ;-o So tense does he become '(# v #)!' that he will often turn to self relief OGC or, if at all possible, the attentions of a corybant to kneel before him _|¯lo and offer succor :Q The skeptic may raise an eyebrow at this assess-
(45) ment /:-) or even yawn :-O but, having myself been that corybant (o)(o) more than once, I know it to be true.

Fragment 4: Epigram

. . .Should you be given a black eye !-(be
(50) grateful for now you may intuit the feelings of the Cyclops @-(or Oedipus after he poked out his own eyes =-(

Fragment 5: Epigram

Don't worry (n~n) Be happy (>w<)

1. In Fragment 1, Xanaxa observed that the humor of apathy was -------.

   A) something she couldn't be bothered with
   B) the opposite of empathy
   C) simply a case of melancholia lite or fatigue
   D) an illusion that shimmers like a puddle of phlegm
   E) not as funny as the other humors

GO TO NEXT PAGE ▷

2. The following mysterious symbols, with no prose attached, were also found on Xanaxa's papyrus:

  _no   OTL   Orz   OTZ   Sto   Jto

With which one of the following symbols should they be associated?

A) @v@
B) =-(
C) (>w<)
D) _|‾|o
E) OGC

3. A fragment by Kriton the Bearded, (:-)## (thought to be the Spartan warrior of Fragment 3), refers cryptically to Xanaxa as :<) and :-D From the context of Fragment 3, what is the best interpretation of Kriton's remarks?

A) Xanaxa has a big nose and no teeth.
B) Xanaxa is stuck up; she's also a blabber-mouth.
C) Xanaxa's eyes are smaller than her mouth and she's from Dallas.
D) Kriton still needs a hug.
E) The meaning cannot be deciphered.

4. Below are three theories. Which one (or ones) best explains the relationship between Xanaxa's symbology and the modern QWERTY keyboard?

  I. The QWERTY keyboard is a development of the ancient Greek KÚ€PTÎ keyboard from which Xanaxa derived her symbols.

  II. Xanaxa also discovered time travel and got her symbols off the internet.

  III. The similarities are a remarkable coincidence.

A) I
B) II
C) III
D) I and III
E) (-_-)

GO TO NEXT PAGE

3   3   3

SECTION 3   **Mathematics**

DIRECTIONS: For each problem in this section there are *n* possible solutions offered, where *n* is the number of the Beethoven symphony that goes "dah-dah-dah-DUM." Choose the correct one. Use any blank space on the page for doodling.

Math Facts

Calories per Costco 18 ounce
chocolate layer cake:1,800

Nutrition Facts
Serving Size: 1 cake (510g)

Amount Per Serving

Calories 1,800 Calories from Fat 792

	% Daily Value*
Total Fat 88g	**135%**
Saturated Fat 32g	**160%**
Trans Fat 0g	
Cholesterol 200mg	**67%**
Sodium 1,840mg	**77%**
Total Carbohydrate 320g	**107%**
Dietary Fiber 16g	**64%**
Sugars 240g	
Protein 24g	**48%**

Vitamin A 0%	•	Vitamin C 0%
Calcium 1%	•	Iron 3%

Calories per can of
Coke Classic: 140

Nutrition Facts
Serving Size: 1 can (12 fl oz)

Amount Per Serving

Calories 140   Calories from Fat 0

	% Daily Value*
Total Fat 0g	**0%**
Saturated Fat 0g	
Trans Fat 0g	
Cholesterol 0mg	**0%**
Sodium 50mg	**2%**
Total Carbohydrate 41g	**14%**
Dietary Fiber 0g	
Sugars 40.5g	
Protein 0g	**0%**

Vitamin A 0%	•	Vitamin C 0%
Calcium 0%	•	Iron 0%

Calories per roll of Mentos: 140

Nutrition Facts
Serving Size: 1 roll (42g)

Amount Per Serving

Calories 140   Calories from Fat 0

	% Daily Value*
Total Fat 0g	**0%**
Saturated Fat 0g	
Trans Fat 0g	
Cholesterol 0mg	**0%**
Sodium 0mg	**0%**
Total Carbohydrate 42g	**14%**
Dietary Fiber 0g	
Sugars 28g	
Protein 0g	**0%**

Vitamin A 0%	•	Vitamin C 0%
Calcium 0%	•	Iron 0%

Calories per quart of
human blood: 480

Nutrition Facts
Serving Size: 1 quart (32 fl oz)

Amount Per Serving

Calories 480   Calories from Fat 311

	% Daily Value*
Total Fat 34.5g	**53%**
Saturated Fat 13.4g	**67%**
Trans Fat 0g	
Cholesterol 120mg	**40%**
Sodium 680mg	**28%**
Total Carbohydrate 1.3g	**0%**
Dietary Fiber 0g	
Sugars 1.3g	
Protein 14.6g	**29%**

Vitamin A 0%	•	Vitamin C 0%
Calcium 1%	•	Iron 36%

GO TO NEXT PAGE

1. Alone and depressed on a Saturday night, Roxanne buys an 18-oz. (1 lb., 2 oz.) Costco chocolate layer cake. Before she knows it, she has eaten all but the slice indicated below.

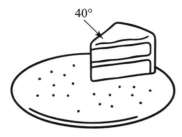

40°

   How much cake has Roxanne stuffed down?

   A) 2 ounces
   B) 14 ounces
   C) 16 ounces
   D) 18 ounces (every last crumb, including the piece above)
   E) 4 lbs., 7 ounces

2. Deathly afraid of blimping out, Roxanne allows herself to retain no more than 200 calories of cake. At 100 calories per ounce, what fraction of the whole cake must she disgorge to stay slim?

   A) $\dfrac{1}{8}$

   B) $\dfrac{1}{4}$

   C) $\dfrac{7}{9}$

   D) $\dfrac{8}{9}$

   E) All of it, including the bits of wrapping that she accidentally devoured.

3. Cliff is convinced he can solve both global warming *and* teen obesity by using all the Coke and Mentos in the world for vehicular power. He can buy a 1.5 liter bottle of Coke for $1.99 and 20 rolls of Mentos for $10. Cliff's experimental vehicle can travel $\dfrac{1}{2}$ mile on one roll of Mentos and a bottle of Coke. What is the cost per mile?

   A) $4.98 / mile
   B) $.49 / mile
   C) $.049 / mile
   D) $9.99 / mile
   E) It cannot be determined due to the clean-up cost of that sticky sludge.

4. There are 3.8 liters in a gallon. How many miles per gallon of Coke can Cliff's experimental car go?

   A) 130 mpg (as good as any moped)
   B) 13 mpg (as bad as any SUV)
   C) 1.3 mpg (way worse than even a military Hummer)
   D) 76 mpg (way better than any hybrid)
   E) .76 mpg (only slightly better than an Abrams tank)

5. If the family gas-guzzler gets 15 miles/gallon of gasoline, how high would the price of gas have to rise for Cliff's idea to make economic sense?

   A) about 75 cents / gallon
   B) $7.48 / gallon
   C) $2.00 / gallon
   D) $1.99 / liter
   E) almost $75 / gallon

GO TO NEXT PAGE ⟶

3   3   3

6. Ethel, 85 years old, tells her husband Sam, 87, "I'm bored. I'm going out. I've decided to be a hooker!" Returning at 3 a.m., she tells Sam "I made $6.72." Sam says "$6.72 *exactly*?" "Absolutely," replies Ethel. "I charged 37 cents for one thing and 10 cents for the other one, but the 37-cent thing was twice as popular." How many 37-cent things did Ethel perform?

GRID-IN

7. Below is a scatterplot where each point on the graph represents a heterosexual couple.

x = the guy's IQ and y = the girl's IQ.

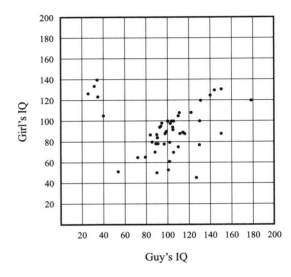

Which of the following statements is supported by the data?

    I. Guys don't like girls who are smarter than they are.

    II. Girls don't like guys who are dumber than they are.

    III. When a smart girl likes a dumb guy, there must be some other factor at work (if you know what I mean).

A) I
B) I or II (but not both)
C) I and III
D) II and III
E) Fascinating, but no conclusion can be drawn.

GO TO NEXT PAGE

8. Prunella, a vampire, works as a technician in a sleep clinic. This evening, although she has already sucked $\frac{3}{8}$ of her nightly requirement of blood, she still has $2\frac{1}{2}$ quarts to go. How much blood does Prunella need to drink each night?

A) 2 quarts

B) 4 quarts

C) $6\frac{2}{3}$ quarts

D) A magnum plus a Bloody Mary chaser

E) 8 quarts

9. Prunella is allergic to type AB-negative blood. If it even touches her fangs, she throws up and has to start all over again. Lucky for her it's found in only 1 percent of the population. If she averages $1\frac{1}{2}$ quarts per victim, how often is her allergy likely to flare up?

A) about once a week
B) about once a month
C) about once a year
D) once in a blue moon
E) Never, if she remembers to take her Benadryl.

10. The Roman Vernal Equinox Games of the year LXXXVIII A.D. showcased Gladiators, Lions and Christians. There were a total of IV Christians participating. If the ratio of Gladiators to Lions was VII : II and the ratio of Lions to Christians was IX : I, how many Gladiators were there?

(You may use a calculator. Or a sundial.)

A) I
B) LIXDIX
C) CXXVI
D) MCMLIV
E) CDMIX

4   4   4

SECTION 4   **Improving Sentences**

DIRECTIONS: The underlined portions of the sentences below may contain errors, from the piddling to the egregious. In some cases the entire sentence is underlined because the whole thing may be messed up. Figure out which of the five alternatives straightens things out the best. Choose answer A if you still prefer the original.

1. Try our Squid Surprise, a mouth-watering seafood rhapsody, expertly served by a waitress steaming hot.

   A) [My favorite!]
   B) expertly served by a steaming hot waitress
   C) hotly served by a steaming waitress expert
   D) served steaming hot by an expert waitress
   E) or just grab a bag of it at the bait shop downstairs

2. And for those of you who are still waffling, we strongly encourage you to neither shit or get off the pot.

   A) [no change—this is good shit]
   B) to neither shit nor get off the pot
   C) to either shit or get off the pot
   D) to either shit or don't shit—whatever
   E) to consider switching to pancakes

3. Strewn with trash after the concert, Lilah gazed across the muddy field.

   A) [Well said!]
   B) Lilah, strewn with trash, gazed across the muddy field after the concert.
   C) After the concert, Lilah, having behaved like trash, lay strewn across the muddy field.
   D) After the concert, Lilah gazed across the muddy, trash-strewn field.
   E) After the concert, trashy and muddy, Lilah felt royally strewed.

4. In a daring move to the hoop, the butt crack was the central feature in Calvin Klein's new line of jeans.

   A) [This is too good to change.]
   B) Calvin Klein's butt crack was the central feature in a new line of jeans.
   C) the butt crack faked left and cruised for the easy lay-up in Calvin Klein jeans.
   D) buttheads and crackheads are featured modeling Calvin Klein's new line of jeans.
   E) Calvin Klein made the butt crack the central feature in his new line of jeans.

5. Knowing the best way to stuff flamingos are two different things.

   A) [It's OK.]
   B) Knowing the two best ways to stuff flamingos are two different things.
   C) Knowing the best way to stuff flamingos and actually stuffing them are two different things.
   D) Knowing two different ways to stuff flamingos is an awesome thing.
   E) Knowing two flamingos makes it a lot harder to stuff them.

GO TO NEXT PAGE

5   5   5

SECTION 5   Improving Paragraphs

DIRECTIONS: The passage below is an unedited draft that needs help. Read it carefully and try to improve it by answering the questions that follow.

---

[1] The voices have commanded me to lead the anointed ones out of danger and to purify the remainder of the sinful horde. [2] Yet those who send me—the Old Ones—whose arrival is at hand, are merciful and offer this warning. [3] When the world least expects, when it lies sleeping, dreaming its wicked dreams, that is when the red hot poker of my anger will do the whoopee dance of vengeance. [4] Thus speak I: repent, for time is short and the road to atonement is steep. [5] Remember, the alternative is . . .

1. Which of the following is the best revision of the underlined segment of sentence [3]?

   When the world least expects, when it lies sleeping, dreaming its wicked dreams, that is when the red hot poker of my anger will do the whoopee dance of vengeance.

   A) [It cannot be improved.]
   B) the red hot poker of my anger will descend like a guillotine.
   C) the red hot poker of my anger will thrust up through your entrails like a sand worm.
   D) the red red robin comes bob, bob, bobbin' along.
   E) I will become very very annoyed and you will know it.

2. Which of the following provides the ending to sentence [5] that is most consistent with the tone of the paragraph?

   Remember, the alternative is . . .

   A) . . . OK, maybe time isn't so short and the road to atonement is <u>not</u> steep after all.
   B) . . . salsa lessons at the Tito Puente Community Center.
   C) . . . a molten sauna in the glowing crucible of my wrath.
   D) . . . that if we don't get the $2 million by 4 p.m., we boil your dog.
   E) . . . wait, where am I? . . . Oh, Auntie Em, there's no place like home!

3. What related issue MOST cries out to be explored by this author?

   A) [no other issue]
   B) What precisely is supposed to happen when the Old Ones arrive?
   C) What happens if they <u>don't</u> arrive?
   D) Who put the author in charge of purifying the sinful horde?
   E) Why is the author so resistant to taking his meds?

GO TO NEXT PAGE >

6   6   6

SECTION 6   Reading Passages

DIRECTIONS: Read the passages below and then answer the questions that follow. The correct response may be as explicit as a thong or as implicit as a burkha.

Passage 1:

This passage was found on a blog at www.digi-taldelinquents.com. The blogger, who goes by the name of Skelter, was recently swept up in a federal cyber-crimes dragnet.

there's like 3 main ways to crash a website. in order of difficulty...

GREEN CIRCLE: if ur a total techno-spazz i rec DoS -- denial of service where u hi-jack 500
(5) or 1,000 PCs at nite and install a bot like bitch-bot or eggdrop to keep pinging the victim so no 1 can get thru to the ip. its so obnoxiously awe-some. i showed my 7-year-old sister this 1 and she crashed Land's End and NPR be4 supper.
(10) dude, even yr parents could do it if they concen-trated. besides the ping flood i also like the mailbomb and also the smurf attack but the best 1 is the pulsing zombie cuz its suttle and hard to detect. but u gotta know more 2 do these.
(15)   BLUE SQUARE: if u know some program-ming u cn hack into the site itself and fuck with their code. either just trash random lines of code and c what happens or u cn do shit like make yahoo's faq link point to yr band's youtube vid
(20) or bignaturals.com. or u cn rewrite shit so like the CNN site will be called CNN SUCKS. lol. 1 thing, tho: ull have to learn to hack passwords which isn't hard if u dont care whose password u get. btw i just put up a new vid on how 2
(25) gather credit card #s. check it.
    BLACK DIAMOND: hacking encrypted sites is only 4 us masters. banks r hard. stock exchanges r harder but not impossible. the algo-rithms r all about factoring large primes which
(30) is cpu intensive so 2 crack a serious cipher u need 1 big computer (and i mean BIG). me & my friends like the los alamos b array or if

that's busy then the fermi lab supercomp that analyzes atomic particle accelerator collisions.
(35) cool box. it takes about 3 weeks (don't miss too much school heh heh) but dude, it's so totally HEROIC to like bust into Bank of America and switch all the funds in the accts around and imagine the wtf!!!!!!! look on everyone's face.
(40) sweeeet.

1. According to the author, what is the best way to crash a large banking website?

   A) Hire a professional website crashing service.
   B) Obtain an exploit from millworm.com.
   C) Hi-jack a government mainframe com-puter.
   D) Deposit 12 trillion dollars in Polish Zlotys and wait.
   E) There is no best way.

2. The writer sees himself as -------.

   A) a suburban mother of four
   B) a Robin Hood, but without the tights
   C) a merry prankster cyber-genius hero
   D) an anti-virus software beta tester
   E) a socially awkward pain in the ass

GO TO NEXT PAGE ⟶

3. Of the "denial of service" attacks mentioned, which is the hardest to detect?

A) ping flood
B) banana attack
C) coronary thrombosis
D) pulsing zombie
E) mail bomb

4. The writer's prevailing emotion throughout this passage is:

A) remorse
B) queasiness and vertigo
C) omnipotent invulnerability
D) impotent powerlessness
E) determination to go snowboarding next weekend

Passage 2

An excerpt from Plastic Maverick, *the life and times of Herman Smill, inventor.*

Herman Smill's fertile mind changed the world. His masterpiece, the synthetic vagina, remains one of the seminal inventions of our age. It freed millions of women from drudgery
(45) and inconvenience on a scale not seen since innovations like the vacuum cleaner and the dishwasher. Perfecting the gadget took a long time, and Smill faced not just technical obstacles, but market skepticism, too. What kind of
(50) pathetic loner would buy such a product? But Herman was a believer and he calmed impatient investors with an inspired slogan: "If I build it, they will come."

Early manufacturing missteps almost
(55) derailed the project. The original V-Pal 4000 had an oversized pump and was plagued with unpredictable pressure spikes and lubricant leakage, resulting in a harsh grip and severe bruising. High-profile lawsuits and stiff fines
(60) nearly broke the company. The stock price drooped and funding all but dried up. (Interestingly, there remains a lusty demand for those defective 4000s and fetishists will pay at least ten times the original price!)
(65) In the end, Smill's persistence and single mindedness paid off. Today, the self-lubricating V-Pal Pocket Edition can be found in the "As Seen on Late-Night TV" aisle in every Walgreen's, Herman Smill is a wealthy man, and
(70) his investors' faith in his genius has been rewarded. As for his personal life, the once awkward and reclusive innovator is enjoying long overdue recognition, but he remains unfazed by endless invitations from starlets and
(75) models. "Fifteen years ago, the feel of a real broad was all I dreamed of. But today, with our new Organic line, who can tell the difference?"

GO TO NEXT PAGE

5. From what kind of drudgery and inconvenience
    did Herman Smill's invention spare women?

    A) washing dishes by hand
    B) severe bruising and stiff fines
    C) filling out the warranty card for the vacuum
        cleaner and dishwasher
    D) changing the batteries in the family vibra-
        tor
    E) uncomfortable and unwelcome sex with
        boorish husbands

6. What kind of a guy is Herman Smill?

    A) a champion of women's rights
    B) a debonair man-about-town
    C) an explorer of the deep mysteries of the
        universe
    D) the natural companion for starlets and
        models
    E) the kind of guy who uses his own product

7. What is the main thrust of this passage?

    A) If you build it, they will come.
    B) If your peg is square and the hole is round,
        don't force it.
    C) Fortunately, guys who use artificial vaginas
        are unlikely to reproduce.
    D) There is a healthy aftermarket for used sex
        toys.
    E) After use, reverse internal surfaces and
        wipe with damp cloth.

GO TO NEXT PAGE

7   7   7

SECTION 7   Analogies

DIRECTIONS: In each question below you are given a pair of words, phrases, or whatevers that are somehow related. From the choices offered, complete the second pair so that they are related in the same way as the first pair

1. trim : haircut :: circumcision : -------

   A) smegma
   B) Mohawk
   C) sex change
   D) nuts in a knot
   E) castration

2. straight : flush :: ------- : full house

   A) flush
   B) out house
   C) Bob Saget
   D) Chinese checkers
   E) bent

3. ration : cation :: ------- : -------

   A) pornographer : photographer
   B) onion : anion
   C) screwy : chewy
   D) pervert : prevert
   E) sucker : succor

4. E = mc² : Einstein :: ------- : -------

   A) Always Low Prices : Kmart

   B) Fee Fi Fo Fum : Jack

   C) $i\hbar \dfrac{\partial \Psi(r,t)}{\partial t} = \hat{H}\Psi(r,t)$: Newton

   D) I Like Big Butts : Jay-Z

   E) Fock You, Ahs-hole : The Terminator

5. crock o'shit : load o'shit :: piece o'shit : -------

   A) pile o'shit
   B) Seamus O'Shit
   C) Oh shit! You actually did it!
   D) Chock Full o'Shit
   E) William O. Shit

6. paycheck : lottery :: ------- : NBA Draft

   A) hot babes
   B) job
   C) the Celts
   D) season ticket
   E) LeBron James

GO TO NEXT PAGE

8   8   8

SECTION 8   Identifying Sentence Errors

DIRECTIONS: Each of the following sentences contains either a single error or no error at all. Select the underlined portion that contains the foozle or, if none, choose E) No error.

---

1. The mind resists, but once you've had the
      A   B

   taste, there's nothing quite, like a piping hot
      C   D

   tureen of cream of leprechaun soup. No error
                            E

2. Then there was the famous night the Amazing
           A   B

   Marocco Brothers screw all six Flying Dubjak
                C

   Sisters and no one fell or got pregnant.
                     D

   No error
   E

3. Despite the pilot's skill, the heat-seeking mis-
                        A

   sile homed in on the plane and flew right up
       B   C

   his tail-pipe. No error
   D   E

4. The old dirty man was arrested for hanging
        A

   around the red little schoolhouse, singing
            B

   "Who's afraid of the bad big wolf?
               C

   La tra tra tra tra." Wrong all
      D   E

5. Miriam explained to her dad that coming home
                       A

   at 3:30 a.m. was normal for all the 10th graders
               B

   she hangs out with, and if he doesn't like it he
       C

   can . . . whatever. No error
        D   E

6. A priest, a rabbi, and a minister sitting on a
                      A

   park bench at 10 p.m. beneath a streetlight
                       B

   examining the centerfold of the April issue of
            C

   Snatch magazine. No error
    D   E

GO TO NEXT PAGE ▷

7. After <u>twenty-seven</u> hours of <u>labor</u>, the obstetri-
           A   B

   cian delivered a <u>tongue</u>, lashing to the attractive
                       C

   technician for her <u>aggressive use of suction</u>.
                          D

   <u>No error</u>
     E

8. A <u>diverse</u> crowd of about 75 <u>gathered</u> at
        A   B

   Baldpate Middle School auditorium on Friday

   night <u>for</u> a teach-in against hate <u>crimes</u>
          C   D

   organized by the Capello County Gay Rights

   Committee. <u>No error</u>
                 E

GO TO NEXT PAGE

9   9   9

SECTION 9   Mathematics

DIRECTIONS: For each problem in this section there are *p* possible solutions offered, where *p* is the number of Lou Bega's big 1999 hit, Mambo #*p*. Choose the correct one. Use any blank space on the page for doodling.

Math Facts

- The volume of a rectangular prism : side × side × side

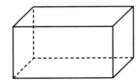

- Pythagoras' theorem: $A^2 + B^2 = C^2$

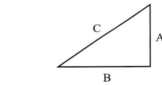

- Terminal velocity for a falling puppet: 100 ft / second

- Average height for NBA players: 6' 7"

GO TO NEXT PAGE >

The Toils of Zebakkuk

Excerpted from an apocryphal Old Testament text, "The Toils of Zebakkuk."

1. Zebakkuk the Midianite dwelt in the Valley of Shamooz with his five wives: Amalech, Bimalech, Comalech, Dumalech, and Emalech.

2. And though his years were 80 in number Zebakkuk was a randy man and lay with each of his wives in turn, a different wife every night.

3. But when Zebakkuk's years did reach 975, his prowess did sometimes flag and his wives grew vexed.

4. One night Bimalech did retire unto her tent and threw back the bed sheet to discover Amalech delighting herself in lascivious posture.

5. Bimalech said, "Amalech, what dost thou?" and Amalech did respond, "What doth it look like I do?"

6. And Amalech did lie with Bimalech and they were satisfied. Nor did they continue to be vexed.

7. When Zebakkuk did behold this new happenstance he was much excited and bent to his marital tasks with renewed vigor. Yet even so the seed within his loins was sore taxed and betimes unreliable of delivery.

8. Therefore after another seven years did Comalech contrive to lie with both Dumalech and Emalech and they did sleep in one big bed, to which Zebakkuk did repair bi-nightly to thrice discharge his connubial contrivance.

9. And it so happened that Zebakkuk's neighbor Methuselah, whose years were but 790, did perceive the toll of encroaching travail upon Zebakkuk and did offer succor, saying,

10. "I see thy wives are much vexed. Let me help thee perform thy spousal assignments."

11. But Zebakkuk would not hear of it, saying, "I would sooner die than let a neighbor plow my ruts and furrows."

12. And thus did it come to pass that on the night of Zebakkuk's thousandth birthday there was great feasting and springing from tent to tent.

13. And at dawn of the next morning Zebakkuk breathed his last and he was drawn up into the bosom of Abraham. Thenceforth did he lie with his ancestors instead of his wives.

14. And there was general wailing and gnashing of teeth among the wives. Yet wide was the smile on the face of Zebakkuk.

1. Consider the situation of Verse 2. Assume that the five wives lay with Zebakkuk in alphabetical order, one per night. If Amalech started the rotation on Monday of Week 1, which wife enjoyed the patriarchal protuberance on Wednesday of Week 5?

   A) Amalech
   B) Bimalech
   C) Comalech
   D) Dumalech
   E) Umathurmalech

2. Scholars have interpreted the events of Verses 4–6 to mean that the conjugal schedule now became a 4-night rotation, with each consort receiving her own rub of the love nub. Under the new arrangement, how much harder did Zebakkuk have to work?

   A) 20%
   B) 25%
   C) 33%
   D) Twice as hard
   E) Hard? Oh please! Solomon had 300 wives. That's a rotation!

GO TO NEXT PAGE

9   **9**   **9**

3. In Verse 8 there is no doubt of the chronicler's intent: Zebakkuk was down to a 2-night rotation. In his sunset years Zebakkuk was now struggling to satisfy 5 wives every 2 nights. Approximately how many times did the patriarch jam his jereboam from his 80th year up until the time of his death?

A) 2,500 times
B) 11,000 times
C) 344,000 times
D) 4,000,000 times
E) All right, that's it! I will no longer be a party to this blasphemous abuse of a sacred text.

4. Two parachutists, Bert and Ernie, simultaneously jump out of a plane flying at an altitude of 20,000 feet. They quickly reach a terminal velocity of 100 feet per second. At 1,000 feet Bert pulls his rip cord and the parachute instantly slows his descent to 20 feet per second. Ernie also pulls his rip cord at 1,000 feet but it fails to open. How much sooner does Bert arrive on the ground than Ernie?

A) 20 seconds
B) 40 seconds
C) They arrive at the same time.
D) -40 seconds
E) 4 seconds

5. The coffin below has an exterior surface area of 58 ½ square feet. The walls of the coffin are 2 inches thick. Inside lies a dead NBA player who is 7 feet 6 inches tall. By how much did the nimrod who ordered the coffin get the interior length wrong?

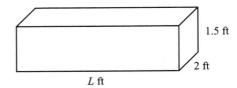

1.5 ft

2 ft

L ft

A) 4 inches too short
B) 6 inches too short
C) 8 inches too long
D) 1 foot too short
E) It's not too short. Just fold him in half.

6. The dead NBA player is being buried. Although a long enough coffin was finally obtained, no one has informed the gravediggers of the non-standard length. While the coffin is being lowered, it catches the edge of the grave, falls in, and now it's stuck (see diagram). The gravediggers want to leave it there and fill in the grave, but if they do, how high will the corner of the coffin project above ground level?

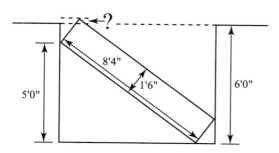

A) 1.2 inches
B) 2.4 inches
C) 6 inches
D) 12 inches
E) None of the above, but can't they find a nice box of peonies to cover it?

7. Three blind mice have had their tails cut off with a carving knife. Blind Mouse A was clever enough to save the severed end. After reattachment surgery, the tail had lost 15% of its original length. If before the operation, the severed end had been 4cm long and the total post-surgical length was 6.8cm, how long was the stump before surgery?

A) 3 cm
B) 4 cm
C) 5 cm
D) 6 inches
E) Who cares? I don't want anything to do with this disgusting problem.

---

8. A police lineup includes five suspects, each accused of one of the following crimes: murder, rape, arson, manslaughter, and jaywalking. If they are arranged in random order, what are the chances that the alleged rapist will be standing next to the suspected arsonist?

A) $\dfrac{1}{5}$

B) $\dfrac{2}{5}$

C) $\dfrac{3}{5}$

D) $\dfrac{4}{5}$

E) Pretty good if they ask nicely.

GO TO NEXT PAGE ⟩

DIRECTIONS: Read the passages below and then answer the questions that follow. The correct response may be as camouflaged as a flounder or as in-your-face as Moby Dick.

Season's Greetings!

Where does the time go? The past year has been an "interesting" one for the O'Dooley Family, to say the least!

(5) Grandpa is doing great! This spring he'll be hosting a young Nigerian exchange-type person named Jane Aboje. Although it's expensive (the Nigerian "government affidavit" alone cost $10,000), it's worth every penny to see him bustling about, redecorating "her room," which used to be our old fallout shelter. He's SO happy!

This summer little Kenny went through a life-changing experience: he fell in love! Her name is Chloe and she's fantastic. We've come to love her like a daughter, though we worry that not everyone is as open-(10) minded as us because she's a sheep. For now they're living at home, both working. He's become a composting evangelist and she continues her work in the dairy and textile industries. Though they haven't set a date, they've located a Unitarian minister who's excited about performing the first human-ungulate ceremony. Stay tuned!

Our Roxanne, ever the seeker, really found herself this year. Putting all her hobbies together, she has (15) been baking up a storm for her geometry outreach project, Polyhedral Bundt Cakes for God. This spring they're planning another big to-do they're calling "Animals are People Too!"—just in time for Kenny and Chloe's wedding. For a parent there's nothing like seeing your children start to "get their act together."

Meanwhile, Big Kenny and I have been busy beavers, trying to save the house from foreclosure. (I kept telling him that a 2% mortgage sounded too gosh-darn good to be true, but you know how stubborn my Ken (20) can be, especially when he's drinking. Oh well. Too late now!) We've really tightened our belt, canceling the trip to Sesame Place and selling the cooking island on eBay. Oh, we also rented out the garage to a psychic and are planning to sell any organs we don't need. K has lost his job at the muffler assembly plant and will concentrate full-time on getting us our share of the bailout. But so far the only "trickle down" we've seen was when his colostomy bag sprang a leak.

(25) On a more somber note, in July we lost Othello, our beloved toy pit bull, when, rummaging through the neighbor's trash, he got his head stuck in a Chinese food container, and wandered blindly through the night, half-crazed with claustrophobia, apparently staggering out onto the New Jersey Turnpike in a pea soup fog. I won't go into the 27-car pile-up he caused. But I must say that this tragedy has put the rest of our petty problems into perspective. The dryer fire, our legal bills, Roxanne's genital warts, these things all (30) pale when I picture poor Othello with strands of lo mein pressed into the tread marks running the length of his pancaked little body. We miss him every day, as I'm sure the families of the other victims do, too.

We send love to each of you in this season of hope and joy. Let us all count our blessings and take comfort in the fact that things will soon get better! Stay well.

The O'Dooleys – Kenny and Felicia, Little Kenny and Roxanne.

(35) P.S. My job at the phone center just got out-sourced to the Philippines. But I'm using my telecom background to try for a job in the 1-900 entertainment field. Wish me luck! When I'm up and running I'll get Little Kenny to Twitter my number to everyone.

GO TO NEXT PAGE

1. The author's purpose in telling the anecdote about Othello (line 25) is mainly to

    A) pad the letter out to a full page.
    B) contrast a tragic death with the petty annoyances of bankruptcy and genital warts.
    C) inform people that she's in the market for a new dog.
    D) warn the reader to dispose of Chinese food containers responsibly.
    E) accidentally demonstrate what an airhead she is.

2. The writer of this passage possesses all of the following EXCEPT

    A) idiotic and unwarranted optimism.
    B) off-the-charts denial.
    C) a husband she should ditch ASAP.
    D) only one kidney.
    E) a clear-eyed view of reality.

3. Given the unsettled state of her family, what could have motivated this woman to send out this letter?

    A) Whadaya mean? What's wrong with the letter?
    B) She enjoys being humiliated.
    C) Tradition is important to her.
    D) She wants to cheer people up.
    E) She's auditioning for the new reality TV show *America's Most Fucked-Up Family.*

GO TO NEXT PAGE

11   11   11

SECTION 11   Essay

DIRECTIONS: Map out and write an essay in which you develop your views on the assigned issue. Support your position any way you choose. Make it AMAZING.

Think Box

The teen years are a time of self-doubt and uncertainty. Many young people lack a stable sense of their own identities and find themselves adrift in value systems that don't fit them. Consequently, all too many succumb to dark thoughts, fascination with self-destructive actions, and deep existential despair.

ASSIGNMENT: Is that all there is? Can you think of any reason at all to carry on?

GO TO NEXT PAGE

STOP
Don't even *think* of turning the page.

BSAT Test 4

Answer Key

Section 1

1 B
2 B
3 D
4 A
5 A
6 E

Section 2

1 D
2 D
3 B
4 C

Section 3

1 C
2 C
3 A
4 C
5 E
6 16
7 C
8 B
9 B
10 C

Section 4

1 E
2 C
3 D
4 E
5 C

Section 5

1 C
2 C
3 E

Section 6

1 C
2 C
3 D
4 C
5 E
6 E
7 A

Section 7

1 E
2 A
3 B
4 E
5 A
6 B

Section 8

1 D
2 C
3 D
4 E
5 E
6 A
7 C
8 D

Section 9

1 A
2 B
3 C
4 D
5 A
6 B
7 B
8 B

Section 10

1 B
2 E
3 C

Calculating Your Scores

Use the work sheet below to arrive at your "Raw Score" for each of the three sections of the test.

To discover your Real Scores and find out what they mean, turn to pages 39-40 and use the "Raw-to-Real Conversion Chart" and the "How-I-Did vs. How-I-Will-Do Chart."

Critical Reading:

Section 1:   Number Correct = _____ ; Number Incorrect = _____

Section 2:   Number Correct = _____ ; Number Incorrect = _____

Section 6:   Number Correct = _____ ; Number Incorrect = _____

Section 10:   Number Correct = _____ ; Number Incorrect = _____

Total Correct = _____ ;   Total Incorrect = _____

_____ − (_____ ÷ 4) = _____
Total Correct   Total Incorrect   RAW SCORE A

Writing Skills:

Section 4:   Number Correct = _____ ; Number Incorrect = _____

Section 5:   Number Correct = _____ ; Number Incorrect = _____

Section 8:   Number Correct = _____ ; Number Incorrect = _____

Section 11:   Essay Score × .4 = _____ ;

Total Correct + Essay = _____ ;   Total Incorrect = _____

_____ − (_____ ÷ 4) = _____
Total Correct + Essay   Total Incorrect   RAW SCORE B

Math & Reasoning:

Section 3:   Number Correct = _____ ; Number Incorrect = _____

Section 7:   Number Correct = _____ ; Number Incorrect = _____

Section 9:   Number Correct = _____ ; Number Incorrect = _____

Total Correct = _____ ;   Total Incorrect = _____

_____ − (_____ ÷ 4) = _____
Total Correct   Total Incorrect   RAW SCORE C

ANSWER EXPLANATIONS

SECTION 1: Sentence Completions

1. Which choice is both a competition and seems to suggest getting wasted (at least to ignorant boys)? Hurling has been called the world's fastest field team sport. It has nothing to do with drinking or vomiting, even though it is Irish. **Answer: B.**

2. <u>Rejection</u> and <u>transplant</u> should suggest surgery. That limits us to B and C. After that, mismatched blood types would seem the best choice. Do testicles have to match? **Answer: B.**

3. Although *C) shit-for-brains* is a possible explanation for the <u>pursuit</u> of <u>a flawed thesis</u> (i.e., an idea that sucks), it does not convey the <u>stubborn and relentless</u> aspect of the quest as well as *D) an idée fixe,* which is just the kind of obsession that happens to brilliant people like Wilbur. **Answer: D.**

4. Reading the answers in order, you strike pay dirt immediately with A, which is the tagline for the famous commercial for Life Call, as seen on late-night TV back when you were still in Power Ranger underpants. Life Call has expired, but the tagline lives on. **Answer: A.**

5. The context tip-off is that Mr. Z is <u>idealistic</u>, which rules out all the rude behaviors in B, C, and E. Regarding D, although an idealist could very well want to get into the principal's pants, the poetry of e. e. cummings is *so* much more uplifting. **Answer: A.**

6. Although we have no idea what a <u>Class III Toy Safety recall</u> is, we can guess that Herman wasn't happy about it. So answer A seems too casual a reaction. However, answers B, C, and D, hinting at suicide, mayhem, or bankruptcy, all seem plausible. **Answer: E.**

SECTION 2: Reading Passage

1. This question is delightful in that it requires no thinking, just functioning eyesight. Look at line 18 and accept our little gift. **Answer: C.**

2. All of the mysterious symbols are variants of the kneeling Corybant, with its characteristic open mouth. **Answer: D.**

3. You can rule out C, since Xanaxa never went to Big D (though she might have gone to Syracuse). Also forget D, since we know from line 35 that "needing a hug" is symbolized by {{{kriton}}}. At first, it would seem that both answers A and B are plausible. However, using a big smile to symbolize insincerity, as in answer A, is a form of sarcasm, whose existence was still centuries in the future. Blabbermouths, though, have existed since the Garden of Eden. **Answer: B.**

4. Lets analyze the three statements. I is preposterous. Even if the ancient Greeks had a keyboard, what would they plug it into? II is even kookier than I. Enough with the time travel. III—a "remarkable coincidence"? There is a famous example of a very low-probability event that applies here: a group of chimps, typing randomly, generating the complete works of Shakespeare. Improbable, but possible. And that means . . . **Answer: C.**

SECTION 3: Mathematics

1. The leftover slice is 40° of a circle, which totals 360°. And $\frac{40°}{360°}$ represents $\frac{1}{9}$ of the circle. So Rox crammed down $\frac{8}{9}$ of an 18-ounce cake, or 16 ounces. **Answer: C.**

2. Rox's pigfest was $\frac{8}{9}$ of the cake, or 16 ounces, which at 100 calories per ounce is 1,600 calories. Getting rid of all but 200 of those calories means hurling up 1,400 calories, or 14 ounces of the entire 18-ounce cake. That's $\frac{14}{18}$, or $\frac{7}{9}$. **Answer: C.**

3. Low-Road, for sure. Just estimate. Since you get $\frac{1}{2}$ mile for a $1.99 bottle of Coke and a 50-cent roll of Mentos, for a whole mile just double it. Only $4.98 / mile is in that range. **Answer: A.**

4. You know from the last question that Cliff's CokeMentoMobile is insanely costly to operate. The stupid thing runs $\frac{1}{2}$ mile on 1.5 liters, or 1 mile on 3 liters, which is a little less than a gallon. So that means a little more than a mile on a full gallon. **Answer: C.**

5. We know that Cliff's "alternative fuel vehicle" costs $4.98 per mile to operate. For the 15 mpg gasoline-powered family car to cost $4.98 per mile to operate, gas would have to cost 15 times as much: $15 \times \$4.98 = \$74.70$, or almost $75 per gallon. **Answer: E.**

6. Set up the equations for Ethel's "things," whatever they are. Suppose x is the 37-cent thing and y is the 10-cent thing. Then:

Ethel's total earnings add up to $6.72, so that is: $.37x + .10y = 6.72$

The 37 cent thing was twice as popular as the 10 cent thing: $2y = x$, or $y = \frac{x}{2}$

So, substitute $\frac{x}{2}$ for y in the first equation and you get $.37x + .10(\frac{x}{2}) = 6.72$.

Multiply both sides by 10 to get $37x + 5x = 672$.

Combine terms and you get $42x = 672$.

And finally divide by 42 for $x = 16$.

So Ethel performed the 37-cent thing 16 times. (Shudder.) **Answer: 16.**

7. We suggest you draw a line with a slope of 45° representing couples whose IQs are equal. Once you've done that, it becomes sadly obvious that guys mainly hook up with girls who are dumber than they are. But what about the possibility that guys *are* attracted to smart girls but smart girls are all into other women? Naahhh. But what about those four little dots in the upper left corner, representing really sharp women pairing off with what appear to be animated tree stumps? "Tree stumps" would seem to be the "some other factor" referred to in III. So, it's I and III. **Answer: C.**

8. Let R be the amount of blood Prunella must suck each night. If Prunella has already sucked $\frac{3}{8}$ of R, then she has $\frac{5}{8}$ to go. So the formula is: $\frac{5}{8}R = 2\frac{1}{2}$ quarts.

Solving for R: $R = (2\frac{1}{2}) / (\frac{5}{8}) = \frac{5}{2} \times \frac{8}{5} = 4$

Prunella's nightly requirement is 4 quarts. **Answer: B.**

9. Since bad blood is found in 1 percent of people, Prunella gets sick from about 1 in every 100 victims. We know that she needs 4 quarts a night. At $1\frac{1}{2}$ quarts per victim, that means she averages around 3 victims per night, or roughly 100 per month. So every month Prunella's bound to come across that one rotten victim who makes her toss her platelets. **Answer: B.**

10. Even if you know absolutely nothing about Roman numerals, you've got a shot. You know there are more Gladiators than anything else, so A can't be right. Answers B and E we can dismiss for inanity, so we're left with only C and D. *Answer D) MCMLIV* should look suspiciously like the year that appears on an old movie underneath the growling lion. This one is 1954, which is overkill for only IV Christians. That leaves answer C, which is correct. You can also solve the problem with math, if you insist. But we don't. **Answer: C.**

SECTION 4: Improving Sentences

1. The modifier "steaming hot" wanders desperately through this problem in search of the right thing to modify. In A and B, it attaches itself unsuccessfully to the waitress. In C it is brutally split into a freestanding adverb and an adjective. In E it goes into hiding. Only in D does it finally settle down, exhausted but content. **Answer: D.**

2. The correct idiom is "to either shit or get off the pot"—presumably so someone else can use it. **Answer: C.**

3. By now you've had plenty of practice with misplaced modifiers. So we'll just outline the general mission on this one: Arrange things such that, after the concert, Lilah is not strewn with trash and the muddy field is. Good luck. **Answer: D.**

4. In this misplaced modifier sentence, the burning question is: Who (or what) made a daring move to the hoop? Answers A, B, and C would have us believe it was a butt crack. In D it's the equally problematic "buttheads and crackheads." Only in E do we find Calvin himself charging down the center lane for a slam dunk line of jeans. **Answer: E.**

5. At first glance, this sentence appears to suffer from a simple subject-verb agreement error. But it's actually more screwed up than that: The subject of the sentence, "Knowing the best way to stuff flamingos," seems to come from a different planet from its predicate, "are two different things." WTF? Your "Ah-hah!" moment should come when you reach C and you realize the real problem: Some idiot left out the words "and actually stuffing them." **Answer: C.**

SECTION 5: Improving Paragraphs

1. After discarding the retarded D and E, concentrate on that red hot poker. Look for a revision that makes the red hot poker behave in its most essential, red-hot-poker-like manner. Red hot pokers DO NOT A) *do the whoopee dance of vengeance* or B) *descend like a guillotine*. However, they *can* easily C) *thrust up through your entrails like a sand worm*. **Answer: C.**

2. First, what is the tone of the paragraph. Try describing it to yourself. For instance:

> biblical prophet-speak . . .
> ravings of a messianic nut job . . .
> megalomaniacal rant . . .

Guided by this mental checklist, you should find it quite easy to ignore asinine ransom notes (as in D), Wizard of Oz references (as in E), and other trivia (as in A and B). In other words home right in on C) *the glowing crucible of my wrath*. **Answer: C.**

3. The truth is, *any* of these issues *could* be explored. But the one screaming question at the very center of this unhinged apocalyptic diatribe is: What's with the voices in the author's head? And on a related note: Which is the more effective anti-psychotic drug—clozapine or risperidone? Either way . . . **Answer: E.**

SECTION 6: Reading Passages

1. The BLACK DIAMOND clearly suggests hopping onto "the Los Alamos B array" or "the fermi lab supercomp." You should know that those are government labs because who else bothers to analyze atomic particles? **Answer: C.**

2. The writer calls himself a "master" in line 27, and "HEROIC" in line 37, where he revels in the havoc caused by his mischief. Therefore, while he may actually be *E) a socially awkward pain in the ass*, the author sees himself as *C) a merry prankster cyber-genius hero*. **Answer: C.**

3. The answer is staring at you in line 13: the *D) pulsing zombie* is "suttle and hard to detect." If you can't find that, you probably couldn't even pull off a ping flood. Sheesh. **Answer: D.**

4. This global psychological assessment should be easy, because this is a type you know intimately. Teen boys think with some primitive part of their paleo-cortex and are universally driven by feelings of *C) omnipotent invulnerability*. **Answer: C.**

5. While not explicit in the text, the answer is easily inferred by anyone but a congenital simpleton. Note for teens: Associating drudgery and inconvenience with sex may shock you. That's because you're young and probably unmarried. Stick around. **Answer: E.**

6. Start by describing Herman Smill in your own words. We'll help you get started: an obsessive nerd, an awkward hermit, a guy with less than no life, a pathetic loner, all of the above. Is this helping? **Answer: E.**

7. The passage is a celebration of Smill's inventiveness and persistence in the face of discouragement. B, C, D, and E may all be true, but they're not the main thrust of the passage. On the other hand, *A) If you build it, they will come* vividly captures the flavor of the first artificial vagina. **Answer: A.**

SECTION 7: Analogies

1. Test sentences:

   Trim is one step short of a full haircut.

   Circumcision is one step short of a full -------.

   While *C) sex change* might be tempting, it involves not just removal, but installation . . . **Answer: E. castration.**

2. Remember all that Texas Hold 'Em you played when you were twelve? That should help you come up with:

   A flush beats a straight.

   A full house beats a -------.

   Answer: A. flush.

3. "Ration" and "cation" are related in an odd way: They are words that look like they rhyme, but don't. "Ration," meaning "portion," is pronounced RAY-shun or RASH-in, while "cation" is pronounced CAT-eye-on and means the negative electrical molecule. Got that? Similarly, "Onion," a fake news outlet, is pronounced UN-yun, while "anion," the *positive* electrical molecule, is pronounced AN-eye-on. Don't even bother trying to find test sentences for a shitstorm like this. Just wrestle it to the ground and move on. **Answer: B. onion : anion.**

4. This analogy is little harder. Try the following test sentence:

   "E = mc²" is a famous quote from Einstein.

   Now try it out on each of the pairs and see if you get lift-off.

   "Always Low Prices" is a famous quote from Kmart. Oops, that was a Wal-mart line.

   "Fee fi fo fum" is a famous quote from Jack. No, that was the Giant.

   "$i\hbar \dfrac{\partial \Psi(\mathbf{r}, t)}{\partial t} = \hat{H}\Psi(\mathbf{r}, t)$" was a famous quote from Newton. Sorry, everyone knows that was Schrödinger's equation.

   "I like big butts," was a famous quote from Jay-Z. Wrong again—Sir Mix-a-Lot.

   "Fock you, Ahs-hole" was a famous line from the Terminator. Finally!

   Answer: E. Fock You, Ahs-hole : The Terminator.

5. Test sentences:

> A crock o' shit is smaller than a load o' shit.
>
> A piece o' shit is smaller than a -------.

Answer: A. pile o' shit.

6. Test sentences:

> You might not want to hear this, son, but a paycheck might be a more reliable source of income than the lottery.
>
> You might not want to hear this, son, but a ------ might be a more reliable source of income than the NBA Draft.

Answer: B. job.

SECTION 8: Identifying Sentence Errors

1. Punctuation! Error! Use a comma when you need a pause, but not, when, you, don't. And here, there shouldn't be one after, "quite." **Answer: D.**

2. Verb form foul-up. Those Amazing Marocco Brothers did the Flying Dubjak Sisters in the past, not the present. That means screw should be screwed. **Answer: C.**

3. Pronoun trouble. Since it's the plane that's emitting the heat for the missile to home in on, the missile surely went up its tail pipe, not the pilot's. **Answer: D.**

4. Faulty idioms. In English, we put adjectives in a certain traditional order (not a traditional certain order, if you see what we mean). For instance, it's always "dirty old bastard," not "old dirty bastard" . . . Oh, wait. What about Ol' Dirty Bastard? Well, that's someone's name, so they can do whatever they want. But otherwise . . . **Answer: E.**

5. Grammatically, the sentence is fine. Even that "whatever" hanging out there by itself. When it comes to dealing with parents, we grant you considerable grammatical leeway. **Answer: E.**

6. A promising beginning for a joke, but the verb form error left our clergymen without a complete sentence. Instead of sitting, how about if they sat while reading Snatch? **Answer: A.**

7. Misleading punctuation. "Delivering a tongue, lashing to the technician" is very different from "delivering a tongue-lashing to the technician." This is a hospital, not a delicatessen. **Answer: C.**

8. Even more misleading punctuation. Oh no! It looks like the Capello County Gay Rights Committee is organizing hate crimes. There's only one way to stop them: Add a comma after "crimes." **Answer: D.**

SECTION 9: Mathematics

1. This is obviously an ancient text passage . . . that turns out to be a math problem (and a tricky one, at that)! Look at it this way:

It's a 5-wife rotation, which means that every 5 days we start over. Figure out which number day is Wednesday of Week #5. If Monday of Week #1 is Day #1, then the last day of Week #4 (Sunday), is the 28th day (4 weeks × 7 days per week = 28 days). And then we're into Week #5:

> Monday is Day #29 Tuesday is Day #30 Wednesday is Day #31

In 31 days Zeb goes through that 5-wife rotation 6 full times and then one more: (5 x 6 = 30 and then 1 more is 31). That's one wife after the last (fifth) wife in the list—in other words, the first one. So on Wednesday of Week #5, *A) Amalech* gets to play Hide the Kielbasa. **Answer: A.**

2. Here's another way of phrasing the question: In any given time period, how many wives must the old codger now boink versus before? For instance, try a period of 100 days. Before this he was doing one wife each day or 100 boinks in 100 days. Now, however, he's doing 5 wives every 4 days, or 125 boinks in 100 days, which is 25% more than before. **Answer: B.**

3. A close reading of the text will allow you to chart Zebakkuk's sexual history. From his 80th year to his 975th year (a total of 895 years), he boinked once per night or 895 × 365.25 = approximately 326,900 times.

Once you've done that calculation you know your answer must be *C) 344,000*. It can't be *D) 4,000,000* because Zeb only lived another 25 years. To reach 4 million boinks in that time he'd have to do it 300 times a day, which only happens in the insect world. **Answer: C.**

4. We can ignore everything that happens until both guys fall to an altitude of 1,000 feet. From there Bert falls at 20 feet per second and poor Ernie continues at 100 feet per second. Bert takes 50 seconds to drift that last 1,000 feet while Ernie's fiery descent lasts a mere 10 seconds. So the answer is *B) 40 seconds*, right? WRONG! Read the question again. "How much sooner does Bert arrive on the ground than Ernie?" But it's *Ernie* who gets there first, so the answer has to be *negative* 40 seconds. If you'd noticed that to begin with, you could have picked the only available negative answer and arrived at the end even faster than Ernie. **Answer: D.**

5. We want to find the length of the coffin using the exterior surface area and two edge dimensions. There's no way to avoid crunching the numbers. Set up the following pain-in-the-ass equation keeping in mind that the coffin has three pairs of matching surfaces for a total of six:

$58.5 = 2 (L \times 1.5)$ sides $+ 2 (L \times 2)$ bottoms $+ 2 (2 \times 1.5)$ ends. Simplifying:

$58.5 = 3L + 4L + 6 = 7L + 6$. Subtracting 6 from both sides, we get:

$52.5 = 7L$. Dividing both sides by 7 gives us:

$7.5 = L$, which converts to 7 feet 6 inches <u>exterior</u> length.

But that's exactly the dead basketballer's height. Oops. The nimrod didn't count on the 2-inch thickness of each coffin wall, leaving the coffin interior a total of 4 inches too short. **Answer: A.**

6. Here's a situation where the Low-Road solution is a <u>lot</u> easier than the High-Road, and a good BSAT-style uneducated guess can save a lot of time.

Low-Road: Look at answers *C) 6 inches* and *D) 12 inches.* The bottom left corner of the coffin is exactly 1 foot below ground level, right? (It's marked as 5 feet from the floor of the 6 foot deep grave.) The angled coffin itself is 1' 6" deep, so that if it were horizontal, the <u>most</u> its top left corner could protrude above ground would be 6 inches. But it's not level, so the answer is something less than 6 inches. Goodbye C and D, leaving just A and B. Now, with that bottom left corner exactly at 1 foot below the surface, for the top corner to stick out only *A) 1.2 inches,* the coffin would have to be pointing almost straight down into the ground. This leaves you with answer *B) 2.4 inches,* which is correct.

Now look at the hellacious High-Road way to choose between A and B. See the diagram below.

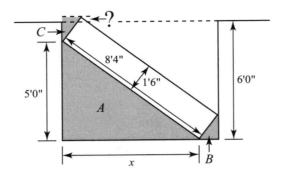

Notice that because the coffin and the grave are rectangles, right triangles A and B are similar (same angles, proportional sides) and B and C are congruent (angles and sides identical). We're looking for the little bit of the long leg of triangle C that's above ground-level, that leg minus 12 inches. First find leg x of triangle A. The length of the coffin (8' 4″) is a hypotenuse of 100 inches and the short leg (5') is 60 inches. That makes it a 3-4-5 triangle (60-80-100) so that $x = 80$ inches or 6' 8″. Now, noting that A and B are similar, we set up the proportion equation:

$$\frac{\text{Long Side A}}{\text{Hypotenuse A}} = \frac{\text{Long Side B}}{\text{Hypotenuse B}}$$

Using the numbers, that's:

$$\frac{80}{100} = \frac{\text{Long Side B}}{1'6''} = \frac{\text{Long Side B}}{18}$$

Solving for Long Side B gives us 14.4 inches, which is also Long Side C. Subtract 12 inches and *voilá!*: 2.4 inches! (A box of peonies would still be nice.) **Answer: B.**

7. Translating the words that describe Blind Mouse A's tail into formulas:

   ORIGINAL = STUMP + 4cm

   ORIGINAL less 15% = 6.8cm

Noting that "ORIGINAL less 15%" is the same as $.85x$ ORIGINAL, we get $.85x$ ORIGINAL = 6.8cm, and substituting from the first formula, $.85x$ (STUMP + 4cm) = 6.8cm. Solving for STUMP, we get .85 STUMP + 3.4cm = 6.8cm, and subtracting 3.4 from both sides, it's .85 STUMP = 3.4cm.

Finally, dividing both sides by .85, we get STUMP = 4cm. The carving knife had cut Blind Mouse A's tail precisely in half. What are the odds? **Answer: B.**

8. The BSAT way to solve this is to imagine that you are the rapist. You can stand in any one of 5 places, which leaves 4 possible places for your friend, the arsonist. Of those 4, for each of the 2 end rapist positions, only 1 adjacent spot for the arsonist remains. For the middle 3 rapist positions, there are 2 possible arsonist spots—1 on either side. So that's $\frac{1}{4}, \frac{2}{4}, \frac{2}{4}, \frac{2}{4}$, and $\frac{1}{4}$. Average those probabilities and you get:

$$(\frac{1}{4} + \frac{2}{4} + \frac{2}{4} + \frac{2}{4} + \frac{1}{4}) / 5 = \frac{2}{5}, \text{ or answer B.}$$

You could do this with factorials and figure out exactly how many overall possibilities there are, etc. But you'd be doing real math then. You sure you want to go there? **Answer: B.**

SECTION 10: Reading Passage

1. Once you've jettisoned the numbskull answers like A, C, and D, you've got to choose between B and E. Per E, the letter does truly demonstrate that the author is an airhead. However, that was not her purpose, which is what the question is asking for. Her purpose was to "put the rest of our petty problems into perspective." Problems? What problems? **Answer: B.**

2. A global question with specific features. Hey, let's make a checklist!

> idiotic and unwarranted optimism
>
> off-the-charts denial
>
> a husband she should ditch ASAP
>
> only one kidney
>
> a clear-eyed view of reality

Now you have a picture of an American original. **Answer: E.**

3. While the O'Dooleys might well have a shot on *E) America's Most Fucked-Up Family,* there's no mention of it in the letter. Too bad. More probably, Felicia simply doesn't have the imagination not to send the annual letter. After all, it's a tradition. **Answer: C.**

PART V

APPENDICES

APPENDIX 1:
Advanced Test-Taking Strategies

Cheating

To cheat or not to cheat? This is the age-old dilemma. In real life 79 percent of people cheat on *something**—their income tax, their true love, their South Beach diet. Cheaters are rarely caught and even more rarely punished. In other words, cheating is a safe and effective way to get ahead. So why not cheat?

Another overlooked advantage: Cheating is exciting, even thrilling. It gets your juices flowing. And flowing juices are what dug the Grand Canyon. Bearing all this in mind, the BSAT has taken a bold step in test design and preparation.

WE EXPECT YOU TO CHEAT ON THE BSAT.

We won't be surprised if, during the exam, you:

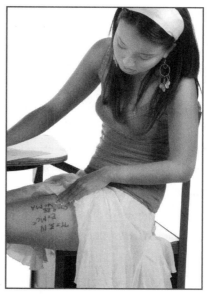

- Discreetly text your peeps for a "lifeline."
- Consult answers you bought online and have woven into the complexity of the rose tattoo on your foot.
- Bring little binoculars to scan your neighbors' bubble sheets for consensus on tough questions.
- Wear an earpiece, Secret Service-style, to receive real-time answers from the nerd you hired to take the test with you.
- Even better, just put that nerd's photo on your ID and send him in your place.

Knock yourself out. We won't try to catch you because, frankly, we think that cheating is part of the rich fabric of real life (on which, we continue to stress, the BSAT is based). Or maybe we're just trying to encourage social collaboration. Yeah, that's it. Social collaboration.

CAVEAT: Even though we expect cheating on the BSAT, in the unlikely event you are caught, *you will be severely punished*. This is fair, because getting caught is a sign of extreme stupidity—about 200 hundreds points worth, which is the penalty we'll deduct from your score. So, as in real life, cheating is fine but getting caught is not.

*This percentage may vary. Actually, we cheated and just made this number up, to help prove our point.

Pharmacological aids

Taking a test when you're high on drugs has its pros and cons. Drugs can make you more creative and give you insights you'd never have in a million years if you weren't totally fucked up. On the other hand, many of these insights take hours to develop and turn out to be irrelevant.

For example, when top student Robert X took the test while tripping on LSD, he had a life-changing experience, likening it to "taking a journey to the center of a potato" and "like having your mind rotted out by this ecstatic pulsing mildew." Though his experience was subjectively positive, we should note that while taking the test, Robert jumped randomly from question to question, getting through about eight of them in three hours, bubbling in the answers on his bellybutton and eventually fixating on a way to conjugate "wow" as a verb. While this is a perfectly valid way to take the test, it is only for those who prize the experience over the result.

If you are an experience junkie like Robert, read on. If, however, you're hung up on the score thing, that's fine, too, and never mind all the fun you're missing. For the former, below is a brief summary of experiences the BSAT produces in combination with some of the most popular substances available.

The BSAT on COCAINE: The first 20 minutes are exciting and empowering, as you discover that you know more math than you thought. However, the drug's short half-life is a problem, so bring plenty and excuse yourself at regular intervals. Otherwise, be prepared for a hard crash and really itchy eyeballs.

The BSAT on POT: Your morning will be characterized by lots of insights into the beauty of the universe. Downside: Your vastly improved ability to spot connections will make it difficult to settle on a single answer, with three or four bubble-ins per question quite typical. Analogies are notorious in this regard—all the answers always seem incredibly right-on.

The BSAT on PEYOTE: Most test takers report a quasi-religious experience, sort of like you're being initiated into a bizarre cult of esoteric knowledge, which in a way you are, aren't you?

The BSAT on ECSTASY: This drug is problematic for test taking because you'll keep asking the DJ to play the techno music louder, when in fact there is no DJ and there is no techno music. Frustrated, you'll end up leaving early to find a party that doesn't suck so bad.

The BSAT on SPEED (meth, crystal meth, Black Beauties, Space Dust, Daffy Dex, and all diet pills): All these variants interact with the BSAT to provide a magnificent feeling of mastery to the point of omnipotence. The only drawback here is when your heart stops, putting a long-term end to the short-term fun. So weigh the trade-offs carefully.

The BSAT on ALCOHOL: Alcohol disinhibits, and that's good on a test that poses the basic question, "How far outside of the box can you go without actually floating away?" We leave dosage questions up to the individual. Just remember that passing out can cost you valuable time.

It turns out that different types of alcoholic beverages provide widely different test experiences:

- **The BSAT on MARGARITAS:** Gives the test a fun festive party atmosphere.

- **The BSAT on MAI TAIS:** Makes it hard to concentrate because you feel like any minute you're going to get lucky and hook up with the person sitting next to you.

- **The BSAT on WHISKEY SOURS:** You feel as witty as Dorothy Parker, right up to the moment you puke.

- **The BSAT on MARTINIS:** Same as whiskey sours, but you feel superior instead of witty.

- **The BSAT on BEER:** Some of the test questions may rankle and make you resent those more privileged.

- **The BSAT on LITE BEER:** Same effect, but you don't resent them quite as much.

- **The BSAT on WINE:** Your insights are more sophisticated than with beer.

Really Advanced Test-Taking Strategies

The following strategies are controversial. Mainly because they hardly ever work. We include them because we know that some of you are desperate, and you should be. But remember: All we can do is make you aware of the available tools. It's up to *you* to fuck things up on your own. Here are some humdingers, in order of futility.

Faking disabilities—Having a learning disability will get you extra time on any test. But you'll need to prove it by having some sort of supporting document from an apparent professional. Just walking in on test day drooling and stuttering won't do it. So where do you get such a supporting document? While we can't endorse any particular agency, we've heard good things about:

- disabilities-warehouse.com
- diplomasfordollars.net
- adhdandcanproveit.com

Religious approaches—Prayer is a surprisingly popular test-taking strategy, one with many creative variations. Some people hedge their bets with multi-denominational rituals (e.g., chanting the Torah on your knees facing Mecca, etc.). Others get a pre-test blessing from their guru. Unfortunately, none of it helps. If you're relying on the faith-based approach you may find that even McDonalds' Hamburger University is a reach.

Curses and the supernatural—It is tempting to engage in the dark arts of conjuring, fulminating, or casting unholy imprecations against college tests and their publishers. Believe us: We've tried it all in our campaign to get the BSAT accepted by the close-knit cabalistic college admissions community. So far it hasn't done shit. But if you have some new Hogwarts-style idea for causing their hair to fall out or their scoring machines to self-destruct, go for it. We're with you. Rabbits' feet, amulets, etc., are not effective.

Pretending you're smarter than you are—This is related to "envisioning success" and other popular forms of magical thinking. You relax and picture yourself achieving things that are normally quite beyond your reach. The problem is that this is the same as giving yourself a placebo or pulling the wool over your own eyes. But, when you lie to yourself, how do you keep yourself from catching on? And when you catch yourself in the lie, how do you deal with the hurtful breach of trust? Next thing you know, you've got a restraining order and you're barred from setting foot within 100 yards of yourself.

On the upside, when you pretend you're smarter than you are and you blow the exam (which you will), you've cleverly laid the groundwork for one of the most satisfying feelings of all: blaming someone else. "This test is biased against me." "Who is this guy Abraham Lincoln anyway?" "I'm gonna shut these fucking charlatans down."

There. Doesn't that feel good?

In Summary

No single strategy is right for everyone. You'll want to experiment. Mix and match. See what works for you. Of all of these strategies, people seem to get the most mileage out of Cheating and/or Drugs. Notice that both can be applied to life—not just tests. To our minds, that proves they're good strategies.

TEST-TAKING DON'TS
- Don't experiment with new drugs during the test.
- Don't take a nap during the test.
- Don't give in to existential despair until after the test.
- Don't fart or, if you must, do it quietly.
- Don't drop your disability: If you limp on the way in, make sure to limp on the way out.

APPENDIX 2:
BSAT List of AMAZING Words
(Words That Aren't as Bad as They Sound)

Word	Pronunciation	What you think it means	What it actually means
acute angina	a-cute ann-JINE-ah	a body part that's better looking than expected	severe heart pain
annular	ANN-yuh-ler	a yearly gathering of assholes	having the form of a ring
asphyxiate	ass-FIX-see-ate	to obsess about someone's butt	to suffocate or smother
asymptote	ASS-im-tote	the fullest part of J-Lo's jeans	a straight line approached by a curve as its equation approaches infinity
circumscribe	sir-cum-SCRIBE	the guy who keeps the official record at a bris	to encircle something
cockatrix	COCK-a-trix	a penis that is pulled out of a hat	a legendary creature, resembling a rooster with a lizard-like tail
congenital	con-GEN-it-ull	gets along well with other genitals	a characteristic that is present at birth
crapulent	CRAP-you-lent	worthless junk but you want it back anyway	sick from drinking or overeating
cummerbund	CUM-er-bund	a cream-filled pastry	a pleated sash worn with a tuxedo
dictum	DICK-tum	the front edge of the scrum (see scrum)	an authoritative declaration
diphthong	DIFF-thong	a skimpy two-piece bathing suit	a speech sound that glides from one vowel sound to another
epistolary	eh-PISS-toe-leh-ree	a jar for the safe-keeping of fluid specimens	a relationship conducted through the exchange of letters
fatuous	FAT-choo-iss	the opposite of thinuous	stupidly foolish
fecund	FECK-und	after first but before fird	fertile, prolific
fistula	FIST-you-la	five fingers where they just don't fit	an abnormal connection between two organs or vessels
formication	for-mih-KAY-shun	screwing on top of the kitchen cabinets	the hallucination that something's crawling all over your skin
fricative	FRICK-uh-tiv	a euphemistic expletive	a kind of speech sound occurring in connection with some consonant sounds like s and th
fungible	FUN-ja-bull	capable of being "funged"	replaceable or substitutable
futtock	FUT-uck	a body part that's gotten used to being treated inappropriately	one of the curved wooden ribs of a ship
glutinous	GLUE-tin-us	pertaining to a butt that keeps jiggling even after the rest of you has stopped	gooey
heinous	HAY-nuss	of or pertaining to the scrum (see also dictum)	atrocious or monstrous
homo erectus	ho-mo ee-RECK-tuss	a chorus boy with excellent balance	a particular, extinct species of human
homogeneous	ho-mo-JEEN-yuss	like Michelangelo	substances in the same material phase

Word	Pronunciation	What you think it means	What it actually means
horology	hor-OL-lo-gee	the academic study of prostitutes	the science of measuring time
infarct	in-FARCT	to take in noxious gas through the colon	bodily tissue that dies due to lack of blood
jugular	JUG-yuh-ler	the same as titular	pertaining to the throat or neck
Klondike	KLON-dike	the northern cousin of an Amazon	a region of western Canada
mandible	MAN-dih-bull	those last drops you have to shake off	the lower jaw bone
mandrill	MAN-drill	the Black & Decker in your pants	a large African baboon
masticate	MASS-teh-cate	to pull on yourself in a sexually suggestive manner	to chew
miasma	my-AZZ-mah	a dangerous build-up of intestinal gases	noxious emission from putrescent organic matter
morass	MORE-ass	what you want when it's still not enough	marshy wet ground or messy entanglement
niggling	NIG-ling	a very small niggle	small and of little importance
pandemonium	pan-duh-MOAN-ee-yum	a Chinese musical instrument that, when pumped, makes a cute growling sound	wild uproar or chaos
peccadillo	peck-a-DILL-o	a phallus you suspect of being of rubber or plastic	a trifling or minor sin or offense
pedantry	PED-an-tree	gallantly seducing a young person	showy display of learning
penal colony	PEE-null CAH-luh-nee	an outpost or settlement of penises	a place of exile for criminals
pissant	PISS-ant	an insect that leaves a moist yellow trail	someone useless, despicable or inconsequential
pithy	PITH-ee	in a hithy fit	succinct or to-the-point
rebut	re-BUTT	gain weight previously lost	to refute by argument
scrum	SCRUM	in front of the bum and just behind the scrotum (see dictum)	the mass formation of a bunch of rugby players
shuttlecock	SHUT-tul-cock	an international playboy	an object struck back and forth in badminton
succubus	SUCK-you-bus	the most popular girl on the ride home from school	a demon or evil spirit
succumb	suck-CUM	what a succubus does	to yield or give in
thespian	THESS-pee-in	one who thinks girls are FABULOUS!	pertaining to acting or the dramatic arts
titillate	TIT-till-late	to wobble back and forth in pairs	pleasurably arouse
titter	TIT-er	a breast man	a restrained laugh
titular	TIT-yuh-ler	the same as jugular	having the title but not the powers
uvula	YOOV-yoo-la	a delicate part of the female anatomy	that tiny punching bag thing hanging down at the back of your throat

Acknowledgements

The authors would like to share blame with the following people, but for whose feedback, suggestions, and misplaced encouragement, the world might have been spared the BSAT. [Any errors in the book are the fault of our editors, who were supposed to catch them. Anything worthwhile in the book is due to us.]

Davy Bridgman-Packer

Elliot Brown

Lisa Clancy

Ted Drachman

Jane Dystel

Michael Fontaine

Eileen Geiger

Miriam Goderich

David Gold

Harriet Goldberg

Eric Goldman

Ari Gold-Parker

David Hendin

Claire Hsu

Ethan Kaplan

Jason Kayser

Cliff Pysher

Jason Rosenberg

Larry Segan

Zach Shevich

Andy Thorne

Rick Treitman

Lily Weitzman

Don Weitzman

The Wexlers

Katie Willingham

Grant Wright

And most especially:

Vicky and Will Forster

Francine, Samantha, and Max Segan

About the Authors

Marc Segan's early experiments with penciling in circles on test forms got him into Princeton, where he majored in beer pong with a minor in Philosophy. Later he quit law school to become an inventor. That led to Hallmark's first musical greeting card, a slew of toys, animated Christmas decorations, weird Nickelodeon alarm clocks, and Disney high-tech animated art. He has also occasionally flirted with seriousness as co-founder of Quadlogic Controls, a leader in green-technology digital electricity metering and as president of the board of New York Stage & Film, producer of Vassar College's Powerhouse theater festival. Marc holds more than 40 patents, the latest for an innovative use of web avatars.

He lives in NYC with his wife, cookbook author and lecturer Francine Segan, and their children, Samantha and Max, both of whom had great success using the BSAT to prepare for the SAT.

John Forster is an award-winning humorist and songwriter whose work has been recorded by Faith Hill, Rosanne Cash, Judy Collins, and Tom Chapin, among many others. His inventive work for children has earned him four Grammy nominations, and his topical songs turn up in places like NPR's Morning Edition and Dr. Demento's radio shows. A graduate of Harvard, John has basically thrown away a perfectly good education in favor of churning out the aforementioned tune-age. His satirical albums include the Indie-Award-winning *Entering Marion*, *Helium*, and *The Official Bootleg Album*. He must also answer for the musicals *Eleanor: An American Love Story*, the perennial *How to Eat Like a Child*, and the musical version of *Freaky Friday*. He lives in the Lower Hudson Valley with his wife and son, beta testers extraordinaire. Sordid career details at www.johnforster.com.